D0422971

F
123   Miller
.M6   Jacksonian aristocracy
(1)

Date Due			

LIBRARY-ALLEGHENY CAMPUS
808 RIDGE AVENUE
PITTSBURGH, PA.   15212

PRINTED IN U.S.A.

JACKSONIAN ARISTOCRACY

Class and Democracy in New York 1830–1860

THE COMMUNITY COLLEGE OF ALLEGHENY COUNTY

ALLEGHENY
CAMPUS

808 RIDGE AVENUE
PITTSBURGH, PA.
15212

LIBRARY

JACKSONIAN ARISTOCRACY

Class and Democracy in New York

1830-1860

———◆———

Douglas T. Miller

New York · OXFORD UNIVERSITY PRESS · 1967

F
123
. m6
(1)

Copyright © 1967 by Oxford University Press, Inc.
Library of Congress Catalogue Card Number: 67-15130

PRINTED IN THE UNITED STATES OF AMERICA

For Sheila

PREFACE

THE uniqueness of American history, particularly in the first half of the nineteenth century, rests primarily on the early triumph of democracy in this country. Native Americans from Franklin to Whitman never tired of proclaiming the virtues of our democratic institutions, and historians have concentrated on the growth of democracy as the central theme in the nation's history. Yet this concentration on the development of democracy in the period before the Civil War is misleading since it overlooks powerful forces that ran counter to this trend and worked toward the stratification of society. In New York State and undoubtedly many other areas of the country, during the period from 1830 to 1860, aristocracy clearly increased in power, causing democracy to weaken.

To write of the rise of aristocracy in Jacksonian America is to contradict traditional beliefs and interpretations. Politically this was the age of democracy as historians have repeatedly emphasized. Writers often disagree about the sources of Jacksonian democracy or about whether democratic reforms were part of the Jacksonian movement or preceded the rise of Jackson, but none question the fact that political democracy made substantial advances in the first half of the nineteenth century. For New York State this democratic triumph was carefully documented nearly fifty years ago in a work that has become a minor classic, *The Decline of Aristocracy in the Politics of New York* (1919) by Dixon Ryan Fox. More recently aspects of Fox's study have been subject to criti-

vii

cal re-evaluation, most notably in Lee Benson's book, *The Concept of Jacksonian Democracy: New York as a Test Case* (1961). But even Benson, who has denied the validity of the traditional concept of Jacksonian democracy, maintains that New York State politics passed through an egalitarian revolution between 1815 and the Civil War.[1]

Most political studies of the Jacksonian era have implied that democracy was victorious not only in the political realm but socially and economically as well. Benson, for example, writes that "after 1815, not only in politics but in all spheres of American life, egalitarianism challenged elitism and, in most spheres and places, egalitarianism won." [2]

This theme has been expressed even more explicitly by writers who have directed their attention to the study of American society during the age of Jackson. In 1927 Carl Russell Fish contributed a volume to the *History of American Life* series covering the years from 1830 to 1850; the central theme of this book is conveyed by its title, *The Rise of the Common Man*. Fish's study has also been criticized by later historians, but his general thesis remains intact. As a recent writer states, "the age of the common man in American history is the period of the early nineteenth century, somewhere between Jefferson and the Civil War, roughly coincident with Andrew Jackson's coming to power and the formation of the Democratic party." [3]

This study does not deny that representative political institutions based on nearly universal white manhood suffrage were the rule from the Jacksonian era to the Civil War. Politics is given very minor consideration here. What is questioned, however, is the assumption that throughout this period democracy meant social and economic equality as well as equal political rights. Even in the early 1830's, when that astute French observer Alexis de Tocqueville noted the prevalence of a general "equality of condition" in America, an economic and social aristocracy was discernible. In 1833 William Gouge, a Jacksonian economist, observed that changing economic conditions were having disturbing social effects. "Through all the operations of business," he wrote, "the effects of an unequal distribution of wealth may be distinctly traced. The rich have the means of rewarding most liberally the professional characters whom they employ and the tradesmen with whom they deal. An aristocracy in one department of society introduces an aristocracy into all." This same year, 1833, Ely Moore, a New York printer and labor leader, wrote that "even in this fair land of freedom, where liberty and equality are guaranteed to all, and where our written constitutions have so wisely provided limitations to power, . . . the twin fiends, *intolerance* and *aristocracy*, presume to rear their hateful crests!" [4]

The United States, of course, had no hereditary nobility in the European sense. Aristocracy in this country could best be defined as consisting of those persons regarded as superior to the rest of the community in such things as wealth, rank, manners, dress, speech, family, and intellect. Of these, wealth was the outstanding criterion for high social standing, and as long as inequalities of wealth were comparatively slight—as was the case in the early 1830's—it was easy for Americans to associate political democracy with equality.

However, the concept of equality itself had a meaning peculiar to America. As a belief it did not imply that the rich should be reduced to the level of the poor. Equality meant that each person should have an equal chance to outstrip his neighbor and become rich himself. As long as America remained a land of small farmers, craftsmen, and merchants there did not appear to be any contradiction between the notion of equality of opportunity and a general equality of condition.

But the three decades preceding the Civil War witnessed a major economic transformation. In these years the revolutions in industry and transportation radically altered the relatively homogeneous middle-class society of the early nineteenth century. Great wealth was created, giving rise to a new plutocratic aristocracy clearly set off from the masses. At the other extreme, heavy immigration and industrialization greatly increased the size of the laboring class while reducing the workers' social mobility and general position. The purpose of this book is to present a history of these important changes from the age of Jackson to the Civil War.

New York State is the major focus of this study. The richest and most populous state in the Union, New York is both representative and prophetic. That is, many of the changes causing the stratification of New York society similarly affected other areas of America; while in other respects New York stands as a forerunner of what was to come. In this latter regard New York City is the best example, presaging the growth of the urban industrial America of the post Civil War Gilded Age.

For encouragement and guidance in the writing of this work, I wish to express my foremost thanks to Gilman M. Ostrander. Professor Ostrander's cordial aid and critical advice were invaluable at every step of the way. I would also like to thank Russel B. Nye and Stuart W. Bruchey for stimulating my original interest in Jacksonian history. For reading all or part of the original manuscript

I wish to thank Professors Ostrander, Nye, Norman Rich, Marjorie Gesner, H. James Henderson, and Mara Wolfgang. To Sheldon Meyer of Oxford University Press I am indebted both for encouragement and for some very helpful editorial comments. In my research I was assisted by the courteous staffs of the New York Public Library, Columbia University Library, the New-York Historical Society, and the libraries of the University of Maine and Michigan State University. In preparing the manuscript for publication I was supported by a Coe Fund Research Grant from the University of Maine. Finally, I wish to express deep gratitude to my wife, Sheila Miller, whose help, criticism, interest, and friendly obstructions have made this work a pleasure.

D. T. M.

East Lansing
January 1967

CONTENTS

1. EQUALITY 3

2. LABOR IN JACKSONIAN NEW YORK 26

3. MANORS AND COUNTING HOUSES 56

4. TO THE NEW WORLD 81

5. FACTORIES AND FORTUNES 106

6. THE WIDENING GAP:
LABOR IN THE FORTIES AND FIFTIES 128

7. THE NEW ARISTOCRACY 155

NOTES 190

BIBLIOGRAPHY 213

INDEX 221

JACKSONIAN ARISTOCRACY

Class and Democracy in New York 1830–1860

1

EQUALITY

> The equality of the United States is no more absolute than that of any other country. There may be less inequality in this nation than in most others, but inequality exists, and, in some respects, with stronger features than it is usual to meet with in the rest of christendom.
>
> —James Fenimore Cooper,
> *The American Democrat* (1838)

E ARLY in 1832 Calvin Colton, a New York journalist and political pamphleteer, wrote that "in America a man may *create* stations and *make* places, and can always find such already open, as might satisfy any reasonable ambition." Colton was writing during the age of Jackson, a period in which enterprise seemed the most general American characteristic as persons optimistically attempted to satisfy their "reasonable ambitions." The opportunity to realize one's aspirations, largely economic, together with political democracy and the fact that there were no great extremes of rich and poor, made equality seem a dynamic reality during the early 1830's.[1]

Foreign observers were particularly struck by the egalitarian aspects of American life, frequently finding equality the single most important factor in shaping this nation's society, manners, and institutions. Alexis de Tocqueville

3

wrote in the introductory chapter of his classic *Democracy in America* that:

> Amongst the novel objects that attracted my attention during my stay in the United States, nothing struck me more forcibly than the general equality of conditions. I readily discovered the prodigious influence which this primary fact exercises on the whole course of society. . . . The more I advanced in the study of American society, the more I perceived that the equality of conditions is the fundamental fact from which all others seem to be derived, and the central point at which all my observations constantly terminated.

Similarly, Tocqueville's fellow countryman, Michael Chevalier, compared American society to Europe stood on its head. "In the United States," he wrote, "the democratic spirit is infused into all the national habits and all the customs of society; it besets and startles at every step the foreigner who, before landing in this country, had no suspicion to what a degree his every nerve and fiber had been steeped in aristocracy by a European education." [2]

American equality was not only noticeable; it was aggressive and boisterous. Historians have often described as an example of triumphant egalitarianism the rough crowds who elbowed their way into the White House at Jackson's first inauguration. Other instances of this forceful spirit are legion. Visiting a Western town, the Duke of Saxe Weimar was nearly pommeled for his presumptuous attempt to hire an entire stagecoach for himself and his valet. On another occasion this same duke went in a hackney-coach to a party in New York City. The next day the driver came for his money, asking the duke whether he was the *man* he had driven the night before, and, on being answered in the affirmative, informed him that *"he* was the *gentleman* what drove him," and that he had come for his half-dollar. Except in the Eastern cities, distinctions in accommodations were rare, and in the smaller towns it was common for an innkeeper to lodge as many as ten or twelve persons in a room, often sleeping two or three in the same bed. More fastidious travelers who requested private quarters were considered unreasonable and were seldom obliged. Like the astonished Ishmael of *Moby-Dick*, a lodger in this period was apt to awaken in the presence of any kind of strange bedfellow. In myriad other ways Americans showed their scorn of aristocratic pretensions. Stage drivers ate at the same table with passengers, and they further asserted their independence, to the disgust of many foreign travelers, by swearing boisterously and refusing to help with baggage. "Boys, and even men," the novelist Cooper complained, "wear their hats in the houses of all classes." [3]

The way in which Americans, in Tocqueville's words, "pounce upon equality as their booty" is perhaps best illustrated by the relationship between servants and their masters. Except in the South, where slaves were used, there was no permanent class of domestic servants. Yet there was a great need and demand for such a class, since housework for a family was arduous and took long hours. Even persons with ample incomes found it difficult to obtain good servants. To help remedy this situation a group of New York City residents in 1825 formed a "Society for the Encouragement of Faithful Domestic Servants." This organization hoped to obtain good servants by offering "liberal premiums to those domestics who conduct well and remain longest in a family"; and thereby "to remedy that restlessness, and love of change in them, which produces so much inconvenience to all house-keepers." The premiums were graded so that the longer one remained in the service of a family the higher his bonus payment would be.[4] But, judging from numerous subsequent complaints, the society seems to have had little success in inducing more persons to enter or remain in domestic service.

Native Americans especially did not want to become servants, for they considered such an occupation degrading. Two things which they most resented were the term "servant" and the wearing of livery. This first objection was bypassed by substituting the term "help" for "servant." Help implied a position of equality, domestic helpers usually hiring themselves out for a limited period only. They did not consider themselves servants and refused to be treated as such. In the smaller towns it was quite common for the help to eat at the same table with their employers, to attend the same church, and in other ways to act as social equals. Even in New York and other cities, where such familiarity between domestics and their employers was less common, the term "servant" was rarely used.

As for livery, whether a formal identifying uniform or merely a maid's dress, most domestics simply refused to wear any. "There are but few native Americans," one foreigner commented, "who would submit to the degradation of wearing a livery, or any other badge of servitude." Another foreign visitor wrote of the American servant that "the man will not wear a livery, any more than he will wear a halter round his neck." Perhaps even more indicative of American egalitarianism than the refusal of domestic servants to wear livery was the fact that policemen, firemen, coachmen, and conductors also resisted all efforts to introduce uniforms.[5]

Both the shortage of servants and their equalitarian pretentions were commented upon in travelers' accounts. "The native men," wrote a Britisher:

> seem averse to servitude, and are rarely to be found in this capacity. The women are somewhat more ready to *help* out; but servants entertain such notions of equality and independence as fit them poorly for this station of life, and tend greatly to abridge the comforts of their employers. . . .

Another Englishman lamented that servants never seemed to be available when wanted. "It seems the servants themselves, or the helps, or hirelings, or whatever name they think it least degrading to go by, do not like being summoned by a ringing of bells. Accordingly, there was often no method left, but to do the things required ourselves." This writer went on to deplore the "total want of good servants in America. . . . Good nurses, men servants, cooks, or any description of female attendants are rarely to be found; and if found, no money will bribe them to stay long in a house, or to behave respectfully there." Americans were so opposed to the concept of servitude that the author of an etiquette book had to assure his readers that with all due deference to republican feelings it was not incorrect to close a letter: "I have the honour to be your very obedient servant." [6]

Dislike of any recognizable signs of social inferiority was reflected in other aspects of American life. Aristocratic gentlemen of the Revolutionary period had been meticulous about their dress: the powder and queues, the cockhats and broad brims, the white-top boots or buckled shoes, the silk stockings, and the close-fitting doeskin knee breeches. But by the 1830's only a few tottering and conservative old gentlemen—relics from an earlier era—

clung to the former styles. Men of all classes dressed in pantaloons, coat and waistcoat, and round hats with narrow brims; short trimmed hair replaced the formal powdered wigs. This is not to say that the dress of a well-to-do gentleman could not be distinguished from the daily attire of a mechanic or laborer, but the marked class distinctions of dress had become less pronounced, and it was not uncommon for lower and middle-class men to appear dressed in the best of fashion, even if their coats and pantaloons were of a poorer quality and their collars and shirts false. One visitor was surprised to see common workers wearing "sleek coats, glossy hats, gay watch-guards, and doe-skin gloves!" [7]

In woman's dress a similar democratization occurred. Powdered hair and long colonial silks were seldom seen in the Jacksonian period. American women, especially in the cities, followed the latest fashions from London and Paris. New York society ladies often spent great sums in procuring their clothing, but no longer were these wives and daughters of the wealthy the only ones elegantly dressed in the latest styles. Fashionable dress was worn by a larger portion of the population than previously, and it was not uncommon to see serving girls or seamstresses promenading Broadway as smartly attired as the daughters of rich merchants.

Public transportation facilities in the Jacksonian era also reflected American egalitarianism. With the introduction of steamboats and steam engines, and the building of canals, turnpikes, and railroads, travel became a commonplace event for the average American, and on most ships, stages, packets, and trains there were no first-class accommodations. A gentleman writing in the mid-1830's deplored the fact that on steamboats and in the newer railroad cars "the rich and the poor, the educated and the ignorant, the polite and the vulgar, all herd on the cabin floor of the steamer, feed at the same table, sit in each others laps, as it were, in the cars. . . . Steam, so useful in many respects, interferes with the comfort of travelling, [and] destroys every salutary distinction in society. . . ." [8]

In Europe established religion was one of the mainstays of aristocracy. But here, where there was no established church, all religions had to fend for themselves. Most church sects, therefore, tended to cater to popular sentiment and reflected the equalitarian spirit of the majority. Even the hierarchical Roman Catholic Church adapted to democracy in the United States. In the older seaboard states certain churches were strongholds of conservatism. In New York the Anglican Church, which had enjoyed official status in the state's lower counties during colonial days, remained largely an upper-class church, its members including many rich merchants and large landholders. The Dutch Reformed Church in areas such as Albany, where descendants of the original Dutch settlers were numerous, also tended to be a church of the elite. But both these churches had declined in relative importance with the spread of the more democratic and emotional religious sects. Evangelical religion made sweeping advances during the early decades of the nineteenth century. The Methodists, utilizing itinerant lay preachers and making converts without regard to social status, made the most spectacular gains. Similar success in increasing membership was achieved by the Baptist and Presbyterian evangelists. So successful were various revivalist preachers in upstate New York that the region became permanently affected by fundamentalist Protestant doctrine. The evangelical sects, instead of upholding privileged orders and becoming bulwarks of aristocracy, tended to be equalitarian and humanitarian and to concern themselves with social problems such as intemperance and slavery.[9]

The American spirit of equality was infectious. Lower-class persons who in Europe did not dare to demand equal rights came to this country with the belief that here all men were free and on even terms, and that, provided they paid the same money, they were as important as any other member of society. When addressed by a commoner upon debarking from a ship in New York harbor, a gentleman complained to his friend that "this fellow here would not have dared to speak to us while on board of the packet; and now he is scarcely in sight of the American soil before he thinks himself just as good as anybody else." [10]

Even foreigners of relatively high social standing in their own countries who settled permanently in the United States often championed equality. A wealthy British gentleman residing in western New York wrote to a friend in England that "we have not more than one in a thousand [here] that retain the degrading principles of the old country; viz., that pride and conceit of being too good to sit at the same table, to eat and drink with their own servants, or those who labour for them." [11] Francis Grund, a German nobleman who emigrated to this country in the late 1820's, became a staunch supporter of political and social equality. In his book *Aristocracy in America* (1839) he ridiculed those Americans who abandoned republican principles and attempted to establish an aristocracy. "I can assure you," he wrote, "that in my own heart I have a much higher respect for the common American, who, in his conduct toward strangers, is solely guided by his own rude notion of dignity, than the *educated gentleman,* who

measures everything, and himself into the bargain, by
the standard of another country." [12]

II

In politics, as with social practices, a similar democratic
spirit prevailed. The victory of Andrew Jackson in the
presidential election of 1828 has generally been viewed
as the triumph of political democracy and the emergence
of the common man as the most significant political force.
America had long been a democracy in terms of voting
rights, but it was not completely so in terms of who was
elected. Most American leaders during the Revolutionary
period and the first decades of the New Republic were
men of the better sort, distinguishable from the ordinary
American by wealth, education, family tradition, dress,
and manners. But by the 1820's aristocratic rule was rapidly receding before the flood of democratic feelings. State
governments were the first to capitulate to the popular will
by introducing universal white manhood suffrage, a reform put into effect by every northern state except Rhode
Island by 1825.

In New York State democratic reform was long overdue
when a Constitutional Convention was convened in 1821
to revise the highly conservative constitution of 1777. The
1777 document had established a dual electorate. Twenty-
pound freeholders and 40-shilling renters could vote for
state assemblymen, but only £100 freeholders might vote
for senators and the governor. It has been estimated that
approximately 78 per cent of adult males could vote for
assemblymen, but only 38.7 per cent for the senators and
the governor. In New York City the percentage of eligible

voters had been even lower. There about 62 per cent of the adult males could qualify to vote for assemblymen, while a mere 24 per cent were eligible to vote for the senators and the governor.[13]

Besides restricting the suffrage, this antiquated constitution further removed the government from the people by providing for a five-man Council of Appointment, which designated persons to fill most of the state's public offices, and for a seven-member Council of Revision having the right to veto popular legislation. Both these councils had become the tools of the party in power and very often went against the will of the people. Popular sentiment had long favored reforms to change the undemocratic aspects of the outmoded constitution, and by 1820 this popular feeling was too strong for politicians to ignore. The split between the followers of Governor De Witt Clinton and the Tammany or Bucktail faction nominally led by Martin Van Buren played into the hands of the populace, since both factions were beginning to find it politically expedient to appear as their champions. Thus when the Constitutional Convention convened at Albany in late August 1821, most of the 126 delegates present favored some degree of amendment.

The elimination of the Council of Appointment and the Council of Revision was carried by unanimous vote. However, when it came to the question of removing property qualifications for voting, there developed what a recent historian has termed "one of the great suffrage debates in American history." [14] A small but distinguished group of old-style Federalists, led by the eloquent Chancellor of the state James Kent, steadfastly opposed further suffrage extension. They held that voting was a privilege and not a right, and that the chief functions of government were the protection of property and of individual freedom, not the forcing of the majority will on a reluctant minority. "The tendency of universal suffrage," stated Kent,

> is to jeopardize the rights of property and the principles of liberty. . . . There is a constant tendency in the poor to covet and to share the plunder of the rich; in the debtor to relax or avoid the obligations of contract; in the majority to tyrannize over the minority, and to trample down their rights. . . .

Kent went on to express the widely held Federalist view that, if universal male suffrage were granted, the cities with their large lower-class population would soon be able to rule the entire state. "New York is destined to be the future London of America, and in less than a century that city, with the operation of universal suffrage, and under skillful management will govern this state. . . ." [15]

In spite of these and other conservative arguments the forces of democracy carried the day. General Erastus Root, one of the leading spokesmen for reform, replied to Kent's aristocratic defense of property. "We have no different estates having different interests, necessary to be guarded from encroachments by the watchful eye of jealousy— We are all of the same estate—all commoners; nor, until we have privileged orders, and aristocratic estates to defend, can this argument apply." [16] This sentiment carried the convention. The vote was given to every white male citizen over twenty-one years of age who had resided one year within the state and six months within his district, and who paid taxes, or worked on the public roads, or served in the militia. The following year, 1822, the people showed their approval of the new democratic document by ratifying it with a majority of over 33,000 votes.[17]

Nor was this the end of political reforms in New York. Four years after the acceptance of the constitution the last restrictions on universal white manhood suffrage were removed; that same year, 1826, the office of justice of the peace was made elective. In 1828 New York voters for the first time voted directly for the presidential electors, and in doing this they expressed their democratic spirit by voting overwhelmingly for Jackson. The final important pre-Civil War democratic reforms were embodied in a new constitution which was approved in 1846. This document extended the earlier reforms. Most state offices were made elective; property qualifications for governer and state senator were abolished; a commission was established to simplify legal forms and judicial proceedings.

In city politics there was a similar trend toward democracy. New York voters won the right to elect their own mayor in 1833; six years later this privilege was extended to other cities within the state. The urban masses, just as James Kent and other old-line Federalists had feared, aggressively expressed their new political position. In 1837 an incident occurred in New York as symbolic of the triumph of the common man in city politics as the rowdy crowds at Jackson's inauguration are in national affairs. It was New Year's Day, and the democratically elected Mayor Cornelius Lawrence (himself a Democrat) was receiving callers in the fashionable New York tradition. What followed is here described by the disapproving aristocrat Philip Hone.

> Formerly gentlemen visited the mayor, saluted him by an honest shake of the hand, paid him the compliment of the day and took their leave. . . . But that respectable functionary is now considered the mayor of a party, and the rabble, considering him "hail fellow well met,"

use his house as a Five Points tavern. . . . The scene yesterday defies description. At ten o'clock the doors were beset by a crowd of importunate *sovereigns,* some of whom had already laid the foundations of *regal* glory, and expected to become *royally* drunk at the hospitable house of His Honor. The rush was tremendous; the tables were taken by storm, the bottles emptied in a moment. Confusion, noise, and quarreling ensued, until the mayor with the assistance of the police cleared the house and locked the doors. . . .[18]

By the 1830's New York, like most states, had become a constitutional democracy—persons had triumphed over property. But probably more important than the legal changes which democratized politics was the less tangible transformation of mode or temper which affected political life. Politics in this period became increasingly a question of creating a popular image and of flattering the common man. The self-made professional politician replaced the high-minded man of wealth as the typical political figure. In New York this new breed of politician was most influentially represented by the Democrat Martin Van Buren and the Anti-Mason and later Whig Thurlow Weed. These men depended for their success on highly disciplined party organizations which could gain wide popular support. Candidates were put up because of their broad appeal; parades, picnics, and fanfare became essential to political life; popular issues were seized upon and adopted as part of party platforms. All this created a new political atmosphere, in which a frontier military figure like Jackson could become a national hero, while a person with the stiff reticence of an Adams became a political anachronism.

Ironically, just when political parties came to play such

a significant role in American life their ideological differences became less important. From 1830 to the present no major American party has openly questioned the basic tenets of democracy. Even a conservative Whig journal admitted in 1836 that universal white male suffrage was unquestioned in America.[19] At a time when the English Chartists were considered extremely radical for advocating universal manhood suffrage, the ballot, a short Parliament and pay for its members, these things were considered indisputable here. Party divisions in the three decades prior to the Civil War occurred over particular issues such as protection versus free trade, states' rights versus a strong federal government, internal improvements, slavery, and immigration—but these issues were fought out within a broadly democratic framework. No aspiring politician after 1830 dared to oppose equal political rights, and henceforth all parties claimed to represent "the people." [20]

Special privilege was greatly weakened in the realm of politics by the triumph of democracy and the reliance on popular support by both major parties. No party was the organ of the "better" classes as the Tories were in England or as the Federalists had been to some measure in the first decades of the New Republic. Publicly, aristocracy was simply not recognized. To be labeled an "aristocrat" or even a "gentleman" became a political handicap, and upper-class persons were coming to realize that if they were to achieve public office and political power they must at least mouth the sacred shibboleths of democracy and cater to the will of the people.

This was best illustrated in the presidential election of 1840, when the Whig party, carefully guided by the New York political boss Thurlow Weed, ran the first truly modern campaign. Every attempt was made to depict the aging General William Henry Harrison, the hero of Tippecanoe who was descended from one of the first families of Virginia and who lived in a fine house along the Ohio, as a man of the people. Taking the Log Cabin and Hard Cider symbols from an anti-Whig article slurring Harrison, the Whigs used these to great effect. Cabins were erected, hard cider was served, and picnics, conventions, song fests, and other circus-like means were used to sell Harrison to the people. The main theme of the Whigs' attack on the Democratic incumbent Van Buren was that he was an aristocrat, living luxuriously in the White House at the people's expense. One campaign pamphlet, entitled "Regal Splendor of the President's Palace," pictured the President as eating French cuisine off gold plates while resting on a "Turkish divan." A popular Whig campaign song went:

> Let Van from his coolers of silver drink wine,
>   And lounge on his cushioned setee,
> Our man on a buckeye bench can recline,
>   Content with hard cider is he.[21]

This sort of campaigning was effective: the voting turnout was immense, and over 800,000 more votes were cast than in the 1836 election. Anti-aristocratic feeling, with a good deal of help from the depression of 1837, swamped Van Buren.

Dixon Wecter, the historian of American Society, called the 1830's the "low water-mark of official Society in America"—formal manners were in almost total eclipse. President Jackson provided his dinner guests with two forks, one silver and one steel—they could take their choice. Jackson himself preferred steel.[22] The President had become the chief symbol of the popular will, and if he was to retain his power he must act in accordance with the mandates of the people.

Numerous Americans of high social standing for the most part simply withdrew from politics altogether, disdaining to contend with the all powerful commoner-constituents. "At the present day," Tocqueville observed,

> the more affluent classes of society are so entirely removed from the direction of political affairs in the United States, that wealth, far from conferring a right to the exercise of power, is rather an obstacle than a means of attaining to it. The wealthy members of the community abandon the lists, through unwillingness to contend, and frequently to contend in vain, against the poorest classes of their fellow-citizens. They concentrate all their enjoyments in the privacy of their homes, where they occupy a rank which cannot be assumed in public; and they constitute a private society in the State, which has its own tastes and its own pleasures.

Unable to resist the forces of democracy by legitimate political means, wealthy citizens often became bitter and, as one contemporary wrote, "frankly expressed . . . their contempt for the government and institutions of America." [23]

III

This anti-political bias on the part of the well-to-do was not just sour grapes—as was true in the later Gilded Age —there were strong economic motives which kept enterprising persons away from politics. Far richer rewards were gained from commerce or industry. Furthermore, retaining political favor was precarious, and dependent on the whims of the capricious public. Holding high public office was not a guarantee that one would be considered of high social standing, whereas great wealth regardless of how gained, was virtually such a guarantee.

In his essay *People of Plenty,* David Potter maintains that political democracies depend for their success on the existence of an economic surplus and a wide distribution of goods. Without this, the promise of that equality which democracy implies would remain unfulfilled, since there would be little possibility of improving one's situation. America in the 1830's had economic abundance sufficient to make advancement seem not merely possible but also quite natural. The traveler Basil Hall noted that here "there is plenty of employment; so that, by the exercise of a moderate share of diligence, the young couple may swell their establishment to any extent they please. . . ." The most important single factor in shaping and sustaining American equality and democracy was this accessibility of wealth.[24]

Society in the Jacksonian era was optimistic and restless. Almost to a man Americans felt that the future would be better than the past, just as democracy was better than monarchy, and steam better than sail. Civilization was progressing and America was in the vanguard. This optimism was shown in energetic enterprises of a hundred kinds—from the reforming of drunkards to the laying of railroads. All was carried out with great haste—meals were gobbled with a rapidity that amazed (and disgusted) foreign visitors; great canals were dug through unpeopled wilds; huge hotels were constructed in towns that were little more than expectations. Behind all this seemingly ceaseless activity was the desire to improve one's position. "The first thing which strikes a traveller in the United

States," wrote Tocqueville, "is the innumerable multitude
of those who seek to throw off their original condition
. . . . No Americans are devoid of a yearning desire to
rise. . . ." [25] The average family had, or expected to have,
its own home; food, drink, clothing, and other necessities
were to be had in abundance. Men generally looked forward to becoming their own boss; women desired to have
servants; and both men and women expected that their
children would be better educated and better off financially than themselves.

Economic opportunity took many forms. One factor was
the abundance of cheap lands. In New York State, except
in the cities and along major rivers and the Erie Canal,
fertile lands were readily available at reasonable prices.
Land speculators had gained control of most of the unset-
tled lands in the western, central, and northern parts of the
state during the first two decades after Independence.
English, Dutch, and French capitalists as well as native
investors purchased sizable tracts, and in this way millions
of acres came under the control of relatively few land job-
bers. Hoping to profit by the rise in land values, these
speculators subdivided their tracts and often built roads,
mills, and schools in an attempt to attract settlers. However, few of the great land magnates realized the profits
they had expected. Some, like Robert Morris and Alexander
Macomb, two of the largest landholders, went bankrupt.
Other speculators, like the English syndicate headed by Sir
William Pulteney, barely got back their initial investments.
The conservative bankers of the Holland Land Company,
who controlled most of the far western part of the state,
realized about 5 per cent per year from their investment,
but they met considerable resistance from the debtor farmers who had settled on their lands. Finally in 1835, after a

mob had sacked one of the company offices, and debtors throughout the Holland purchase area had refused to pay their outstanding debts, these Dutch bankers sold their holdings.[26]

By the 1830's thousands of freehold farmers had come into possession of their own lands. Land speculators who retained large tracts were eager to sell parcels of property to bona fide settlers, and on many occasions generous credit terms were granted. The ready availability of land mitigated against the establishment of a landed aristocracy. Great rural estates were, of course, still extant, especially in the valleys of the Hudson and Mohawk rivers, but these were the exceptions. Most farmers were their own masters, and small farms worked by a single family, with perhaps the help of one or two hired hands, were the general rule.[27]

Farmers were sturdy and independent as American tradition would have them, but they were also conservative, poorly educated, overworked, underpaid, and living barely above subsistence level. During the second quarter of the nineteenth century farmers turned more to raising particular cash crops and, gradually, to improving agricultural techniques. The average farmer's profits nevertheless remained small. While more persons were engaged in agriculture than in any other occupation, many ambitious Americans began to turn to more rapidly rewarding occupations in the areas of commerce and manufacturing. Tocqueville noted this trend. "The cultivation of the ground," he wrote, "promises an almost certain result of his [the farmer's] exertions, but a slow one. . . . Agriculture is therefore only suited to those who have already large superfluous wealth, or to those whose penury bids them only seek a bare subsistence. . . . Thus democracy leads men to prefer one kind of labour to another; and whilst it diverts them from agriculture, it encourages their taste for commerce and manufactures." [28]

The completion of the Erie Canal in 1825 opened up new vistas to many New Yorkers. For some it was merely a better system for transporting goods to market, but to the imaginative and ambitious it was a stimulus to new enterprises. The canal, Levi Beardsley recalled, "enlarged the views, and removed many prejudices against internal improvements, so that men began to believe things possible which they did not fully comprehend. . . ." [29] The success of the canal and other innovations and improvements in transportation gave to the ordinary American a new optimism and spirit of enterprise. Society was in a state of flux, or, as it seemed to some contemporaries, in a state of chaos. All around them people saw examples of successful individuals who had amassed small fortunes through shrewd investments in commerce, manufacturing, real estate, or any number of other projects.

The times favored risk and gambling, and everyone was out to accumulate riches. "Americans," wrote a contemporary, "boast of their skill in money making; and as it is the only standard of dignity, and nobility, and worth . . . they endeavor to obtain it by every possible means." [30] Wealth was considered a sufficient enough end in itself to sanction various shady practices and even to praise these questionable acts as "sharp" dealings or as examples of "Yankee ingenuity." Wealth was a symbol of status in America, and while money was not the only criterion of social standing it was the most easily recognized.

It was largely the search for wealth that made Americans the most mobile people in the world. "In the United States," wrote Tocqueville, "a man builds a house to spend his latter years in it, and he sells it before the roof is on:

he plants a garden, and lets it just as the trees are coming into bearing: he brings a field into tillage, and leaves other men to gather the crops: he embraces a profession, and gives it up: he settles in a place, which he soon afterwards leaves to carry his changeable longings elsewhere." [31] America was an open society with an expanding economy. Distinctions of rank were not clear-cut, special legal privileges were uncommon, hereditary property was subdivided, and education and freedom were widely diffused. As a result the struggle for wealth was the dominating passion.

"Rags to riches" was not a fairy tale; it was an accepted truth. Poor-boy-made-good examples abounded. John Jacob Astor, probably the richest man in America, started out as an impoverished immigrant, while President Jackson's own career was an example of what could be accomplished by an energetic and enterprising American. The Jacksons and Astors of society were not thought of as extraordinary persons; they were merely examples of what *any* American could achieve with the right amounts of pluck and luck.

The availability of wealth and the common belief that anyone could succeed colored the American notion of equality. Poor persons often ranted against the "moneyed aristocracy" but seldom with class bitterness. Almost no one wanted to rid the nation of inequality by taking from the rich and giving to the poor; instead, people wanted the right to become rich themselves. Equality was not looked upon as a leveling process; it meant equality of opportunity in the race for riches. As one writer put it: "True republicanism requires that every man shall have an equal chance—that every man shall be free to become as unequal as he can." [32] Equality meant that all men could become gentlemen, not that all gentlemen would be eliminated. This gave Americans a dynamic view of class structure. There was a strong awareness of class in the Jacksonian era, but class levels were regarded as rungs to be climbed rather than as permanent ranks. This is why mobility and change were such important aspects of American life. Michael Chevalier noted that "in general, the American is little disposed to be contented, his idea of equality is to be inferior to none, but he endeavors to rise in only one direction. His only means, like his only thought is to subdue the material world. . . ." [33]

In the pursuit of wealth, unfortunately, failures were more frequent than fortunes, and for many the American dream of wealth became a nightmare of frustrated aspirations. Even successful individuals were goaded on by a mild discontent; few were satisfied with past accomplishments. In reflecting on American life a somewhat disaffected contemporary wrote that:

> Every one is tugging, trying, scheming to advance—to get ahead. It is a great scramble, in which all are troubled and none are satisfied. In Europe, the poor man, as a rule, knows that he must remain poor, and he submits to his lot, and tries to make the best of it. . . . Not so in America. Every other little ragged boy dreams of being President or millionaire. The dream may be a pleasant one while it lasts, but what of the disappointing reality? What of the excited, restless, feverish life spent in the pursuit of phantoms? [34]

Similarly, in reading Tocqueville's analysis of American society one recognizes the picture of an enterprising people who were extremely anxious, restless, impatient, and unstable. "Democratic institutions," he wrote, "awaken and foster a passion for equality which they can never entirely satisfy." People felt that they had the opportunity of rising to the level of their fellow citizens and they were disappointed by their failure to reach any "level." Like a mule

pursuing an outstretched carrot, Americans constantly
sought an equality which

> perpetually retires from before them, yet without hiding
> itself from their sight, and in retiring draws them on. At
> every moment they think they are about to grasp it; it
> escapes from their hold. They are near enough to see its
> charms, but too far off to enjoy them; and before they
> have fully tasted its delights, they die. . . . In demo-
> cratic ages enjoyments are more intense than in the ages
> of aristocracy, and especially the number of those who
> partake in them is larger: but, on the other hand, it
> must be admitted that man's hopes and his desires are
> oftener blasted, the soul is more stricken and perturbed,
> and care itself more keen.[35]

Success was not a fixed goal; it was advancement to a
higher level. Therefore, a person's achievement was meas-
ured less by what he possessed than by what he had gained.
Even the well-to-do individual who did not increase his
wealth at a reasonable rate often considered himself a failure, while the poor man who failed to progress could not
blame his bad fortune on society—he alone was at fault.

This stress on individual achievement ran counter to
the concept of equality, but in expanding Jacksonian
America "equality of opportunity" was the slogan that
seemingly reconciled these conflicting ideals. The dream of
rags to riches ("from log cabin to White House") meant, in
effect, unobstructed freedom of enterprise within a framework of democratic political rights. Each individual, it
was assumed, was at liberty to use his abilities to become
socially and economically unequal. Under these circumstances men of talent and drive advanced quickly to positions of wealth and power. Even in the egalitarian 'thirties
acute observers noted growing inequalities in American
society.[36]

2

LABOR IN JACKSONIAN NEW YORK

That our citizens are yearly departing from the simplicity of
our republican institutions, is a complaint made by many whose
opinions deserve attention, and is evinced by the increasing
arrogance of those termed the higher classes, and the servil-
ity of those denominated the lower, which must be evident to
all who are accustomed to observe what is passing around them.

—*The Working Man's Advocate*,
New York, February 20, 1830

LEISURE was a luxury in which few persons indulged in
Jacksonian America. Most men, including the wealthy,
made money by their own toil. Even gentlemen inheriting
sufficient wealth to live comfortably felt a compulsion to
engage in some sort of useful, and usually financially rewarding, enterprise. Work was not viewed as a bar to gentility. To be totally idle, on the other hand, was regarded
as being virtually outside of society. Because of this attitude labor was not looked on with scorn.[1]

Respect for labor in the early 1830's was conditioned by
the fact that this country up to that time had never had an
excess of workers. This scarcity of laborers meant that
workers received comparatively higher wages here than
workers in Europe. Numerous foreign travelers commented
on this fact. In 1830, S. H. Collins, an English author of
a guidebook for prospective emigrants to America, wrote

that the United States was the best country in the world for workers; here they would earn four or five times what they could in Europe. This was a highly exaggerated estimate, but it certainly was true that a worker was generally paid more here than in Britain or any other European country.[2]

Michael Chevalier on arriving in New York in 1833 was struck by the prosperous appearance of the laboring classes:

> The United States are certainly the land of promise for the worker and the peasant. What a contrast between our Europe and this America! After landing in New York, I thought every day was Sunday, for the whole population that throngs Broadway seemed to be arrayed in their Sunday's best. None of those countenances ghastly with the privations or the foul air of Paris; nothing like our wretched scavengers, our ragmen, and corresponding classes of the other sex. Every man was warmly clad in an outer garment; every woman had her cloak and bonnet of the latest Paris fashion.

Chevalier went on to relate the story of an Irishman, recently arrived in America, who showed his employer a letter he had just written to his family. On reading it the employer exclaimed, "But, Patrick, why do you say that you have meat three times a week, when you have it three times a day?" "Why?" replied Pat, "because if I told them that, they would never believe me." [3]

Other Europeans gave similar testimony. John Parks, an English immigrant working as an apprentice carpenter in New York, wrote in the late 'twenties that "the labouring people live by the best of provisions; *there is no such thing as a poor industrious man in New York.*" "Mechanics of all kinds in this country," observed an Irish gentleman, "would do remarkably well." [4]

Comparatively speaking, foreign observers found that farm workers also fared better in the New World than in the Old. Contrasting the conditions under which farm hands worked in England and New York State in the late 'thirties, James Silk Buckingham found that the latter had all the advantages. New York farm laborers earned nearly a dollar per day, half again as much as their English counterparts. They paid no tithes; they were not harassed by game laws; they had the advantage of accessible schools for their children; they lived in much more substantial cottages. "The consequence is, that the farm-labourers and their families are all well-fed, well-dressed, well-educated in all the ordinary elements of knowledge, intelligent in conversation, agreeable in manners, and as superior to the corresponding class of farm-labourers in England as all these advantages can indicate." [5]

The lack of beggars, thieves, and persons on poor relief in the towns and cities of America also impressed foreign visitors familiar with the impoverished classes of Europe. An English immigrant residing in a western New York village wrote in 1828: "I have been *poor master* of this town for many years, and I find it is a rare thing for a resident to become an annual town charge. In the circle of my acquaintance I know of no one who takes the trouble of locking or barring their doors by night, for thieving is so uncommon that they think it entirely useless and unnecessary." [6]

The accounts of foreign travelers attest that working conditions in Jacksonian America were better than in Europe. However, even the most thorough of these analyses tend toward superficiality and overgeneralization. In discussing working conditions foreign authors shed light upon the broad differences between Europe and America, but they do not adequately treat the position of the American worker in relation to other classes of society. By the 1830's class lines were already tightening, while working conditions were worsening in the face of economic changes that were radically altering American society.

II

Before examining what working conditions actually existed in Jacksonian New York it is necessary to analyze the groups composing the working classes. Workers themselves in the period made a broad distinction between the "productive" and the "nonproductive" classes. The productive classes included all those whose work had tangible utility, or, in the words of the New York Working Men's party, "all that support society by useful employment." The term "workingmen" was used synonymously with "productive" classes, and was applied to small merchants, clerks, and subprofessionals as well as to common laborers. A more particular term current during the 'thirties (and indeed during the next two decades) was that of "mechanic." It generally referred to skilled artisans working at a craft within the apprenticeship system. Capitalists, speculators, bankers, lawyers, importers and exporters, auctioneers, absentee owners, political enemies, and others more or less removed from direct manufacture composed, in the eyes of the workers, the nonproductive classes. In some respects these broad divisions separated labor from capital. But this separation was never too sharply drawn in Jacksonian New York. Workers, especially the skilled artisans or mechanics, did not like to think of themselves as a distinct class.[7]

In 1830 the percentage of wage workers was small, and few of those in this category intended to remain there.

The English factory system with its clear-cut division between employer and employee was in its infancy in America. Only in the cotton textile industry was this system well established. Those making up the bulk of the wage workers included unskilled laborers (largely immigrants employed at heavy digging or construction work), farm hands, domestic servants, women working either in their homes or in small factories, and skilled mechanics employed by master craftsmen. These workers, with the possible exception of some unskilled laborers, looked forward to an independent status as farm owners, shopkeepers, master craftsmen employing their own workers, or, if women, to becoming the wives of successful men.[8]

Not all wage workers, of course, were able to realize this ambition of achieving an independent station. This became increasingly true as transportation improved, industry expanded, and a permanent wage-earning class developed. Working conditions were worst at this time for unskilled laborers and for factory operatives, a category which in New York State included many women and children. However, the first major awakening of workers to their special class interests, occurring in the late 1820's, did not come as a reaction to the factory system. The labor movements arose primarily as a protest by skilled mechanics against economic changes that threatened their position in society.

Traditionally, the apprenticeship system in which skilled mechanics were employed allowed for a good deal of vertical mobility. The various ranks from apprentice through journeyman to master were like rungs of a ladder to be climbed by the ambitious artisan. For this reason there was not a sharp split between the employees and their employers. The first unions, or "trade associations" as they were commonly called, reflected this closeness. Organizations of artisans such as printers, bakers, tailors, cobblers, cordwainers, and carpenters flourished in New York and other cities and towns during the late eighteenth and early nineteenth centuries. They often represented both journeymen and masters, and their functions included paying accident, sickness, and death benefits, promoting inventions and improvements, assisting young journeymen to become independent producers through loans, setting wages and prices, and adjudicating in disputes between members. In short, a trade association was similar to a medieval guild, acting as a benevolent organization and as a regulatory power. Workers within this craft system did not think of themselves as mere wage earners. They sold a product, not their labor. The concept of a fair price and a fair wage prevailed. Generally masters and journeymen worked in the same small shop producing goods ordered for the local market.[9]

After the mid-1820's, however, new forces were breaking down this harmonious system, much to the detriment of the artisan's position. The revolutionary improvements in transportation, the growth of cities, and the enlargement of credit economically changed America. Canals, turnpikes, and later railways united the rapidly growing population, creating large markets for manufactured goods. The small craft shop of a master and his two or three journeymen and apprentices could no longer adequately supply this type of market. To meet new needs industries expanded and came more under the control of the middleman—the merchant-capitalist.

The heyday of the merchant-capitalist occurred during the transition from the era of handicraft and domestic production for a limited clientele to the full-scale factory system mass-producing goods for broad distribution. The dates of this shift vary from industry to industry. In some enterprises, such as textiles, the factory system was dominant by the 1830's, whereas in the manufacture of clothing the factory did not surpass the output of tailors until the early 1850's. But generally speaking, in New York the shift from handicraft to factory production took place in the two decades from the mid-1820's to the mid-1840's, and in this period the merchant-capitalist thrived.[10]

Essentially he was a middleman combining several functions. He bought and sold; he dealt with cash and credit. His chief interest was making money. He seldom owned a shop or a mill in which artisans were employed. He distributed raw materials and bought back the finished products. These in turn would be distributed and sold over an extensive area. To make his profit the merchant-capitalist depended on purchasing goods at the lowest price possible and selling them cheaply but in quantity.[11]

The effect of these middlemen on the apprenticeship system was to make the skill of the journeyman less important and to make him less independent. Master craftsmen, owning their own shops, no longer made goods to order for a local market. To survive they were forced to sell directly to a merchant-capitalist at the latter's price. The merchant, who was himself often engaged in cutthroat competition with other capitalists, bought wherever goods were cheapest. Thus, to sell a product the local employer had to price his goods as low as any rival. Numerous tactics were used to decrease production costs, all of which were injurious to the interests of skilled workers. One method of reducing costs was to encourage piece work. Instead of manufacturing an entire product such as a shoe or a table, several workers would be employed to do particular tasks. One might cut a leather pattern or a table leg. Another would sew or sand or nail. In this way production was speeded up while expenses were greatly reduced.

Another cost-reducing practice hurtful to the trained mechanic was the hiring of less skilled, and therefore cheaper, workers. This was possible since performing piece work did not require highly trained artisans. Employers began using the cheapest available labor sources—children, women, prisoners, recent immigrants, and unskilled laborers. Journeymen were no longer paid for the product they made; rather they received a daily wage. If they organized and demanded higher pay, they were often dismissed. One practice employers used was to take on numerous apprentices and then drop them at the stage when they would normally have become journeymen at a higher salary.

Under these pressures the apprenticeship system deteriorated. The growing power of the merchant-capitalist to control markets and set prices drove a wedge between masters and journeymen, employers and employees. The master was compelled in many instances to become a virtual sweatshop operator since his only profit was the difference between the price he received from the capitalist and that which he paid his workers. Those masters who attempted to maintain the old system and wages were soon forced out of business.

Skilled artisans reacted angrily to what they considered to be infringements of their rights. Pushed into the position of mere wage workers selling their labor and not a product, they became aware that their interests were antagonistic to those of their employers. As early as 1817, the New York printers' society expelled a master on the grounds that "this society is a society of *journeymen* printers; and as the interests of the journeymen are *separate* and in some respects *opposite* to those of the employers, we deem it improper that they should have any voice or influence in our deliberations." [12]

By 1830 the split between labor and capital had become more recognizable. The pro-labor New York *Evening Journal*, February 18, 1830, attacked the "monopolists and capitalists" who usurped the rights of mechanics, "abridging their privileges by opposing them in their business with the advantage of a large capital." The article went on to assail the practice of hiring unskilled cheap labor, stating that "men who are no mechanics . . . are engaged in mechanical concerns . . . at the expense of the interest of the legitimate mechanics; and in many cases, preventing the industrious, enterprising, but perhaps indigent mechanic, from following his trade to advantage, or from following it at all." This editorial concluded with a defense of the apprenticeship system and the concept of advancement traditionally associated with it. "The ideas of an apprentice are constantly buoyed up by the prospect, not only of being franchised from his indentures, but by a desire to become a proprietor himself; which is . . . necessary alike to master and apprentice, for it increases and strengthens the appetite to become . . . adept, and gives a zest to all his efforts."

In the labor or pro-labor writings of the late 1820's and the 1830's an increasingly defensive attitude is discernible. Wage workers felt somehow that they were not highly esteemed and that their social status was waning. "Who is most respected, who is considered as belonging to the higher class?" asked the friend of labor, Orestes Brownson. "He who labors most and is most useful? No. Under the present order of things to be respectable you must be idle or be able to live upon the vices or misfortunes of others." [13] A writer for the *Evening Journal* bemoaned that "although the Mechanics are the most useful and powerful body of men in the community, and . . . as respectable as any other class, they are . . . considered in many points inferior. . . . Is it a stain upon the character to gain an honest livelihood by useful industry? . . . There are more real gentlemen among this than any other class." [14] This feeling on the part of mechanics that their social status was waning gave great impetus to the labor movements of the late 1820's and the 1830's.

The trade associations formed by skilled mechanics in the 'twenties reflected the growing gap between capital and labor. In New York City and in many of the smaller towns within the state, stable trade organizations were formed among printers, cabinetmakers, carpenters, hatters, tailors, shoemakers, and others. These societies retained many of the mutual aid features of the earlier craft unions, but the major emphasis shifted to direct economic action. More and more these skilled workers attempted to maintain and improve their position through such weapons as strikes and boycotts.[15]

One of the most persistent of mechanics' demands was for a shorter work week. The standard day of labor at this time was the traditional one of sunrise to sunset. This system, which had been taken over from agriculture, was baneful to industrial laborers. Workers were aware that some free time was necessary if they were to advance in society. A group of mechanics stated in 1835: "We have been too long subjected to the odious, cruel, unjust, and tyrannical system which compels the operative Mechanic to exhaust his physical and mental powers by excessive toil, until he has no desire but to eat and sleep, and in many

cases he has no power to do either from extreme debility."
Naturally the work day was relatively short in winter since
there were fewer hours of daylight. But wages were paid
on a daily rate regardless of the season of year. Therefore,
employers found it advantageous to get as much work
as possible done in the spring, summer, and fall. During
these seasons the average work day was from 12 to 15 hours.
Not only was this a great strain on workers, but the system
also made it economically advantageous for employers to
lay off workers in the winter when not as much work could
be obtained for the same wages.[16]

Another frequent labor protest was against imprisonment for debt. In 1830 the number of persons annually imprisoned in New York State for this offense was estimated
at 10,000. Some were in prison for debts as small as twenty-
five cents. In 1829 George Evans, the editor of *The Working Man's Advocate,* assessed the number of persons in
prison for debts of five dollars or less in New York City
alone at nearly a thousand.[17] Debtors' prisons were noto-
riously overcrowded and unsanitary; no provision was made
for food, clothing, bedding, or other necessities, except
through charity.

In addition to these demands, the workingmen's movement persistently advocated free public education. This
reform measure was closely associated with the desire of
workers to improve their standing, or at least that of their
children. New York State had what amounted to two school
systems: private schools for the children of parents who
could afford to pay tuition, and charity schools for all
others. Schooling was not compulsory and thousands of
children received no formal education. In 1829 the Public
School Society of New York estimated that 24,000 city
children between the ages of five and fifteen were not en-

rolled in any school. As late as 1833, the number of children in that age group not in school in the entire state was estimated to be 80,000. The worst aspect of New York's education laws was that free education at the charity schools was granted only if the parents of a child signed a pauper's oath. Many poor parents, being too proud to sign this socially degrading oath, kept their children at home.[18]

The struggle for free public education was consciously aimed at aiding equality of opportunity. The Rochester *Spirit of the Age* blamed the "aristocracy of wealth" for opposing "a *general system of education,* by which the children of the poor would alike be enabled to enter life, *equal* in all respects. . . ." [19] A meeting of "Mechanics and other Working Men" held in New York in December 1829 drew up a pamphlet calling for a system of education "that shall unite under the same roof the children of the poor man and the rich, the widow's charge and the orphan, where the road to distinction shall be superior industry, virtue and acquirements, without reference to descent." "We believe," the pamphlet continued, "that our existing system of education, if continued, under which many are deprived of all or nearly all its advantages, and which tends in a greater or less degree to separate the children of the poor man and the rich, will eventually lead us into all the distinctions that exist under despotic governments, and destroy our political liberties." [20]

The New York State militia system also came in for strong criticism by organized workers. Like the educational arrangements the militia system was harder on the poor than on the rich. The law called for periodic drills and parades at which all males of militia age were required to attend. These lasted anywhere from one to three days, during which time the worker lost his wages. Furthermore, participants were expected to provide their own arms and other equipment, imposing an additional financial burden on those least able to pay. Nonattendance was punished by a fine or, if one was unable to pay that, by imprisonment. In New York the wealthier classes generally chose to pay the fine, which was twelve dollars, rather than attend. "It is high time," the *Mechanics' Press* editorialized, "that this expensive and useless mock of pageantry and parade was done away. For our own part we never *could* see what peculiar advantage there was to peaceful citizens, in perambulating dusty streets, sweating under a musket or performing a hundred *mere showy* evolutions that are seldom if ever necessary in actual warfare, to the great detriment of their business and loss of time, which can ill be spared from the working man's necessary avocations." [21]

Workers were also hurt by the fluctuating values of paper currency. It was not uncommon for employers to buy discounted bank notes with which they paid their employees. Laborers had to accept this currency at face value, even though some notes were discounted as much as 50 per cent or were totally unnegotiable. In manufacturing towns workers were frequently paid in tickets redeemable only at stores owned and operated by the employer, where the prices were generally higher than elsewhere.[22] These factors helped cause the widespread hatred of paper money and banks among workers.

The enmity workers felt for banks was linked with a more general distrust of any privileged institution. Banks were a form of chartered monopoly accorded special legal privileges by state law in the case of those banks chartered by the New York Assembly, or by federal law in the case of the Second Bank of the United States. Workers and other classes not directly benefited by banks attacked these institutions as impediments to economic equality. Other chartered corporations were similarly opposed as monopolies whose "all exclusive privileges, or powers, or facilities, for the accumulation of wealth, or the exclusive use and enjoyment of the bounties of Providence secured to individuals or combinations of men by legislative enactments, the free and uninterrupted enjoyment of which are denied by laws to other members of the same community." [23]

These general reforms which mechanics felt would bring them the benefits of equal citizenship had not been achieved through trade union activity in the 'twenties. Unions had been blocked by employer associations using such methods as black-listing, physical force, and, most effectively, court action. English common law traditionally held that whenever two or more persons conspired to do something jointly, even when an individual was entitled to take such an action, the public interest was endangered and therefore the action was an illegal conspiracy. This common-law definition of conspiracy was applied by American courts to mean that any combination of workers who aimed to raise their wages or shorten their hours through united action was illegal. In the 1820's six conspiracy trials are recorded, including one against the New York hatters in 1823 and one against the Buffalo tailors in 1824. All these cases were decided in favor of the employers.[24]

In this light it was natural that skilled workers, many of whom were newly enfranchised, turned in the late 'twenties to direct political action. A strike of building trade workers in Philadelphia for a ten-hour day led to the formation of a general Mechanics Union of Trade Associations in 1827, the first city-wide combination of unions. Subsequently this group formed the Working Men's Labor party, which in 1828 made considerable local gains. The success

of the Philadelphia Labor party, together with depressed
economic conditions, stimulated New York City mechanics
to organize politically in 1829.

Led by Thomas Skidmore, a machinist and radical labor
spokesman, New York workers held several mass meetings
in the spring of that year. A Committee of Fifty was ap-
pointed to assist mechanics in achieving a standard ten-
hour work day. Skidmore and the Committee also turned
to broader political issues. Believing that society's evils
stemmed from unequal division of property, Skidmore drew
up a plan calling for equal land distribution.[25] At a general
gathering of workingmen in October 1829, Skidmore's
plan was not enthusiastically received; however, a separate
recommendation calling for independent political action
was heartily endorsed. A State Assembly slate was nomi-
nated and the new New York Working Men's party began
a vigorous two-week campaign for the November election.
The Tammany and Masonic newspapers denounced the
"Workies" as atheists, infidels, agrarians, and foreign rabble, but the election results were highly encouraging for
members of this inexperienced party. One candidate, a
carpenter named Ebenezer Ford, was elected to the Assembly, and every other candidate on the slate made a
respectable showing, receiving at least 6000 of the 21,000
votes cast.[26]

Early in 1830 the workingmen's movement spread
throughout upstate New York. Organizations of "farmers,
mechanics, and workingmen" won local elections at Albany,
Troy, Syracuse, and Canandaigua that spring. Workers'
parties were also active in Schenectady, Rochester, Ithaca,
Auburn, Geneva, Batavia, Palmyra, Utica, Kingsbury, and
Glens Falls. In August 1830 a state convention representing
most of New York's mechanics' parties met in Syracuse to

nominate a candidate for governor and other state offices.[27]

In spite of the rapid spread of the workingmen's movement in the state, labor parties were on the decline before the 1830 convention met. The New York City party from the beginning had been plagued by doctrinal disputes which split the party. Skidmore's scheme for equal distribution of property had not met with general approval. As a result he and a handful of followers seceded, forming the Equal Rights party, and thereby weakening labor's unity. A second splintering occurred over labor's education plank. One faction headed by Robert Dale Owen, son of the English reformer, and George Henry Evans, the editor of *The Working Man's Advocate,* championed a system of "state guardianship," in which all children would be placed in state boarding schools and given equal education, dress, and housing at public expense. Repelled by the extremes of the Owenite program, a third faction headed by Noah Cook and Henry G. Guyon separated and formed still another party.[28]

When the state convention met in Syracuse the dissension within the New York City party proved disastrous. Rival delegations attended the meeting, and professional politicians of the major parties, taking advantage of the dissidence, were able to win most of the workers' support by pledging to back many of labor's aims. During the next two years workingmen's parties remained active in New York, but their vote dwindled, and most workers virtually gave up the idea of independent political action.

The failure of labor to organize a politically successful third party is significant. Workers had no real basis for the establishment of such a party since class lines were not clearly drawn. Laborers still did not think of themselves as a separate class, especially the skilled artisans who made up the majority of organized labor. They considered themselves as broadly democratic, opposed only to the few aristocrats who held work in contempt. Their aims were to increase the dignity and status of toil as much as to improve actual working conditions. Many members of the New York Working Men's party resented the scornful denunciations heaped upon them by "respectable" politicians and journalists. Such epithets as "levelers," "Dirty Shirt party," "mob," and "ring-streaked and speckled rabble" implied a permanent lower-class position which few workers were willing to accept. The membership of the Working Men's party, although chiefly drawn from the ranks of craft workers, represented a wide segment of society from unskilled laborers to professional people. The single characteristic most common to members was the desire to get ahead—to gain greater equality of opportunity and thus to be able to participate more fully in American prosperity. Walter Hugins, the historian of the New York Working Men's party, concluded after studying the biographies of fifty New York labor leaders that none of these men considered himself to be part of a permanent working class. "Disparate and diverse as their origins and careers might be, they seemed to share the desire for change, a striving for self-improvement." [29]

The rejection by workingmen of radical panaceas such as Skidmore's plan for equal division of property similarly attests to the basically middle-class attitudes of most organized workers. This measure ran counter to the fundamental aim of mechanics which was to acquire property and wealth. As the General Executive Committee of the Working Men's party declared, "we expect the reward of our toil, and consider the right to individual property, the strongest incentive to industry." [30]

Workers formed unions and political parties early in the Jacksonian era largely as a reaction to the altering economic situation which adversely affected their social status. They felt that opportunities were being closed to them, and organized in an attempt to make the American ideal of social and economic advancement more of an actuality. The major demands of labor—the ten-hour day, free public education, abolition of imprisonment for debt, reform of the militia system, elimination of special privileges and monopolies, and reform of the banking system—were not exclusively for the benefit of the working class. These objectives had broad popular support in Jacksonian America. They helped skilled workers, small shopkeepers and businessmen, professional persons, and most individuals not directly benefited by some special privilege. Numerous grievances against vested interests existed and created wide support to the reform measures initiated by organized labor. The keynote of labor's demands was not a proletarian hatred of capitalist society, but the desire for an equal chance to share the fruits of capitalism.

That labor's demands were not strictly those of a single class is illustrated by the fact that several worker-supported measures won broad backing, were taken up by the two major parties, and were adopted during the Jacksonian era. While the Working Men's party was campaigning in 1830, for example, the Tammany Democrats threw their support behind the workers' demand to abolish imprisonment for debt. Two years later the New York State legislature enacted this reform. Abolition of the militia system followed more slowly; in 1830 a New York State bill aimed at reducing the time spent in militia training from two whole days to one afternoon, failed of passage. In 1836, however, the New York legislature, with two-party support,

overwhelmingly passed a measure which reduced the fine
for nonappearance at drill to a token sum. In practice this
put militia drill on a voluntary basis.[31]

The workers' demand for a standard ten-hour day, supported by both unions and the workingmen's political
movement, met with some success in the skilled trades. As
early as 1829, New York City's mechanics won the shorter
day. In 1835, after a series of bitter strikes by artisans
in such upstate cities as Albany, Troy, Schenectady, Batavia
and Seneca Falls, the ten-hour day was more generally
established. However, unlike other gains, the ten-hour day
was not enacted into law, and for the majority of wage
workers there were longer hours throughout the 1830's.[32]

Labor demands for free public education made steady
progress in New York, winning a much wider base of support than the ten-hour program. This movement was in
accord with the reform spirit of the age—which led to the
establishment of free public schools in New England, in
Pennsylvania, in New Jersey and in Ohio during the
'thirties—and humanitarians joined with workers in attempting to improve the educational system. Although
educational schemes were hotly debated throughout the
'thirties, a genuine free public school system was not
established until 1842 in New York City, and not until
1849 elsewhere in the state.

The crusade against monopoly and privileged banking
institutions became a national crusade centered in the
Democratic party, and leading to the defeat of the "Mon-
ster" Bank of the United States. In New York State the
circulation of notes valued at less than five dollars was
outlawed in 1836. Two years later, with Whig support,
New York enacted the nation's first free banking law,
removing banks from the realm of chartered monopolies.

These measures were a triumph for the workingman as well as a general advance for free enterprise.

III

Despite the genuine gains for democracy brought about at least in part by the workingmen's movement, workers continued to feel that their social and economic status was declining. Achievements such as the abolishment of imprisonment for debt and the ending of compulsory militia service, although helpful, did not offset the over-all economic changes which were reducing formerly independent craftsmen to the level of wage earners. Because of this, trade union activity, which had declined while labor was active in politics, revived in the early 'thirties. Mechanics took up the struggle with employers in a more militant fashion than ever before.

Far more than earlier movements the struggle of the 'thirties centered on the economic interest of workers as opposed to their employers. "The time has now arrived," declared the leader of the New York Typographical Association in 1833, "for the mechanics of our city to arise in their strength and determine that they will no longer submit to the thraldom which they have patiently borne for many years, nor suffer employers to appropriate an undue share of the avails of the labourer to his disadvantage." [33]

Inflation, which accompanied the return of prosperity in the 'thirties, was also an important factor contributing to renewed trade union activity. The period from 1832 to 1837 was one of unprecedented speculation accompanied by an extravagant rise of prices. Jackson's veto of the bank bill and his subsequent withdrawal of funds from the Second National Bank, as well as Bank President Biddle's

questionable behavior, helped unleash an inflationary
spiral. One hundred and ninety-four new banks were
founded between 1834 and 1837; the amount of money in
circulation rose by more than 75 per cent. From 1834 to
1836 the cost of living soared an estimated 66 per cent.
For example, flour rose during this period from five dollars a barrel to twelve dollars. Real estate values increased
by more than 220 per cent, and rents advanced accordingly.
The excess of paper currency issued by banks drove specie
out of circulation. Workers were forced to accept at face
value paper bills which could only be spent at a discount.
The smaller notes, with which workers largely dealt, were
the most questionable. Labor newspapers complained
against this "fictitious capital" that robbed workers and
created an "indolent aristocracy." [34] Wages did not keep
pace with this inflationary spiral, and many workers were
reduced to poverty.

Trade associations were revived in all the formally
organized crafts during the period from 1832 to 1837, and
numerous additional trades were unionized for the first
time, including New York cabinetmakers and silk hatters.
Nor was it only skilled workers who organized at this time.
Unions were formed among all classes of workers. In New
York there appeared the Ladies' Shoebinders and the Female Union Association. Elsewhere in the city and upstate
unskilled factory workers took the initial steps toward
unionization.[35]

The rapid multiplication of trade societies led quite
naturally to attempts to broaden and unite the entire labor
movement. New York City workers paved the way for
closer co-operation between unions by organizing in 1833
the General Trades' Union, a city-wide federation of unions. By 1836, fifty-two trade societies were associated with

this General Union. In Albany, Troy, Schenectady, and other upstate cities similar central trades' councils were formed. A beginning was even made in the establishment of a national labor movement. In 1834 representatives of trade societies from New York, Brooklyn, Philadelphia, Boston, Poughkeepsie, and Newark met in Manhattan and organized the National Trades' Union, which hoped to aid in founding unions throughout the country and to promote the general welfare of the laboring classes. However, labor's interests were still too local and their organization too loose to permit an effective national movement, and the National Trades' Union never amounted to much.[36]

Nevertheless, organized labor was extremely active and vigorous in the mid-1830's. In the country as a whole there were more than two hundred active trade associations, with membership estimated at anywhere from 100,000 to 300,000. In New York more than two-thirds of the city's workers were said to be union members. The chief weapon of labor at this time was the strike. Contemporary accounts record over 160 such work stoppages between 1833 and 1837, most of which were for higher wages.[37]

But, as in the 'twenties, employers also organized to curb the power of labor. In New York employers of curriers and leather workers mutually agreed not to employ "any man who is known to be a member of . . . any society which has for its object the direction of terms or prices for which workmen shall engage themselves." [38] By 1836 there were at least eight such employers' associations in the city. Black-listing of union members was the most common means used against labor. But the conservative courts, as previously, proved to be the employers' greatest ally.

In 1829 the New York State Assembly passed a statute

making it a conspiracy "to commit any act injurious to
public morals or to trade or commerce." At the time this
was not aimed specifically against organized workers, but
by interpretation it became the employers' strongest
weapon against the trades' unions. The first use of this
law was in the Geneva shoemakers' case of 1835. Journeymen shoemakers had organized there and adopted a wage
scale, agreeing not to work for less, and not to work in the
same shop with anyone who did. The shoemakers struck
a shop employing a man at a lower wage, and the master
had the workers indicted under the 1829 statute. The
case went to the State Supreme Court, where the shoemakers were found guilty of conspiracy, since their action
was "injurious to trade or commerce." The decision went
on to imply that it was illegal to combine to raise wages.
The precedent established by this decision seemed to
leave organized labor in New York State virtually power-
less.[39]

Following the case against the Geneva shoemakers, employers of striking journeymen tailors in New York had
twenty pickets arrested for conspiracy. As in the shoemakers' trial, the tailors were found guilty. Ogden Edwards,
the presiding judge, stigmatized trades' unions as "illegal
combinations." This decision outraged New York workers, and in the week that elapsed between the verdict and
the sentence preparations were made for massive protests.
A leaflet decorated with coffins which called on workingmen to attend court on the day the tailors were to be sen-
tenced was circulated. "On Monday, June 6, 1836, these
Freemen are to receive their sentence, to gratify the hellish
appetites of the Aristocracy. On Monday, the Liberty of
the Workingmen will be interred! Judge Edwards is to
chant the Requiem! Go! Go! Go! every Freeman, every

Workingman, and hear the melancholy sound of the earth on the Coffin of Equality!" The appeal of the unionists was stated in distinctly class-conscious terms. The circular went on to proclaim:

> The *Rich* Against the *Poor*
> Judge Edwards, the tool of the aristocracy, against the people! Mechanics and Workingmen! A deadly blow has been struck at your Liberty! . . . The Freemen of the North are now on the level with the slaves of the South! With no other privileges than laboring, that drones may fatten on your life-blood!

The courtroom was filled to overflowing when sentence was pronounced against the tailors; a week later a mass meeting of workingmen drew over 27,000 persons to City Hall Park, where Judge Edwards was burned in effigy.[40]

The reaction against the decision in the Tailors' Case was so strong that it probably influenced subsequent decisions in which unions were involved. At any rate, less than three weeks after the Tailors' Case decision, Hudson shoemakers who had been enforcing a closed shop were found not guilty of conspiracy. And in a famous Massachusetts Supreme Court decision of 1840 (Commonwealth *v.* Hunt), Chief Justice Lemuel Shaw declared trade unions to be legal organizations. This Massachusetts decision soon established a precedent in New York and most other states.

Well before Judge Shaw rendered his precedent-setting decision, however, trade unions had virtually ceased to exist. In 1837 the prosperous conditions that buoyed up the labor movement came to an abrupt end. Speculation, over-expansion, and other questionable economic practices punctured the bubble of prosperity, with the result that prices plummeted and business stagnated. Hard times swept the nation as Americans experienced the most severe depression they had yet known. For laborers, wage reductions or unemployment became the general rule. Forced to choose between starving or working for a pittance, most workers decided on the latter. Unions were abandoned out of fear of employer retaliation, and all but a handful of the trade associations folded up, along with the city-wide federations and the labor papers.[41]

The gains of the labor movement of the late 'twenties and 'thirties proved at best to be only a temporary check against labor's weakening position. Its long-range reforms and immediate specific gains in terms of wages and hours were illusory and, in many cases, short-lived victories. Skilled workers were fighting a losing battle against the major economic forces of the industrial revolution which rapidly made many of the traditional trades obsolete.

IV

The labor movement had aimed primarily at improving the position of skilled craftsmen working in the apprenticeship system. This system was collapsing, and the mechanic was being reduced to the level of a wage worker. However, the condition of the skilled artisan was actually much better than that of the growing number of unskilled laborers. It remains to examine the conditions under which the noncraft workers toiled in the Jacksonian period.

By 1830 less than half of those designated as workingmen were accomplished artisans, and the proportion of noncraft labor grew yearly as factories and machines replaced handicraft shops and craftsmen. Working conditions for those not in the apprenticeship system were generally worse than those endured by journeymen—wages were lower, employment was less secure, and redress of grievances was nearly impossible. There was, in the words of the humanitarian Mathew Carey, a large class of laborers "whose services are so inadequately remunerated, owing to the excess of labour beyond the demand for it, that they can barely support themselves while in good health and fully employed, and, of course when sick or unemployed, must perish, unless relieved by charitable individuals, benevolent societies, or the guardians of the poor." [42]

The average city laborer, Carey estimated, earned about seventy-five cents per day or $4.50 a week. If he missed only eight weeks of work from want of employment or illness he would not earn enough to supply a family of four with even the barest necessities. Yet many of this class had much larger families and various emergency expenses. Their employment even more often than that of skilled workers was on a seasonal basis. For example, unskilled construction workers such as hod carriers were generally laid off in the winter and averaged less than 225 working days yearly. Even when winter employment was available, wages were lower since there was always an excess of labor. [43]

Perhaps the most oppressed workers were the Irish peasants and other unskilled laborers hired to do construction work on canals, turnpikes, and railroads. This toil was hard, low paying, unhealthy, and seasonal. In the wintertime workers able to find jobs rarely averaged more than five dollars a month; sometimes during that season men worked for board alone. The following description of canal work was given in 1833:

LIBRARY - Allegheny Campus

Thousands of our labouring people travel hundreds of miles in quest of employment on canals, at 62, 75, and 87 cents per day, paying a dollar and a half or two dollars a week for their board, leaving families behind, depending on them for support. They labour frequently in marshy grounds which destroys their health, often irrevocably. They return to their poor families—with ruined constitutions, with a sorry pittance, most laboriously earned, and take to their beds sick and unable to work. Hundreds are swept off annually, many of them leaving numerous and helpless families. Notwithstanding their wretched fate, their places are quickly supplied by others, although death stares them in the face.[44]

There were countless other laboring positions in which long hours, low pay, and deplorable conditions belied a land of opportunity. In the cities and towns many unskilled workers were needed for such tasks as loading and unloading boats and carts, carrying wood, coal, ice, and bricks, taking care of horses and stables, and performing sundry odd jobs. Some persons not only worked laboriously for poor pay, but also were socially degraded by their position; domestic servants, nurses, charwomen, laundresses, cooks, waiters, barbers, and coach-drivers were among those thus stigmatized. Some of the hardest conditions were to be found on ships. Sailors received better pay than unskilled laborers (about twenty-five dollars a month), but the harsh discipline and back-breaking work were, judging from contemporary accounts, all but unbearable.[45] Farm laborers received about ten dollars per month plus room and board, or a dollar per day without it, but were generally driven hard from sunrise to sunset.

For a woman needing employment because she was a widow or a spinster, or because her husband's earnings were insufficient, or because she was the daughter of impoverished parents, opportunities were rare. She could take in washing or sewing, do domestic work, open a boarding house, work in a factory, or become a prostitute. None of these options was very rewarding or inspiring. Women who did industrial work at home such as binding shoes or sewing pre-cut pantaloons averaged about ten cents per day. Housework paid better, but was considered socially debasing, besides requiring hard work and long hours. In New York City the ready-made clothing industry was highly organized. Sweatshop conditions were the rule. Carey calculated that seamstresses working a full week could on the average sew nine shirts. Prices paid for this work varied from six to ten cents per shirt, giving these women a wage of fifty-four to ninety cents a week "for the incessant application of a human body, during thirteen or fourteen hours a day, for the payment of rent, the purchase of food, clothes, drink, soap, candles and fuel!" [46] A New York doctor attributed the growth of prostitution in the city to the poor pay in the needle trades:

> My profession affords me many and unpleasant opportunities of knowing the wants of those unfortunate females, who try to earn an honest subsistence by the needle, and to witness the struggles often made by honest pride and destitution. *I could cite many instances of young and even middle-aged women, who have been "lost to virtue," apparently by no other cause than the lowness of wages, and* THE ABSOLUTE IMPOSSIBILITY OF PROCURING THE NECESSARIES OF LIFE BY HONEST INDUSTRY.[47]

The distress of the laboring classes was greatest during times of economic recession. This was particularly so in winter. Employment was scarce, wages were lower, and expenses higher. In New York, as Horace Greeley observed, "legions of laborers, servants, etc., are annually dismissed in Autumn from the farms, country-seats, and watering places of the suburban districts, and drift down to the city . . . vaguely hoping to find work here, which a small portion of them do: the rest live on the good-nature of relatives, if such they have here, or on credit from boarding-houses, landlords, or grocers, so long as they can; and then make their choice between roguery and beggary. . . ." [48]

Even summers sometimes brought unusual hardships. In the summer of 1832 and again in 1834, Asiatic cholera epidemics ravaged New York State, killing thousands, especially in overcrowded city areas. Mechanics and laborers were the most severely affected. Living generally in heavily populated slums or shanty towns, workers were susceptible to contagious diseases. Unlike the wealthier classes they could not afford to flee the cities for safer rural locations. Furthermore these epidemics brought business in New York City and elsewhere nearly to a standstill, throwing thousands out of work who ordinarily looked to the summer as a time of full employment. [49]

Well before the panic of 1837 plunged New York's working classes into an extended period of hard times, there were signs that changing economic conditions were creating permanent inequalities in New York society. The skilled worker, as has been shown, was losing ground socially and economically, while the position of the unskilled laborer was by any standard already abominable. The labor movement in both its unionist and political phases could not in the long run stay labor's decline. The revolutions in industry and transportation were transforming American life. It was becoming clearer every day that the Jeffersonian ideal of a nation composed of independent yeomen and craftsmen was not possible. Workers themselves were increasingly aware that the American ideal of equality was rapidly receding.

3

---◆•••◆---

MANORS AND COUNTING HOUSES

The great error into which nearly all foreigners and most Americans fall, who write or speak of society in this country, arises from confounding the political with the social system. In most countries, in England, France, and all those nations whose government is monarchial or aristocratic, these systems are indeed similar. . . . But in America the two systems are totally unconnected, and altogether different in character. In remodelling the form of the administration, society remained unrepublican. There is perfect freedom of political privilege, all are the same upon hustings, or at a political meeting; but this equality does not extend to the drawing-room. None are excluded from the highest councils of the nation, but it does not follow that all can enter into the highest ranks of society. In point of fact, we think that there is more exclusiveness in the society of this country, than there is in that even of England—far more than there is in France.

—*The Laws of Etiquette* (1836)

THE United States had no hereditary ranks and distinctions. Here there was no titled nobility possessing definite legal and social privileges. Government was democratic; there was no established church; laws of primogeniture and entail had long been abolished. Before the law all men, at least in theory, were equal, and the road to social and economic advancement was open to everyone.

However, American equality was that of legal rights and not a general condition of society. As Tocqueville wrote,

"I know of no country . . . where profounder contempt is expressed for the theory of permanent equality of property." Recognizable class distinctions existed in this country and were accepted by all ranks of society. The terms "lady" and "gentleman," for example, were used discriminately. A contemporary wrote, "The appellation of saleslady to a sales-woman would have been held as a joke, and would have been resented by the recipient of the term." In both the fictional and nonfictional writings of the period quite sharp class demarcations were taken for granted. Such class references as the following two selected at random from N. T. Hubbard's *Autobiography* were typical: "The General was highly respected by all classes of his fellow citizens"; or "Our company was composed of the best class of young men. . . ." It seems evident then that Americans recognized various social ranks. Classes could be distinguished by such factors as wealth, dress, speech, manners, education, and general way of life.[1]

The most important single criterion for high social standing was wealth. "The avarice of an American, in general," observed a Britisher, "is nothing more than the passion of ambition directed to the acquisition of wealth as the only means of attaining distinction in the state of society in which he is placed." Wealth has always been related to gentlemanliness. It provides a distinguishing feature in itself while at the same time bestowing on its possessor the leisure and means to cultivate social refinements. The lack of permanent hereditary distinctions made material success that much more important. This factor gave a mercantile tone to our best society which foreign gentlemen often derided. A German nobleman remarked sarcastically that by watching the manner in which an American lady curtsied to the gentlemen who were presented to her, one was "able to distinguish the capitalist from the poor beginner, or unsuccessful speculator, as effectually as if their property has been announced with their names. Every additional thousand produces a new smile." [2]

Historically, no aristocracy has rested on wealth alone. America was no exception. Family was an important consideration. In New York, well-known Hudson Valley families such as the Van Rensselaers, Livingstons, and Schuylers formed a landed gentry inheriting both property and position. Lesser landholders such as the Coopers of Cooperstown or the Peter Smiths of Peterboro were in a similar position. In New York City, family background was equally significant. Knickerbocker society was tightly knit. Its leading members were merchants, professional men, and literary people; some were well-to-do, others were not, but all were from respected families. This society, according to contemporaries, was very exclusive and difficult for a stranger to break into regardless of his wealth. [3]

The theoretical concept of aristocracy had been widely discussed during the early years after the Revolution. Class concepts had to be reconciled to the new democratic Republic. Federalists, fearing mob rule or anarchy, favored retaining the aristocratic element of society, believing that an hereditary elite was the best safeguard against the evils of democracy. Republicans opposed this view; Jefferson, their chief spokesman, attempted to weld aristocracy to democracy in his theory of a natural aristocracy based on talent and not birth. Aristocracy became a political issue, and with the triumph of the Jeffersonian Republicans the basis for gentlemanliness was theoretically broadened. Based on natural selection it was no longer the hoarded property of a single class. Federalism withered, and with it the concept of a hereditary upper class suffered a setback.

But side by side with the notion of an aristocracy of talent the idea of birth as a determining factor persisted. Once a family had achieved high social standing the chances of their children's inheriting this position were good. Children not only fell heir to wealth and property, they also acquired many of the tastes, habits, and refinements of their parents. Furthermore people tended to associate with others of similar position and interests. Thus, as the novelist Cooper wrote: "The day laborer will not mingle with the slave; the skilful mechanic feels his superiority over the mere laborer, claims higher wages and has a pride in his craft; the man in trade justly fancies that his habits elevate him above the mechanic, so far as social position is concerned, and the man of refinement, with his education, tastes, and sentiments, is superior to all." [4] The social milieu in which one was raised often determined one's future status. In spite of popular belief, the carpenter's son was not likely to become a bank president, nor was the frontier Indian fighter apt to end up in the White House.

But sometimes these things did happen, and they happened frequently enough to make the Jeffersonian ideal of an aristocracy of talent seem an actuality. There was sufficient social mobility in America to make it impossible for any one group to form a permanent upper class. The prominent position of the New York landed gentry was steadily challenged by rising merchants, shippers, speculators, and western landholders. These persons in turn were not secure in their own social position. Some went bankrupt because of overspeculation or changing economic conditions; others were outstripped by rising competitors.

Social gradations were precarious, not being regulated according to fixed titles and ranks. While there were persons of high and low standing, most Americans, especially those not at the top, believed that these positions reflected an accidental and perhaps temporary situation.

American democracy, far from mitigating competition for social status, intensified it. The concept of equality placed an overwhelming emphasis on "getting ahead," no matter what the accidents of birth, wealth, or class happened to be. Achievement was more important than inheritance, and Americans of all ranks felt compelled to demonstrate their success. Foreign observers were surprised at the conspicuous way in which persons in this country flaunted their wealth, even workers tried to "make a show."

The very competition for status made it extremely difficult for one to know just how much he had achieved. Successful persons wondered if they had arrived, or if they were fairly certain of their immediate position, they were plagued with doubts as to whether they could maintain their rank and pass it on to their children. In a traditionally aristocratic society class distinctions are generally known and consequently do not need continual emphasis. However, in America the stress on equality and opportunity made people class-conscious. Those with claims to a higher status felt a necessity to assert those claims for fear of losing the right to it. High society in the United States, noted a European nobleman, was "characterized by a spirit of exclusiveness and persecution unknown in any other country." American aristocrats, this observer continued, are just one or two steps removed from the masses; they "think themselves beset by dogs, and are continually kicking for fear of being bitten." [5]

Aristocracies have been tolerated generally because they either protect the lower classes or have little contact with them. But in America the aristocrat was not the protector of the common man; rather, he was in continual struggle for power with him. Nor could incessant contact between classes be avoided. Hence class relations were often characterized by sharp bitterness. The rich, instead of being supportive of and kindly to the lower classes, arrogantly claimed a rank which the poor were unwilling to grant; bolstered by high notions of equality and provoked by the arrogance of the well-to-do, the poor in their turn angrily attacked "that noxious weed of aristocracy" in terms that a European laboring man would not offer his equals.[6]

> Your state of society [said the German Francis Grund to an American aristocrat] is such, that, in the ordinary intercourse with your fellow-citizens, you must necessarily offend more than you can gratify; and the mortifications which two-thirds of the whole population are constantly suffering from the small portion distinguished from the rest by nothing but success in business, must add to the natural jealousies felt by the labouring classes of all countries with regard to the rich. The distinction between the different orders of society may be more *apparent* in England, . . . but they are, nevertheless, far less offensive than yours.[7]

New York's upper classes did not form a unified estate. There were various coteries of aristocratic persons. In the cities the best society was commercially centered, but also included professional persons such as eminent doctors, lawyers, literary figures, ministers, and professors. Even the frontier communities of western New York had their own local aristocracies composed of large landholders, merchants and industrialists, and lawyer-politicians.

In 1828 Basil Hall, traveling by stage over the rough plank roads west of Syracuse, came upon a thriving town in the midst of the wilderness. "Driver," he called, "what is the name of this village?" "Camillus, sir." "And what is that great building?" "That is the seminary—the poly-tecnic." "And that great stone house?" "Oh, that is the wool-factory." The English novelist Charles Augustus Murray, journeying across western New York a few years after Hall, was surprised at seeing so many mansions which stood out from ordinary farms in size and luxuriance. He stayed at a handsome estate along the Genesee River south of Rochester, "which," in his words, "many of the proud-est nobility of Europe might look upon with envy. . . ." [8] Seminaries, factories, and magnificent manors suggest a society concerned with social distinctions. As an historian writing about New York's upper Susquehanna Valley in this period concluded: "There is no evidence of a desire to establish a classless society. Established families imitated the habits of high society as it was in New York City and other established Eastern communities." [9]

II

The general trend was for aristocracy to grow stronger in New York during the three decades preceding the Civil War, but there was one exception. The most privileged group in colonial New York, the landed gentry of the Hudson Valley, was by the age of Jackson waning in power and importance. In 1830 this landed elite was still an in-fluential coterie composed of a few families closely con-nected through intermarriage and common interests, and indirectly holding sway over nearly two million acres of land and an estimated 300,000 persons.[10] However, these aristocrats were becoming land-poor at a time when cities such as New York were beginning to produce the greatest wealth in the nation.

To encourage colonialization of New Netherlands the Dutch West India Company in the seventeenth century had attempted to establish patroonships along the Hudson. Large land grants were made to members of the company who would establish an American colony of fifty or more persons within four years. Those establishing such a settlement were granted the title of patroon and had full property rights as well as civil and military control over the people. In short it was a form of feudalism in which the patroon had baronial authority over his tenants. However, of the five patroonships created only one, that of Kiliaen Van Rensselaer, survived more than a few years, though a number of large estates, not officially patroonships, were extant when the English took control of New Netherlands from the Dutch in 1664. Under the English the Van Rensselaer patroonship was transformed in title to a manor, and the patroon became the lord of the manor. Dutch landlords were allowed to retain their holdings, while the English continued the policy of large land grants, creating nine additional manors and numerous smaller but still substantial estates. In this way the English hoped to build up a powerful landed aristocracy which would, in the words of the last colonial governor, "counterpoise in some measure the general levelling spirit that so prevails in some of His Majesty's governments." [11]

From the beginning, however, this type of transplanted feudalism had met with resistance. On a number of occasions actual armed clashes took place between tenants and their landlords. In 1766, for example, there were a series of tenant rebellions from southern Westchester County to

Albany which were not suppressed until British troops had been brought in.[12]

During the period of the Revolution the power of the large landholders was somewhat reduced. They were stripped of their baronial honors and lost some of their special legal privileges and feudal rights. Entail and primogeniture were outlawed, thus ensuring the eventual partition of the great estates. Small gains in freehold ownership were also made with the breaking up of the estates of those manor lords who had served the Tory cause during the war. The large holdings of the DeLanceys, Philipses, and Johnsons were confiscated, bought up by speculators, and in many cases sold in smaller divisions to farm families.

Despite gains for agrarian democracy, the large landholders continued to dominate the Hudson Valley in the years following the Revolution. Many of the confiscated lands were bought up by these landlords who were thus able to augment their already large holdings. The number of tenants or leaseholders was greatly increased, and for the first time this system was utilized by landlords in the Mohawk and upper Delaware valleys, and as far west as the Genesee Valley. Leases varied from manor to manor; most were termed "durable," since they were held in perpetuity. Generally the lessee was required to pay a certain yearly rent either in money, crops, service, or some combination of the three. On the Van Rensselaer estate tenant farmers paid 10 to 14 bushels of winter wheat per 100 acres, plus four fat fowls, and one day's work with a team of horses or oxen. In addition, landlords generally reserved the rights to timber, mill sites, water power, minerals, and other resources. When a leasehold was sold by a tenant the landlord was entitled to receive one-quarter or one-third of the amount realized from the sale.[13]

Among the chief families composing the Hudson River gentry in Jacksonian times were the Livingstons, Morrises, and Jays of British descent, and the Van Rensselaers, Hardenberghs, Verplancks, Van Cortlandts, and Schuylers of Dutch origin. Of these the Van Rensselaers were by far the most important. Their manor, Rensselaerwyck, in the family since 1629, embraced all of Rensselaer and Albany counties and part of Columbia county. In 1838 between 60,000 and 100,000 tenants farmed these extensive lands, supervised by the eighth patroon, Stephen Van Rensselaer III, one of the most socially prominent men in the state.[14]

By the Jacksonian period Van Rensselaer had been lord of Rensselaerwyck for over sixty years. During this time the tenancy system had been extended; much of the formerly uncultivated uplands had been leased out. However, like most of the Hudson Valley gentry, Van Rensselaer was not a harsh landlord, since any insistence on enforcing all of the remaining feudal rights would have made it difficult for him to obtain tenants. Because of this nearly all feudal obligations had fallen into disuse. Most tenants were assessed a simple money rent, and even this payment was not always collected by the "Good Patroon." On the other hand, Van Rensselaer never sold lands outright and had his agents keep a strict account of all unpaid rent. When he died in January, 1839, the amount of rent in arrears was nearly $400,000.[15]

Although it was not considered so at the time, the death of Stephen Van Rensselaer III marked the end of an era. His passing affected not only his own tenants but the entire tenancy system. This form of land tenure, though not strictly enforced, was anachronistic in Jacksonian America. Unrest among tenant farmers desiring freehold ownership had long been widespread, and periodic clashes between land agents and renters were common. Major dissension on the part of the Van Rensselaer tenants had probably been averted during the latter years of the Good Patroon's life only because of his forbearance in collecting back rents. Tenants accustomed to this leniency did not think that they would ever be called upon to pay their arrearages; few could afford to pay; almost none were willing. But the old patroon had contracted various debts during his long life; and, not wanting to diminish the inheritance of his two sons, Stephen and William, he left a will requiring that his creditors be paid from the uncollected rents.[16]

On hearing of this plan farmers held protest meetings. A committee representing the lessees of western Albany County was brusquely turned away in their attempt to meet with Stephen Van Rensselaer IV, who had inherited his father's holdings west of the Hudson. Angered by this treatment, tenants, on July 4, 1839, held a mass meeting at Berne, the highest point in the Helderberg mountains of Albany County. A declaration of independence from landlord rule was drawn up proclaiming: "We will take up the ball of the Revolution where our fathers stopped it and roll it to the final consummation of freedom and independence of the masses." [17]

Stephen Van Rensselaer met this declaration by sending a sheriff with writs of ejection against several of the tenants' leaders. But the sheriff, Michael Artcher, and his deputy, Daniel Leonard, were manhandled by the embittered tenants, now organized into armed bands determined to resist the implementation of the deceased patroon's will. In December 1839 the farmers, or Anti-Renters as they were now called, successfully turned back a posse of five hundred men led by Sheriff Artcher and including such persons as former Governor William Marcy and John Van

Buren, the President's son. The Sheriff then appealed to Governor William Seward to call out the state militia and restore law and order. Seven hundred militia men were sent to the Helderberg hills; at the same time the Governor issued a proclamation warning the Anti-Renters of the seriousness of their resistance. Under these pressures the tenants gave in without battle, and several of their leaders were evicted from their farms.[18]

But the will to resist the landlords was not broken. Tenants continued to refuse payment of their back rents and and even stopped paying rents altogether. Disguised as Indians and dressed in calico they harassed sheriffs, deputies, and land agents, using the traditional American method of tarring and feathering.

> Oh hark! in the mountains I hear a great roar;
> Those Helderberg farmers are at it once more,
> With their war whoops and Indians most wickedly bent
> On shaving Van Rensselaer out of his rent;
>> And the way they make war
>> Is to feather and tar
> Every unfortunate law-seeking gent,
> Who by landlord or sheriff among them is sent. . . .[19]

From Rensselaerwyck the Anti-Rent movement quickly spread throughout the Hudson Valley. Tenants turned Indians terrorized the land. On one occasion late in 1844 three companies of state militia were sent to the town of Hudson, where angry farmers threatened to storm the jail to release one of their leaders, Smith Boughton, known as Big Thunder. A year later, following the murder of an undersheriff at an eviction sale, Governor Silas Wright declared Delaware County to be in a state of insurrection.[20]

The Anti-Rent movement became highly organized in the early 'forties at the town, county, and eventually state

levels. Anti-Renters printed their own newspapers, held
conventions, drew up pamphlets and petitions, and elected
representatives to the state legislature. They became an
important political force, and in 1845 candidates endorsed
by the Anti-Renters were quite successful. Both major
parties now seemed willing to bend over backwards to
grant the rebellious renters relief from landlord rule.
Legislative enactments outlawed the landlord's right to
seize the goods of a defaulting tenant, and a tax was levied
on rent income. In 1846 a constitutional convention
amended New York's Constitution, making illegal any future lease of agricultural land for a period longer than
twelve years.[21]

The election of 1846 was advantageous for Anti-Renters.
Both the Whig and Democratic parties were wracked with
dissension, and this gave the Anti-Rent block of votes more
power than their numerical strength warranted. John
Young, the Whig candidate for governor, promised if
elected to free imprisoned Anti-Rent leaders. At a convention in Albany the Anti-Rent party gave their endorse-
ment to Young; this proved decisive. Good as his word,
when elected Young had those Anti-Renters in prison re-
leased. In 1848, Young, again courting Anti-Rent support
in hopes of re-election, asked the legislature for the power
to investigate the legality of the landlords' titles. In spite
of large-scale landlord lobbying against this measure, the
legislature quickly passed the test of title bill.[22]

Fearing the outcome of any legal action and sensing that
popular sentiment was running against them, manor lords
began selling out their interests. The days of the landed
gentry's dominance of the Hudson Valley were numbered.
Seventeen landed proprietors started selling their holdings
in 1845; that same year Stephen Van Rensselaer put his

Albany County lands up for sale. By 1850 the Manor of Rensselaerwyck was no more; many of the leases had been sold outright to tenants; others were purchased by speculators who vainly hoped to perpetuate the formerly profitable tenancy system.

The courts aided this downfall. In 1850 the New York Supreme Court held that the hated quarter sales, whereby a tenant who sold his farm paid one-fourth or one-third of the price to the landlord, were unconstitutional. This decision implied that the tenants were in effect freehold owners of their land. The same year the Supreme Court also declared the Van Rensselaer title invalid. This decision increased the willingness of the manor aristocrats to sell out. And, even though the Court of Appeals reversed the invalidation two years later on a technicality, the position of the landlords was not improved since the courts continued to regard the tenants as the rightful owners of the soil.[23]

Controversy over titles and leases continued sporadically throughout the nineteenth century. As late as the 1880's there was an episode of violence when a deputy sheriff was shot trying to dispossess a Helderberg farmer. But in general freeholds had replaced leaseholds by the time of the Civil War, and the era of the manor aristocrats was over.

III

The decline of New York's landed gentry in no way diminished aristocracy in the Empire State. A few persons such as the novelist James Fenimore Cooper staunchly maintained that the only true gentility was based on landed property.[24] But even in the 1830's Cooper's dream of a splendid yet democratic gentry leading and serving the people was as much a myth as the Jeffersonian ideal of a yeoman Republic. Both visions were based on the assumption that America was and would remain a rural agrarian society. Yet rapid transportation and widespread commerce, industries, and urban areas thwarted the agrarian dream and altered the American notion of aristocracy. While the countryside was becoming less aristocratic it was rapidly giving way in relative importance within the state to the cities, in terms of both wealth and population. Well before the heirs of the last patroon sold their interests in Rensselaerwyck, the image of the aristocrat had changed from the traditional patriarchal squire to the wealthy plutocrat—the city-centered merchant or industrialist more concerned with drawing rooms and counting houses than manors and tenants. Unlike the landed aristocrats, whose position as an elite group steadily declined before the forces of democracy, capitalist-aristocrats thrived under the laissez-faire economic conditions prevalent in Jacksonian America.

New York City in 1830 seemed far removed from the generally quiet farms and manors of rural New York. All was hustle and bustle in the metropolis; everything was given over to business and speculation as residents attempted to outstrip one another in their quest after the "Almighty Dollar." [25] Gotham had grown from a mere 33,000 inhabitants in 1790 to over 200,000 forty years later. In this same period New York became the undisputed commercial center of the New World, greatly surpassing the nearest rivals—Philadelphia, Boston, and Baltimore.[26] Foreign visitors were impressed with the city. Michael Chevalier praised New York as the "Queen of the Atlantic Coast." Even the otherwise virulent Mrs. Trollope found scarcely anything caustic to say about Gotham; in fact she praised it roundly. "I must . . . declare," she wrote, "that I think New York one of the finest cities I ever saw, and as much superior to every other in the Union (Philadelphia not excepted,) as London to Liverpool, or Paris to Rouen. . . . Situated on an island, which I think it will one day cover, it rises, like Venice, from the sea, and like that fairest of cities in the days of her glory, receives into its lap tribute of all the riches of the earth." [27]

At the time Mrs. Trollope visited the city in 1831, New York far from covered Manhattan Island. The city was compact, extending from the southernmost point at the Battery north along the Hudson for about two miles and along the East River for approximately two and a half miles. Canal Street marked the northern limit in the late 1820's; beyond that were several separate villages—Greenwich, Chelsea, Bloomingdale, Manhattanville, and Harlem —and scattered farms and elegant country seats. The streets were generally narrow and crooked, although a great deal of labor and money had already been expended to implement the regular broad and wide street pattern north of the old city. In 1828 lots could still be purchased in the present Times Square area for less than $700; further north for as little as $60.[28]

The chief thoroughfare, which New Yorkers never tired of showing off, was Broadway. Running from the Battery north to Bleecker Street, Broadway was the most fashionable promenade in the Union. The Southern travel writer, Mrs. Anne Royall, visiting New York in the late 1820's, exclaimed: "It is impossible to give even an idea of the beauty and fashion displayed in Broadway on a fine day; the number of females, the richness and variety of dress, comprising all that can be conceived of wealth or skill, mocks description." Broadway shops were the "self-appointed dictators of fashion." Wheeler, Tryon and Derby, Brundage, or Elmendorf furnished the aspiring beau's clothes; boots were obtained from Kimball and Rogers; a St. John was the only acceptable hat.[29] Americans were fond of comparing Broadway to London's Regent Street. Foreign visitors were more fond of describing the scavenging pigs that still roamed the streets or the uneven pavement. But most visitors were impressed. Mrs. Trollope wrote that "this noble street may vie with any I ever saw, for its length and breadth, its handsome shops, neat awnings, excellent *trottoir*, and well-dressed pedestrians." [30]

In her New York visit Mrs. Trollope was struck by the refinement and elegance of the city's upper classes. "We saw enough," she wrote, "to convince us that there is society to be met with in New York, which would be deemed delightful any where." Other accounts attest to the truth of this. A native New Yorker writing in the 1830's pointed out that "there is an old aristocracy in this city, which is not generally understood. There is no strata of society so difficult to approach or reach." [31] This aristocracy was composed chiefly of the leading mercantile families, most of whom had been established for a generation or more. The origins of these leading families varied; some such as the Beekmans, Van Cortlandts, Dyckmans, or Brevoorts were of Dutch descent and were closely associated with the Hudson Valley manor lords. Upper-class families of English stock included among others the Aspinwalls, Howlands, Kings, Wards, Grinnells, Macys, and Whitneys; of French Huguenot origin were such wealthy families as the Lorillards, Jumels, Laws, and Pintards. Collectively these old families composed New York's highest class, or what was generally termed Knickerbocker society.[32]

The following description of Knickerbocker New York as it existed in the early 1830's was given by A. C. Dayton, himself a member of Knickerbocker society:

> There were circles naturally formed by congeniality of tastes and similarity of daily occupation, which could not be entered by a mere golden key. The applicant for admission must possess the requisite affinities and bear the unmistakable evidences which, the world over, proclaim the gentleman by sentiment and education. This idea of aristocracy pervaded Gotham and was derived from the staunch Knickerbocker stock; it underlay and formed the foundation of New York society. The good old fathers and their *Madames* were great sticklers for form and ceremony; their ruffles and cuffs were starched, and unwittingly imparted to the wearers an air of dignified composure that would check the merest approach to familiarity from their juniors. . . .[33]

At the period to which Dayton refers New York was small enough so that the leading members of society were well known. "In 1830," a contemporary noted, "a New Yorker of no very extended acquaintance could tell the names of all the principle merchants, and where they lived." The leading commercial persons were well-to-do, but few were extremely wealthy. Probably only one New Yorker was worth over a million dollars; that was the immigrant fur magnate John Jacob Astor, whose estate was valued at several times that amount. The only others close to being millionaires were Robert Lenox, John Coster, Stephen Whitney, and Nat Prime.[34]

The style in which New York fashionables lived in the early 1830's was comfortable, dignified, and often elegant, but seldom ostentatious. Few persons in this period felt socially compelled to maintain private equipages. Abram

Dayton could recall only two four-in-hand teams around New York in the early 'thirties; one belonged to John Hunt of Hunter's Island near New Rochelle, "a gentleman of leisure and large wealth"; the other was maintained by Henry Marx, a noted and dashing man-about-town known as "Dandy" Marx. Among others having private equipages were Philip Hone, the wealthy ex-mayor and diarist, and the distinguished Dr. Valentine Mott.[35]

One reason for the scarcity of family carriages was the fact that most well-to-do New Yorkers lived in the lower part of the city, within walking distance of their offices or places of employment. Fashionable residences flanked Battery Park and Bowling Green. Here some of the oldest and wealthiest families lived, including the Primes, Whitneys, Clintons, Schencks, and Schermerhorns. Slightly further north in the area around City Hall Park other fashionable families dwelled. This was especially true after the Astor House opened on Broadway opposite the Park in May 1836. This luxury hotel was the most elegant in America and the wonder of the age. Costing more than $400,000, its marble structure was six stories high, contained 390 rooms, and boasted of such extravagant features as gas lights, running water, seventeen bathrooms, and two showers. In this neighborhood lived such well-known families as the Hones, Motts, Carters, Haggerties, Austins, Beekmans, and Hosacks.[36]

The mansions of Knickerbocker New York showed no great variety and were rather humble compared with those built after 1840. Most were of brick with painted shutters. They were narrow and deep to fit the general pattern of city lots. On the first floor was found the formal reception room, used only on infrequent occasions such as funerals and weddings, the kitchen, and the dining room. The second floor contained the commonly used parlour or sitting room, where ladies would receive their callers, sometimes a library, and often a bedroom. The third floor was exclusively given over to bedrooms. The attic provided the servants' quarters, while the basement served as a nursery. Furnishings were ornate and, to present-day tastes, overdone; mahogany and rosewood, silk and satin, marble and gilt were found in abundance.[37]

As New York's population grew and commerce flourished, the lower part of the city was increasingly surrendered to business. Wall Street, Pearl Street, Water Street, and Broad Street were almost totally taken over by warehouses, shops, banks and offices. An exodus to the more northerly parts of the city, which continued until well after the Civil War, was begun by people of fashion. As the rich moved further north, working-class persons began taking up residence in the vacated mansions of lower Manhattan. But where formerly one family had lived, twenty or fifty, or even a hundred were crowded.[38] Some well-to-do families, of course, lagged behind in the northern migration, and there developed that curious juxtaposition often commented upon by foreign visitors of mansions and tenements existing within a few blocks of one another or even side by side.

By the mid-'thirties one of the most exclusive residential areas in the city was St. John's Park. This park bordering Hudson, Laight, Varick, and Beach streets was owned in common by the abutting residents who had keys to the iron gates. A contemporary called it "one of the very highly aristocratic portions of the city." But even this location proved too southerly as society continued its northern march. St. John's Park declined in prominence, and in 1869 the land was purchased by the New York Central and Hudson River Railroad. A depot and freight store-house replaced the stately trees and winding walks.[39]

In the late 1830's the rallying cry of fashionables was "above Bleecker." More splendid mansions than the city had yet known were built about Washington Square, along Fifth Avenue, University Place, Lafayette Place, and Astor Place. Union Square became a dignified residential area, and north of that the private Gramercy Park, established by Samuel Ruggles in 1831, was the site of a fashionable building boom. The "old down town burgomasters," noted Philip Hone in 1836, were "marching reluctantly north to pitch their tents in places which in their time, were orchards, cornfields or morasses, a pretty smart distance from town." Hone, himself, was no exception; he moved from the crowded lower city opposite City Hall Park up-town to a new location just south of Astor Place.[40]

Certain institutions were traditional mainstays of aristo-cratic society in New York City. The Episcopal Church was such an establishment. As the tax-supported church in colonial days it was the church of the ruling class and the elite in general. This situation did not change with dis-establishment. Episcopal churches in the city were well endowed, especially Trinity, which was one of the major landholders in Manhattan. But the most elite congrega-tion in the 1830's was that which gathered in old Grace Church at the corner of Broadway and Rector Street. Grace, in the words of a member, was "the chosen shrine of the *crème de la crème,* among that portion of society who especially affect the imposing ritual of Episcopacy." [41]

Another institution which upheld New York society was Columbia College. From its founding as Kings Col-lege, Columbia had been closely associated with order, tradition, paternal benevolence, and the Episcopal Church.

In political matters the college's leanings had been Federalist, and by the 1830's were Whig. Its trustees and presidents were almost always gentlemen of rank and wealth. The student body was comprised largely of the sons of New York's leading families.[42]

One institution which became an aristocratic stronghold was the Union Club, organized in 1836 along the lines of an exclusive London club. Its charter members included many of New York's most eminent citizens. The richly furnished clubhouse at 343 Broadway opened in 1837 with "good servants, and above all a most *recherché chef de cuisine.*" In the 1840's and 1850's the Union Club flourished, and others were patterned after it. Prior to its founding select coteries of the city's society were in the habit of meeting on certain occasions in special rooms of the principal hotels. At Washington Hall and the City Hotel distinct social sets met. Although these gatherings were not formally organized they were as well defined and almost as exclusive as private clubs.[43]

Social life in New York revolved around elegant parties and formal balls, both privately given or run by subscription at one of the leading hotels. Hone described a fashionable private party which, he assured his diary, was *"quelque chose distingué."* The mansion in which the gathering was held Hone described as the finest house in New York, "furnished and fitted up in a style of the utmost magnificence—painted ceilings, gilded moldings, rich satin ottomans, curtains in the last Parisian taste, and splendid mirrors. . . . On this occasion, all the science of all the accomplished *artistes* was put in requisition; decorators, cooks, and confectioners vied with each other, and each in his vocation seemed to have produced the *ne plus ultra.* . . ."[44]

Francis Grund wrote that American aristocrats did not seem to like their own country. This seems applicable to New York socialites, who in many ways scorned anything American. These aristocrats aped European fashions in everything from the cut of their clothes to language and manners. A work of art or a style of dress was not favored with fashionable approval unless it was known to be in vogue in London or Paris. New York advertisers capitalized on this by referring to the European success of their particular luxury product. For example Brewster, Lawrence, and Company, coachmakers, advertised "that in addition to their usual variety of work, they have now for sale Carriages, constructed on the English plan, and of the newest London fashion. . . ." [45]

Often at fashionable gatherings democracy and American notions of equality were ridiculed. "All that I have been able to see in the United States," wrote Grund, "convinces me that the wealthy classes are in no other country so much opposed to the existing government. . . ." "I have no objection to liberty in the abstract," commented a New York lady at a society soiree. "I think all men, with the exception of our negroes, ought to be free; but I cannot bear the ridiculous notion of equality which seems to have taken hold of our people. . . ." [46] Abroad well-to-do Americans desirous of receiving introductions to courts or to London's fashionable West End circles attempted to atone for American democracy by admiring every form of European despotism. [47]

Socially aspiring Americans, in the words of a contemporary observer, "worship everything in the shape of a nobleman, until, by continually talking about nobility, they imagine themselves to belong to it." Anyone possessing a title was doted on. Persons went to great lengths to establish impressive genealogies; coats of arms were hunted up or created; old European portraits were purchased to form galleries of ancestors.[48]

All this, of course, reflected the fact that class distinctions were at best tenuous. Trade, industry, and wild speculation flooded the ranks of the wealthy in the 1830's, and newly rich individuals, usually prodded by aspiring wives, craved social recognition. As a result, the closed and established circles of New York society began to give way to a society-page "High Society," typical of wealthy industrialized countries. Sheer display of wealth, often made in a tasteless and vulgar way, became for the first time a major means of gaining social notoriety and rank. James Kirke Paulding, the sophisticated Knickerbocker satirist, ridiculed this tendency among the New York rich:

Mr. ———— has a fine house, the inside of which looks like an upholsterer's shop, and lives in style. He gave me an invitation to dinner, at a fortnight's notice, where I ate out of a set of China, my lady assured me cost seven hundred dollars, and drank out of glasses that cost a guinea a piece. In short, there was nothing on the table of which I did not learn the value, most especially the wine, some of which mine entertainer gave the company his word of honour, stood him eight dollars a bottle, besides the interest, and was half a century old.[49]

Since social rankings were precarious, people competed recklessly to be in the "Best Society." Individuals who had "arrived" were jealous of their position and attempted to keep others from achieving an equal status. This made High Society very cutthroat. "It is almost impossible for an educated European," wrote Grund, "to conceive the degree of rudeness, insolence, and effrontery, and the total want of consideration for the feeling of others, which I have often seen practised in what is called the 'first society' of the United States." [50] Aristocracy became in many respects nothing but a wealthy overgrown bourgeoisie, composed of persons who had been more successful in business than their fellow citizens.

But this is not to imply that class divisions were lessening or that aristocracy was declining. New York society was probably less democratic in Jackson's time than in Washington's. By the later period there were substantial commercial fortunes, factories, the beginnings of an urban proletariat, and a class-conscious labor movement. Aristocracy in New York was in a state of transition. The class of gentry was declining, but the rise of the wealthy capitalists more than offset this. In the period between the Revolution and the mid-1820's New Yorkers had become a more homogeneous middle-class society. But after that time this trend was reversed, and by the late 1830's the Jacksonian ideal of a classless egalitarian society was rapidly receding in the face of changing social and economic realities.

4

TO THE NEW WORLD

We have been recently, before and during the famine, in
Irish towns and cities, and we have no hesitation in saying
. . . that there is more thorough Irish degradation in the
single city of New York than in all of them put together. As
to the peasantry of Ireland, let them be never mentioned in
the same day with this degenerate lodging-house population;
no amount of physical suffering ought ever be compared with
the moral degradation of the transplanted city Celt, which our
police reports exhibit every day of the week. . . . There is
often a more intimate sympathy between the Alabama planter
and his African *slave* than between a Yankee employer and his
Irish *help*. The Irishman may by industry, put "something to
the fore," but he never can in these old States become a proprietor, or feel that easy sense of equality, without which liberty
itself is but the liberty of the Arab—the *freedom* of wander-
ing over a social desert, where the barren privilege prevails
without any of its real advantages.

—*American Celt* [New York], 1855

No factor contributed more to the stratification of
Northern society than the heavy influx of foreigners
in the three decades before the Civil War. By the 'forties
and 'fifties mass immigration had created a more than adequate supply of cheap labor to man the expanding factories, to perform the heavy construction work, and to fill
the need for domestic servants and other menials. Wealthy
capitalists generally profited from the labor of immigrants,

but for native workers these newcomers represented a threat to their social and economic position. As foreigners came in increasing numbers, wages for large numbers of workers dropped or failed to keep pace with rising living costs. In New York and many other cities and factory towns, living conditions for immigrant and native workers alike often deteriorated to the point where the difference between the industrial slums of the Old World and those of the New virtually disappeared. Native Americans of all ranks tended to feel superior to new immigrants. This class-conscious feeling together with the obvious economic inferiority of the majority of immigrants presented a strong challenge to egalitarian America, and came close to creating permanent class stratifications in the two decades before the Civil War.

I

Between 1815 and the Civil War over five and a half million Europeans entered the United States. Coming largely from western, northern, and central Europe, this immigration reached record heights in the period from the early 1840's to the late 1850's. Numerically, the great flood of immigrants after 1880 far outstripped the antebellum influx, but, relative to the total population, immigration during the two decades prior to the Civil War was the largest in American history. Both Europe and America were greatly affected by the movement.[1]

Historians are aware of the huge impact that the immigration of the 1840's and 1850's had on this country. However, few of them have sufficiently emphasized the fact that for over half a century following the Revolution immigration was not a major factor in American growth.

This lack of newcomers up to the Jacksonian era had nearly as great an effect on American society as the large influx of immigrants did a few decades later. At the time of the Revolution the population totaled slightly over three million; by the first election of Andrew Jackson in 1828 the population stood at well over ten million; yet during this period fewer than 400,000 immigrants arrived in the country.[2]

The Napoleonic wars were the chief factor in limiting the number of foreigners entering the United States during the formative years of the young Republic. Between 1790 and 1815 less than 250,000 immigrants arrived, averaging about 10,000 yearly. With the return of peace to the Western world, immigration immediately increased in volume, only to be sharply checked by the economic recession which the United States experienced in 1819. Though the economy picked up quickly in the 'twenties, the dream of America as a land of opportunity had not yet captivated the imagination of lower-class Europeans enough to stimulate a major exodus. For one thing the revolutions in transportation and industry which were to transform America and absorb numerous foreign workers were only beginning. Then, too, the trip across the Atlantic was long, dangerous, and costly. Finally, since the number of foreigners here was small in the 'twenties newcomers seldom had the consolation of joining friends and relatives on arrival, something which greatly eased the transition from European to American life for many at a later period. Arrivals averaged less than 14,000 annually in the 'twenties, and the type of immigrants tended to be substantial farmers, merchants or craftsmen, who were fairly easily assimilated into American life.[3]

By 1830 the great majority of foreign-born were naturalized citizens and had been absorbed into the expanding economy without causing drastic wage reductions.[4] It is no mere coincidence that the great growth of political, social, and economic democracy which culminated in the Jacksonian period took place at a time when European immigration to the United States was at a low point.

Periods of heavy immigration, from colonial times until the restrictive laws of the 1920's, have always increased class consciousness. An aristocracy is only possible where there exists an inferior group willing to perform the most menial tasks. Slaves, indentured servants, and redemptioners provided such a class in colonial times. The penniless Irish and Germans were to provide such a class in the 1840's and 1850's. During the early years of the New Nation the accidental circumstances reducing European immigration proved a strong stimulus to the growth of democracy, weakening aristocracy in America. By the time of Jackson, as Tocqueville and others observed, the United States was a fairly homogeneous middle-class society.[5]

While the lack of large-scale immigration was one of the underlying factors furthering the growth of democracy, it was during the Jacksonian period, at a time when equality seemed triumphant, that immigration picked up sharply. In the year that Jackson first won the presidency, 1828, some 30,000 registered passengers entered the United States. During 1832, the year Old Hickory was locked in a death struggle with Biddle's Bank, over 50,000 aliens arrived, and the total was to fall below that figure only twice before the Civil War. Taking the 1830's as a whole, immigration reached nearly 600,000—almost quadruple that of the 'twenties. By the time Jackson retired from office in 1837, increased immigration already presented a clear challenge to the egalitarian ideals of American society. Yet this was only the beginning of the great pre-Civil War migration.[6]

There were many reasons for this phenomenal movement of peoples. To lower-class Europeans, the United States appeared not only as the most democratic state in the Western world, but also as a land of unbounded economic opportunity. The mythic proportions which these factors of "democracy" and "opportunity" had acquired had a tremendous appeal to Europeans, who were frustrated economically and socially in the more settled societies of the Old World. America was looked upon as a new Eden, a classless land of plenty where the individual was master of his own destiny. It is undeniable that the majority of persons contemplating leaving Europe were drawn primarily by the hope of economic advancement, inspired by reports of abundant cheap land and higher wages.

American opportunities would not have led to emigration on such a scale had it not been for the strong discontent in Europe with existing conditions. After the French Revolution the aspirations of the ordinary European had been greatly raised; yet many found their yearnings frustrated, making them more receptive to the idea of America as a promised land. The remnants of feudalism were disappearing while more efficient methods in agriculture and industry were being introduced, and for many middle- and upper-class citizens this meant vast new economic opportunities. For millions who were less fortunate, however, these changes brought suffering. The industrial revolution, developing first in England in the mid-eighteenth century and spreading from there to the Continent during the late eighteenth and early nineteenth centuries, by destroying the domestic system of manufacture adversely affected skilled artisans. These changes brought poverty, ill-health, and insecurity to thousands of workers.[7]

For those Europeans who might have hoped to escape the evils of industrial life by remaining in rural areas, life was equally difficult. The expanding urban-industrial society made more efficient methods of agricultural production imperative. Changes in the rural economy took a variety of forms. In England and the Scandinavian countries the enclosure movement, which had been going on for several centuries, ended the communal system of agriculture and created larger and more efficient farm units. In Ireland and along the Rhine in southwest Germany a similar consolidation of holdings by large landowners had been taking place since the mid-eighteenth century. In all of these areas the rural tenant class was being displaced from the land. Even the small farm owner, because of competition from large-scale farms, found his status declining and his hold on the land weakening. The result was that many rural peasants were forced to become farm laborers, to move to the new factory towns in search of employment, or to emigrate.[8]

The majority of pre-Civil War immigrants were Irish and German. Without doubt the worst economic and social conditions in western Europe during the first half of the nineteenth century were in Ireland, where a changing agrarian economy was further complicated by absentee landlordism, an exploding population, and religious and political strife. The nadir of Irish fortunes came between 1845 and 1849, when the potato crop (the major peasant staple) suffered a series of crop-reducing blights. The resulting famine changed Irish emigration which had grown steadily since 1815 into a mass movement. Altogether in the fourteen-year period from 1841 to 1855, about 1.6 million Irish left for the United States, nearly one-fifth of the entire population.[9]

Second in numbers to the Irish were the Germans. By the outbreak of the Civil War there were more than 1.3 million German-born persons living in the United States. The great German immigration, unlike that of the Irish, was not touched off by any single episode comparable to the famine. The German exodus was never the full-scale flight from poverty and starvation that typified Irish emigration during the famine years; the Germans entering the United States in the 1850's in record numbers were much better off than the Irish. Immigration records reveal that the average German entering New York City in the 'fifties arrived with about $125 in cash, not a lavish sum but a good deal more than the average Irishman.[10]

II

Irish, German, and to a lesser extent English, French, and Scandinavian immigrants were attracted to America by a dream of equality and opportunity. But for many foreigners this dream remained unfulfilled or took on nightmare aspects. On the journey across the Atlantic immigrants suffered untold physical hardships. When disease spread among steerage passengers the mortality rate was often shockingly high. Reports in the New York newspapers of deaths on immigrant ships were quite matter of fact. "The packet ship Isaac Webb," reported the *New York Daily Tribune* in February 1851, "is detained at Quarantine, on account of sickness among her passengers, having had 47 deaths on the passage." A few months earlier the *Tribune* told of a German immigrant family of five, all of whom perished at sea except for a five-year-old girl.[11] As might be expected, the conditions on the ships coming from Ireland and Liverpool during the Irish famine were the most notorious. These packets, commonly referred to as "coffin ships," were, in the words of a contemporary, "charnel-houses . . . in which cruelty to *mere Irish* ceased to be a sin." [12]

Even though an immigrant survived the horrors of steerage passage, his ordeal was far from over. Upon landing at its American destination the emigrant ship was besieged by runners in the employ of hotels and boarding houses, railroads, steamship companies, land agents, and other concerns hoping to profit at the expense of the newcomers. The following description of the system was given by the *New York Daily Tribune,* November 10, 1853:

> Such a scene of confusion and violence, of cheating, and swearing, and noise, and plundering, I have never witnessed. . . . The whole tribe of runners, hackmen, and tavern-keepers were combined to fleece the immigrant and often to ruin or sell the virtue of the unprotected girls. The worst cheating was always with the luggage. Tickets would be sold at a fair rate, and then the luggage be charged by weight. Weight, of course, was an arbitrary matter with these strangers; so that the poor foreigner, what with his cart-hire, and luggage expenses, would lose his whole little property before getting out of the city.

Most European immigrants entered this country through the port of New York—more than two-thirds of the more than five and a half million aliens who arrived in America between 1815 and 1860. Nor do these figures tell the whole story, since numerous immigrants entered New York after debarking on the New Jersey side of the Hudson.[13] The prominence of New York as a port of entry undoubtedly meant that the mass immigration of the 1840's and 1850's had a more significant impact on New York State than any other American region. According to the New York State Census of 1855, over one-quarter of all the state's residents were foreign-born. In New York City the foreign-born composed almost half the population, and other cities in the state had a comparably large percentage.[14]

Persons arriving in New York were particularly preyed upon, for relieving the new arrival of his remaining money and possessions was a well-developed science there. Competition between runners, who were on commission, was keen and often involved violence. One New Yorker described the runners as "big-fisted, double-jointed 'shoulder hitters,' who pride themselves on travelling through life 'on their muscle'; semi-savages of civilization, and far more dangerous than the real, inasmuch as they possess greater scope for evil. . . ."[15]

Of the many thousand tenement houses that existed in New York by the mid-1840's, none were worse than those which specialized in housing recently arrived immigrants. There were many such hostelries in the area around lower Greenwich Street and in the vicinity of the East River docks. Once a newcomer was induced by runners or simple ignorance into one of these houses, he seldom escaped the landlord's clutches until his resources were exhausted. It was customary for the landlord of such an establishment to lock up a boarder's luggage, supposedly for safekeeping, but actually to keep it from its owner in case of default of payment. Not only were thousands of immigrants fleeced of their last savings, they were also housed miserably. A writer in the 1850's described one of these boarding houses as being subdivided into numerous small rooms, "each one being filthy and noisome in the extreme, infested with all manner of vermin, and holding as many straw mattresses, ragged quilts, and dirty blankets as sufficed for the nocturnal requirements of the boarders—eight or ten of whom, without regard to sex or age, were crowded into spaces fit only for one or two." [16]

Various attempts were made by private groups, the city, and the state to aid and advise the newly arrived. A German Emigrant Society had been organized in the late eighteenth century; a similar Irish society was founded in 1841. In 1847, New York established the Board of Commissioners of Emigration. These societies adopted the methods of the runners, boarding immigrant ships in an attempt to give sound advice about such things as baggage, boarding houses, jobs, and rail or canal tickets. In addition to this, the Board from its inception required the captain of a vessel to file a passenger list for each voyage, and to put up a bond for each person or to pay one dollar per person to the New York City Health Commissioner to cover possible costs for hospitalization or relief.[17]

These measures were of some help, but it was not until the Board of Commissioners acquired Castle Garden, an old fort at the tip of the Battery, as an immigrant landing depot in 1855 that the situation really improved. Here the runners could be successfully combated, since they were not allowed within the confines of the Castle without special permission. In the old fort the Board established railroad ticket offices, a money exchange, a city-run baggage delivery service, and a general information desk. From 1855 until immigration was put under federal regulation in 1890 and Ellis Island came into use, those entering the United States via New York harbor first set foot in the New World at Castle Garden.[18]

Despite the various private and public agencies established to assist the immigrant, the lot of those landing in New York remained difficult. Nearly every guidebook published for prospective European emigrants contained a note of warning not to linger in New York City. In 1832 an American author urged:

> Never let the poor and destitute emigrant stop in New York—it will be his ruin. But let him push into the country: he may find employment somewhere, if he is honest and willing to work.

In 1850 a writer similarly cautioned prospective emigrants that "there will be very little likelihood of the stranger finding employment in New York, the place being already crowded with mechanics, labourers, and loiterers." Later writers were even more emphatic in urging immigrants to avoid New York and other large eastern cities.[19]

The advice to "face toward the setting sun," as one emigrant agent put it, was difficult to follow. The way in which foreigners thronged into the city and remained, alarmed many native Americans. During the Irish famine year of 1848, the Alms House Commissioner lamented that "the City of New York seems to be the desired residence of all emigration." [20]

The Irish were particularly prone to herding into New York and other east coast cities. The reasons of these agrarian peasants for congregating in the cities are varied. Most arrived virtually penniless, and to buy transportation to the West was more than they could afford. Even those with sufficient funds for rail or canal tickets seldom had enough money to purchase land. Furthermore, the agricultural methods of the Irish peasant, who seldom knew more than potato farming, were scarcely suitable to American conditions. Added to this was the congeniality of living with their countrymen and having a Catholic Church in close proximity. As one Irishman put it:

> There were old friends and former companions or acquaintances to be met with at every street-corner; and there was news to give, and news to receive—too often . . . in the liquor-store or dram-shop kept by a countryman. . . . Then the chapel was handy, and a Christian wouldn't be overtaken for want of a priest; then there was the schooling convenient for the children, poor things. . . .[21]

By 1860 there were over 204,000 Irish in New York; they could be found throughout the city, but were concentrated most heavily in Manhattan's Lower East Side. Living in cramped tenements, cellars, or other cheap lodging houses, the New York Irish formed an easily exploited menial class.[22]

German immigrants in general were quite different. They tended to be more industrious, patient, and thrifty. Also, many came to America with enough money to travel west and buy land. Although many more Germans than Irish went into farming, nevertheless, thousands of Germans did press into New York and other cities. By the outbreak of the Civil War there were over 120,000 New Yorkers of German birth. The sizable German section of the city ran along the Bowery from Houston Street to 14th and east to First Avenue. In this area, known as *Kleindeutschland*, language, dress, shops, schools, and churches were all characteristically German.[23]

The lot of the urban immigrants varied from nationality to nationality and individual to individual. But on the whole their economic and social conditions were poor. Most of New York's tenement and cellar dwellers were foreign-born. One block in the notorious Five Points area in the 1850's is a good illustration; living there were 812 Irish, 218 Germans, 186 Italians, 189 Poles, 12 French, 9 English, 7 Portuguese, 2 Welsh, 39 Negroes, and 10 native Americans.[24]

The city's foreign-born in general suffered from poor housing, lack of job opportunities, and discrimination. These included such minority groups as the Italians, Poles, and Portuguese. The following description by a native American of Italian life in the 'fifties reflects both the immigrants' bad living and working conditions and the native's feelings of superiority:

> Here [the Five Points area], in large tenement-houses, were packed hundreds of poor Italians, mostly engaged in carrying through the city and country "the everlasting hand-organ," or selling statuettes. In the same room I would find monkeys, children, men and women, with organs and plastercasts, all huddled together; but the women contriving still, in crowded rooms, to roll their dirty macaroni, and all talking excitedly; a bedlam of sounds, and a combination of odors from garlic, monkeys, and most dirty human persons.[25]

Probably the Chinese lived under the worst conditions of any foreign group in New York. By the Civil War there were some 200 Chinese living in the city, barely managing to make a living by selling tea or candy or cigars. Sometimes they got dock jobs, but were likely to be beaten up by the Irish or Germans for attempting this. One reporter described a Chinese rooming house with fifteen or more persons living in a room with narrow shelves coming out of the wall for beds, similar to steerage berths on ships.[26]

By far the largest immigrant group in New York was the Irish, many of whom knew no trade and had little education and almost no money. They came to form the largest source of unskilled labor in the city. A British immigrant commented on this in the 1850's. "The Celtic Irish," he wrote, "do very much more than their share of the hard work, and are by no means overpaid. A New Yorker will immediately compare the wages of the Irish labourer in Ireland and in America as a matter of cash; but the real question is the sort of life that the labourer leads." [27]

The sort of life the Irish led in New York was hard indeed. Discrimination was an everyday occurrence as the phrase, common in job advertisements for clerks and other white-collar positions, "No Irish need apply," indicates. It was customary to see such signs as early as the 1830's. The type of employment open to the Irish was heavy construction work. "Who digs the canals of America, and builds the foundations of her railways?" asked a writer in the 'thirties. "They are almost exclusively Irish labourers . . . ignorant, groveling, intemperate, addicted to fighting. They go from a bad condition on this side of the Atlantic [the Irish side], to make themselves worse, if possible, on the other." [28] Besides supplying the hard labor for internal improvements, they did much of the pick and shovel work within the city, excavating, leveling, building docks and quays, filling in swamps, digging drains, wells, and sewers. The Irish supplied the labor for the building of the New York and Harlem Railroad, completed in the 1830's, and for the construction of the Croton waterworks and aqueduct which first brought a fresh supply of water to New York in 1842. As Charles Dickens remarked after seeing two Irish workers on Broadway during his 1842 visit: "It would be hard to keep your model republics going, without the countrymen and countrywomen of those two labourers. For who else would dig, and delve, and drudge, and do domestic work, and make canals and roads, and execute great lines of Internal Improvements!" [29]

Other Irishmen found work as longshoremen, cartmen, porters, or hod carriers. In these lines unemployment was common; it was not unusual for a man to have to wait around a pier or a construction project for several days before finding a few hours' work. Irish lads hawking newspapers—"ragged, barefooted, and pertinacious"—were a familiar sight from dawn to dusk throughout the city. Irish women filled the growing need for domestic servants, while others found employment in the needle trades.[30]

German-Americans in New York, Rochester, Buffalo, and other cities were sometimes able to achieve a higher position than the Irish; a number were skilled artisans and found work in a variety of trades from bookbinding to violin making. But the fortune of the majority who remained in the cities was not much better than that of other immigrant groups. Charles Loring Brace, a writer on New York social conditions in the 1850's, was shocked at the poverty of many Germans living in East Side slums, earning a meager subsistence by gathering and selling rags and bones. Brace felt the contrast to be very great between the clean farms of southern Germany and the New World slums with "dirty yards piled high with bones and flaunting with rags, and the air smelling of carrion. . . ." [31]

Want among foreigners was commonplace. The *Tribune* of January 25, 1850, described "a large number of destitute immigrants" who out of charity had been housed in a basement hall of the police office at New York's Tombs Prison. "It was a sad and sorry sight," commented the *Tribune* reporter, "to witness these poor outcasts, who had expected a better state of things on their arrival in a foreign country, subjected to such misery." "Have we as a people,"

asked the Reverend Stephen Byrne, "paid sufficient attention to the proper establishing of ourselves in a state, not
merely of prosperity, but of simple competency or independence in this great country? Let the crowded tenement-
houses of the Eastern cities, where the very atmosphere is
poisoned by the occupancy in one house of from twenty to
forty families, and where morality itself is greatly endangered on account of associations that cannot be avoided,
answer. Let the unnamed and unnumbered graves along
the canals and railroads of the United States, answer. Let
the forlorn and forgotten creatures who, having neither
homes or friends, lie down and die in common hospitals
of the country, answer." [32]

One of the problems was that within the city the large
numbers arriving from Europe in the 'thirties and, in
increasing numbers, in the 'forties and 'fifties, glutted the
labor market, causing both greater unemployment and
lower wages than in the less populous areas of the country.
Because of this, pauperism greatly increased in the period
between 1830 and 1860. During the Irish famine year of
1847 an estimated 100,000 person received some form of
public charity in New York; this was close to one-quarter
of the city's population. The following year the Alms
House Commissioner reported that we have "in our midst,
among the multitude of our population, a greater proportion of the truly necessitous, than any other place in the
United States. The *resort* of the world must, of necessity,
be the *refuge* for the poor. It is, therefore, our unavoidable
lot to be compelled to contribute more largely to the cause
of charity than others, and yet with all the extent of the
City's bounty, how many pass their winters in the most
appalling misery." [33] Nor was this simply a phenomenon
of the Irish famine years. In 1855, New York State re-

ported an all-time high in the number of paupers treated at public expense, over 200,000. This represented a rise of more than 700 per cent in twenty years. "Both in the City and State of New York," it was stated, "the proportion of poverty and pauperism is yearly increasing." [34] Commenting on the prevalence of poverty, slums, and bad working conditions in New York, a British writer and long-time resident of Gotham declared: "It is curious and sad to see how young and insolent New York follows exactly in the tracks of old cities of effete, tyrannized, priest-ridden Europe—to use the language of young America; sometimes even going ahead." [35]

Outside Manhattan the prospects of success for the newcomer were relatively better. The rate of dispersion of foreigners landing in New York City increased in each succeeding decade from 1820 to 1860. Many settled within the state. In all the towns and cities from New York to Albany, and from Albany to Buffalo following the route of the Erie Canal, immigrants were to be found.[36]

Just how much better off than the city dweller, if at all, those who settled in rural New York were is hard to estimate. The advice offered by writers of immigrant guide books was overwhelmingly in favor of the newcomers' going to the country and taking up farming. But, for New York State at least, it is questionable how sound this counsel was. For one thing, arable land near any of the major routes of transportation, such as the Erie Canal, was expensive. In 1850 a traveler reported that improved lands in the Mohawk Valley near the Canal cost as much as $70 an acre. Even forty miles away from the canal land prices were as high as $35 an acre.[37]

Not only were land prices high, but chances of making a living on the land were not promising for new farmers.

Throughout the period under consideration, from 1830 to 1860, the percentage of the population engaged in agriculture was declining. As early as 1844 only 44 per cent of the state's population were so occupied, and rural areas throughout these decades grew at a very slow rate. For example, a close study which a recent historian has made of New York State's upper Susquehanna Valley reveals that by 1830 the valley contained 85,500 inhabitants, a number that was not surpassed until 1860, when 86,000 were reported.[38]

Thus, the number of foreign-born who settled in New York State and acquired their own farms was relatively small, and there were very few Irish among them. It has been estimated that less than 10 per cent of the Irish arriving in America prior to the Civil War engaged in agriculture, and of those who did most did so as hired farm laborers.[39] English and German immigrants, frequently having larger financial resources than the Irish, were more likely to be in husbandry, and many did acquire farms in New York. The Yankee tendency to move on in search of new lands and opportunities very often placed improved farms on the market. German settlers became noted for following in the wake of Yankee migrations, taking up old farms and further improving them. German farmers tended to be hard-working and thrifty. Many, through industry and the application of economical farm methods, were able to make a living, but few became rich.[40]

For the majority of immigrants who remained in New York State, farming was not the solution to their economic problems. Many were as impoverished as the New York City immigrant. One finds, for example, that throughout the state the Irish were generally employed in poor paying and unskilled non-farming jobs. They did the heaviest work for the least pay. They dug the canals and built the railroads; they provided a cheap labor force for the factories. In northern New York they lumbered and quarried; at Port Henry, Trout River, Clayton, Ausable Forks, and Rogersfield, they manned the iron mines. At Codyville, Black Brook, and Brasher Falls they worked in tanneries. Throughout central New York former Irish canal workers were settled. In Utica and Binghamton they did construction and factory work; in Syracuse they were employed in the salt mines. The shack replaced the tenement, but the lot of the upstate Irish was not too different from that of the city Irish.[41]

Comparisons made between other immigrant groups within New York City and elsewhere in the state show similar results. German settlers were found in large numbers in most of the upstate cities, especially Rochester and Buffalo. In Buffalo the 1855 New York Census reported 30,000 Germans out of a total population of 74,000. As in New York, many Germans were successful as skilled craftsmen and mechanics, but more made livings as common laborers. German slums in western New York cities rivaled those in Manhattan.[42]

III

It is generally held by present-day historians that immigration did not adversely affect the American economy in regard to such factors as workers' wages or social mobility. The coming of the immigrants is viewed as a dynamic force, operating from below, helping to push persons from the earlier lower ranks to higher job levels. As one of the leading historians of immigration, Oscar Handlin, writes: "Immigration . . . endowed the social structure with fluidity. In an expanding culture it was difficult to preserve fixed forms, to establish rigid class distinctions that might limit opportunities. Diversity and mobility became characteristic features of life in the United States." [43]

Over an extended period the Handlin thesis is undoubtedly true. However, if one considers only the effects of heavy immigration on the single generation preceding the Civil War a contrary picture emerges. As the historian of the Irish movement in these years writes: with heavy immigration "the gulf between classes widened perceptibly, ushering in the modern age of acute class consciousness and the wage struggle." During the two decades preceding the Civil War the United States moved from a condition of fluidity toward a state of stratification.[44] The evidence regarding New York State during the period supports these conclusions.

A good illustration of the adverse economic effects of mass immigration is the general reduction in workers' real wages between the 1830's and the outbreak of the Civil War. A frequent complaint during this period was that recent immigrants, working for a pittance, made it difficult for other workers to gain decent wages, or, in some cases, even to find work. A writer in 1850 fretted that Germans working for low wages had "caused a great reduction in the price of labour." He described a German who, speaking no English, arrived in Buffalo and took away from a native American a job chopping firewood. Because of this sort of thing, the writer concluded, the Germans "are utterly disliked by the labouring Yankees, and, indeed by all except those who employ them." [45]

Grumblings of this sort were well-founded. Wages for an unskilled laborer dropped from an average of a dollar a day in the early 1830's to less than seventy-five cents a day a decade later. Wages of skilled workers, although less affected, dropped also. That immigrants took only jobs that native Americans scorned was simply not true. In many instances Yankee workers, such as the Buffalo wood-chopper, were put out of jobs by foreigners willing to work for less, or else were forced to accept reduced pay. This was true not merely of unskilled jobs, but even in some of the craft trades. As one newspaper writer bemoaned in 1844:

> Our labouring men, native and naturalized, are met at every turn and every avenue of employment, with re-cently imported workmen from the low wages countries of the world. Our public improvements, railroads, and canals are thronged with foreigners. They fill our large cities, reduce the wages of labor, and increase the hard-ships of the old settlers.[46]

Much of the impetus underlying nativist reaction to immi-gration in the 1840's and 1850's was economic in nature.

Heavy immigration also contributed to the boom-bust cycle of the American economy, which greatly hurt the laboring classes. During prosperous times such as the mid-'thirties, increasing immigration helped prolong the boom by keeping labor available and wages low. But once a depression set in, as it did in 1837 and again in the late 1850's, its severity was much greater and longer lasting because of the numerous unemployed and destitute im-migrants.[47]

Large-scale immigration also made unified action on the part of labor difficult. After the collapse of the New York labor movement in 1837, the increasing availability of low-priced Irish and German laborers greatly hindered the effective revival of unions. Similarly, this labor surplus tended to counteract the safety-valve effect of cheap land

and the frontier in drawing off workers from New York and other eastern cities. After 1840 the magnitude of the emigration to America came close to creating a permanent semi-pauperized working class.[48]

Not only political nativists, but Americans as a whole, regarded recent immigrants as inferior beings, little better than the Negro. Immigrants, observed a contemporary, "are singled out and kept apart, from the mere circumstances of their birth, as a distinct and inferior caste—denounced in the degrading vocabulary of every native American, as unworthy of a more intimate fellowship with him, and in no wise fitted for the enjoyment of that rational freedom and independence, which at another time he claims as of man's inheritance—the inborn right of every human being." [49] Even an Irish emigrant agent felt compelled to warn his fellow countrymen not to be too proud and think that America was a land of freedom where one man was as good as another. "It is true," he wrote, "that at the legal tribunal and at the voting booth all are equal, but there the equality ends. . . . Every demand for a fellowship with respectable society, grounded upon the *law* of the land, will be rejected with contempt. . . ." [50] This class feeling, coupled with the fact that immigrants as a whole filled the most menial positions in society, made social stratifications more pronounced.

This is well illustrated by the changing status of domestic servants. Prior to the flood of foreign immigration in the 1840's and 1850's, native Americans were mainly employed as domestic servants; they were called and generally treated as "help," not as servants, and class lines were not tightly drawn.[51] But by the mid-'forties the Irish came to form the most numerous and important group engaged in domestic employment. German women also entered this profession in growing numbers and by the early 'fifties were second only to the Irish. With the increased use of the foreign-born, class lines tightened, and fewer native Americans entered into service. The term "servant" was once more introduced and the wearing of livery—the hated badge of servitude—became common. No longer was domestic service a temporary position. These workers came to be a semi-permanent class of domestics, serving the needs of the wealthier classes.[52]

Few foreigners, unless they came to America with wealth or special skills, rose above menial, subordinate positions during this period. They generally ate and drank better than in Europe, but this was usually the extent of their advancement. As a British resident in America wrote: "but a very limited proportion indeed of the numbers—the many thousands who annually migrate to the United States, ever reach to mediocrity, much less to affluence or station. . . ."[53]

Not finding the promised plenty that they had been led to expect, many immigrants repented of ever having come to America. A Welshman living in New York wrote of his fellow immigrants: "The chief want and disadvantage which I saw among them was the scarcity of circulating money; they were ready enough to worship the DOLLAR, could they have seen one." "I have encountered many of my fellow-countrymen," he concluded, "who would go back to their native land if they could, but Oh! without having the means. . . ."[54]

After seeing the poor prospects for immigrants, Francis Wyse, a Britisher who spent several years in the United States during the 1840's, wrote a three-volume work *America, Its Realities and Resources*, which aimed at dissuading future Europeans from emigrating. Wyse was critical of the two standard economic motives for migrating to this country—cheap land and high wages. There was abundant land, he admitted, but the expenses and difficulties involved in creating a successful farm he found "almost insurmountable" for a poor man. As for wages, although somewhat higher than in England, Wyse saw that much employment was seasonal and that living expenses were higher. All too often the immigrant was left "at the end of a laborious struggle, with scarcely any better prospects than when he first started; and certainly without making any very rapid advance in that independence, and increased wealth, which he was so confidently promised as a corollary to his labours at the outset." [55]

The second generation, of course, had better prospects of advancement than did their parents, but even here social and economic improvement was the exception rather than the rule. A study of the relative status of first- and second-generation immigrants in New York's predominantly foreign Sixth and Tenth Wards, based upon the New York State Census of 1855, reveals that out of 201 second-generation immigrants, largely Irish and German, only 44, or less than 22 per cent, attained a higher status than their parents. [56] This is not to say that pre-Civil War immigrants did not eventually rise; the Civil War helped the Irish and Germans both economically and socially. But generally it was not until the massive foreign influx from southern and eastern Europe in the late nineteenth century that the older immigrant groups made substantial improvements. [57]

New York's upper classes were not threatened by immigration. Rather it was the reverse; large-scale immigration bestowed prosperity on them. From the mid-'forties on, the newcomers brought a seemingly endless supply of unskilled, cheap labor, making possible the full introduction of factory production to the profit of some, but to the detriment of both native and foreign laborers. Yearly more and more workers found themselves in the category of permanent wage-earners, while social positions became more fixed and distinct.

5

◄••••►

FACTORIES AND FORTUNES

As the conditions of men constituting the nation become more and more equal, the demand for manufactured commodities becomes more general and more extensive; and the cheapness which places these objects within the reach of slender fortunes becomes a great element of success. Hence there are every day more men of great opulence and education who devote their wealth and knowledge to manufactures; and who seek, by opening large establishments, and by strict division of labour, to meet the fresh demands which are made on all sides. Thus, in proportion as the mass of the nation turns to democracy, that particular class which is engaged in manufactures becomes more aristocratic. Men grow more alike in the one—more different in the other; and inequality increases in the less numerous class, in the same ratio in which it decreases in the community.

—Alexis de Tocquerville,
Democracy in America (1840)

B Y the eve of the Civil War, America had passed through the most important early stages of the industrial revolution. In 1840 the total value of manufactured goods produced in the United States was less than $500 million; twenty years later this figure stood at nearly $2 billion, and the country was well on the way to becoming the world's leading industrial nation.

The impact of industrialization on American society was very great in the three decades before the Civil War.

The spread of factories hastened the decline of domestic and craft shop manufacturers. The demand for skilled artisans lessened, while the ranks of the unskilled were filled with recent immigrants. Cities multiplied, experiencing their greatest relative growth in the nation's history during the 1840's and 1850's. In the latter decade New York became the first American city to pass the million mark in population. These changes made all the problems associated with an urban-industrial society clearly apparent. Slums, crime, and filth spread in the burgeoning cities. The persistent encroachment of machines and mass production made workers in the skilled trades feel severely threatened. As factories grew there was a steady trend toward concentrating production in larger and larger units controlled by absentee owners. "The wealthy monopolists," complained a reporter in 1849, "are anxious to crush those who are doing a small business and get them out of the way, in order that they may fix prices to suit themselves." [1]

Industrialization caused class lines to tighten and class consciousness to increase. Great wealth was created through manufacturing, but it was seldom shared by the growing number of factory operatives, who showed signs of becoming a permanent wage-earning class. At the other extreme, the triumph of industrialization created a new capitalist aristocracy whose fortunes and power far outstripped that of any earlier elite group in America.

I

The real beginning of the factory system in New York, as in the country at large, came during the Napoleonic wars. Cut off from imports by the restrictive legislation of

Jefferson and Madison and blockaded by Britain following the outbreak of war in 1812, Americans were forced to manufacture their own commodities. Many well-to-do merchants and shippers, suffering from the drop in trade, turned to manufacturing for the first time. By the end of the War of 1812, the factory system had a foothold.[2]

America's infant factories faced a severe test after 1815. British merchants and manufacturers, anxious to regain the American market and nip American competition in the bud, dumped enormous quantities of goods in this country at low prices. As Henry Brougham said in Parliament: "It is worth while to incur a loss upon the first exportation in order, by a glut, to stifle in the cradle those rising manufactures in the United States which the war has forced into existence contrary to the natural course of things."[3] Importations rose in value from $13 million in 1813 to $147 million in 1816. The bulk of these goods entered the United States by way of New York harbor. This caused a brisk rise in New York's commercial activity and was particularly advantageous to auction companies. But many of the manufacturing firms within the city and the state seemed doomed because of this British competition.[4]

To offset the glut of British goods on the American market, manufacturers beseeched the state and national governments for relief. An American Society for the Encouragement of Domestic Manufacturers was established in New York City in 1816 to advocate protective tariffs. From Oneida County a group of cotton and woolen manufacturers warned that an investment of $600,000 was endangered. Elsewhere in the state similar complaints from manufacturing interests were heard.[5] Strong postwar nationalism together with the lack of organized opposition to tariff protection led to the passage by Congress in 1816 of the first avowedly protective tariff in American history.

In 1824 and again in 1828 the tariff was revised upward. The "Tariff of Abominations" of 1828 was the high-water mark of pre-Civil War protection; after this, strong opposition from the Southern planters and other agrarian and commercial interests necessitated compromise between protection and free trade. But even wth the lower tariff duties of 1833, 1846, and 1857, the principle of protection of domestic industry was maintained to the benefit of manufacturers in New York and elsewhere.[6]

Although manufacturing in the Empire State suffered from the fact that New York City was the nation's chief commercial and importing center, the state itself was far-sighted in aiding manufacturing interests. Well before the close of hostilities with Britain in 1815, New York State had adopted a policy patronizing to industrial interests. As early as 1790, the legislature granted an earthenware manufacturer a loan, declaring that "the establishment of useful manufactures is closely connected with the public weal" and that "it is desirous to encourage the same." Legislative loans to individuals or corporations engaged in manufacturing became fairly common. Between 1812 and 1816, for example, twenty-eight state loans were authorized amounting to $143,500; these went chiefly to firms making cotton and woolen cloth and iron products.[7]

New York was also the first state to pass a general incorporation law, in 1811. The law permitted manufacturing firms to be chartered, providing they filed certain basic information and their capital was not over $100,000. Prior to this, special legislative acts were necessary to create a corporation, and the corporate form of business enterprise was used primarily in public fields such as banking, utilities, transportation, and insurance. The law of 1811 allowed manufacturers to take advantage of the corporate structure; between that date and 1818, one hundred and twenty-nine charters were granted to New York manufacturing firms. By 1830 a fair number of firms had incorporated, many of which were capitalized at well over the original $100,000 limit.[8]

The completion of the Erie Canal, announced by a relay of cannons from Buffalo to New York on October 26, 1825, opened a new chapter in the state's history. The great success of Governor DeWitt Clinton's famed ditch not only started a national boom in canal construction, but also speeded the industrial revolution by opening up vast new markets to manufactured goods. The Canal stimulated manufacturing along its entire route. In the West, primary manufactures such as grain and saw milling were encouraged, while in the East, secondary manufactures such as the making of boots and shoes, vehicles, implements, stoves, and textiles were given a boost. It is significant that for several decades after 1825, the Great Lakes Basin developed no industrial towns comparable to Pittsburgh, Lexington, and Cincinnati along the Ohio River system, for it remained dependent on New York City and the manufacturing districts located along the Hudson and Mohawk valleys to supply the kind of articles that the Ohio River cities furnished to the settlers of the Mississippi Valley. The Canal set in motion a current of trade highly favorable to a variety of industries along its course and in New York City. From the West came an endless supply of raw materials—iron ore, lead, wool, leather, lumber, grain, and potash. Less than one per cent of the west-to-east canal freight was classified as manufactured, and this included a good deal of whiskey, while the overwhelming percentage of cargoes hauled from east to west were manufactured products.[9]

By the late 1820's manufacturing in New York State was thriving. James Hardie, in a book on New York City written in 1827, boasted that the city's yearly output of cotton cloth had risen from less than 3000 yards in 1812 to nearly 1,175,000 yards in 1825. "Other factories," he reported, "have advanced in at least an equal ratio, and new ones are almost daily springing into existence." Five years later, another New Yorker exclaimed:

> The whole region, from east to west of the State, presents one bustling, stirring, scene, not unlike a May-day hive of bees—all moved to activity by their connexions with the city of New York, which receives their products, and renders them their delicacies.[10]

During the mid-1820's the profits of shippers and commercial auctioneers declined as prices of imports dropped. The formerly lucrative China trade went into a slump as the markets for Oriental luxury goods became saturated. Shippers and merchants began investing in other enterprises, among which manufacturing was important. Between 1826 and 1830 John Jacob Astor took his money out of ocean commerce. In 1834 he invested $60,000 in Philip Hone's Matteawan Company to expand its textile mills. Hone, the fashionable ex-Mayor of New York City, was himself an example of a person who, having made his fortune in the New York auction business, invested his funds chiefly in mining, manufacturing, and transportation.[11] Many other merchants and shippers began employing their capital similarly.

In Jacksonian New York the factory system was not yet

dominant. In all but a few industries handicraft and domestic production prevailed. However, the days of the
craft shop and home manufacturing were numbered. Until
the nation-wide depression of the late 'thirties caused a
temporary setback, factory production grew rapidly. By
the mid-'thirties, in the manufacture of textiles, clothing,
and shoes the factory had surpassed the craft shop and the
home.[12] The largest factories in the 'thirties were those
producing cotton textiles. In 1831 New York had 112 cotton mills; only Massachusetts, with 250, and Rhode Island, with 116, had more. Already there was a tendency
for larger mills to dominate the industry.[13]

New York's woolen production similarly came to be
established firmly on a factory basis in this period. In 1831
the state's woolen mills were collectively capitalized at
nearly $900,000 and employed over 1200 workers. Nine
years later in 1840, the woolen factories showed a significant increase. By the latter date these mills represented a
capital investment estimated at about $3.5 million and
employed nearly 4650 workers. This rapid gain in the
wool industry was made while the number of factories decreased, illustrating the tendency of the larger concerns
to dominate the field.[14]

As factory production came to dominate the textile industry, household manufacture markedly dropped off. By
the 'fifties, not only in textiles, but in every other field,
household manufactures were almost wholly superseded by
factory-made goods.[15] Along with the decline of household
manufactures, small craft shops also waned. In some cases
the handicrafts traditionally found in towns and villages
simply disappeared. In other instances they were transformed into larger units. Thus the cabinetmaker's shop
could become a furniture factory, a blacksmith shop could

become an engine works or a stove manufacture.[16] By 1840 the process of transformation from craft production to factory was far from complete, but it was well under way. Where transportation was best, household and craft manufactures were fewest. In most New York cities and villages, however, small shops and mills continued to exist, although larger factories were becoming more common.[17]

According to the United States Census of 1840, New York State annually produced manufactured goods valued at $96 million. In that year the total amount invested in manufactures in the state (exclusive of iron works, which were classified with mines) was over $55.25 million. Both in annual production and in capital investment in manufacturing, New York led every other state. New York City alone produced goods valued at nearly $23.4 million, an increase of 242 per cent over the rather unreliable figures given in the State Census of 1835. The leading manufacturing enterprises in 1840 were cotton factories, woolen mills, iron works, distilleries, and tanneries. Within New York City over two-thirds of those gainfully employed were engaged in some sort of manufacture; the figure for the remainder of the state was 25 per cent. Clearly the factory system was well on its way to dominating New York's economy.[18]

II

The two decades between the panics of 1837 and 1857 were years of phenomenal economic growth in New York and the nation. It was during this period that factories began returning sufficient profits to supply a good share of the necessary capital for future development and expansion. The growth of major industries was maintained by plowing back part of these profits and by attracting European capital. In this way the industrial revolution became self-sustaining, no longer dependent on government as the chief supplier of capital. During these years the United States, particularly in the Middle Atlantic and New England states, built up what a recent economist has termed the "social overhead capital" necessary for carrying through the industrial revolution. Americans were being propelled toward the modern world in which the wealth of the factory would far overshadow the riches of the soil. By 1850 the value of manufactured goods already surpassed that of agricultural products.[19]

In value of output, number of workers engaged in manufacturing, and diversity of industrial production, New York continued to lead every other state in the three decades preceding the Civil War.[20] The pre-eminence of New York owed much to the state's natural and man-made advantages. It had the finest harbor on the Atlantic Coast, as well as the most central and economical route to the West along the gateway of the Hudson and Mohawk valleys. Long the commercial leader of the nation, as well as its financial center, New York had more investment capital available than any other state. Since New York City was the port of entry for the great majority of immigrants, the state's industries had a more than adequate supply of cheap labor. In addition, New York had an ample food supply, many natural resources, and favorable corporation laws.

After 1840, railroads came to play an extremely significant role in New York's economic development. Far more than turnpikes or canals, railroads broke down local self-sufficiency and encouraged commercial farming and manufacturing. The Mohawk and Hudson Railroad had been incorporated in 1826 with the "Good Patroon" Stephen Van Rennsselaer as its first president. Five years later the engine "DeWitt Clinton" was pulling the first trains on a sixteen-mile stretch from Albany to Schenectady. At the time this was the second operational railroad in the country. Railroads were viewed chiefly as supplements to the waterways of the state. By 1840, however, railroads had passed their experimental stage; their advantages in speed, dependability, and year-round service were now recognized. In 1841 New York had over a thousand miles of tracks, more than one-fourth of the total track mileage in the country. With the completion of the Attica to Buffalo line on November 24, 1842, it was possible to travel across the state from Albany to Buffalo by train.[21]

In the 'forties railroads began to gain a larger percentage of the freight carried in the state. But until 1851 the New York legislature banned freight shipments on rail lines bordering the canal routes except in winter. When this ban was lifted, railroads transported practically all freight with the exception of bulky raw materials such as lumber and grain. In 1853, Erastus Corning, a wealthy Albany merchant, combined the various short lines across the state and their branches into the New York Central Company, which provided direct rail service from Albany to Buffalo and had connections with lines from Boston and New York in the East and with lines running along the south shore of Lake Erie, reaching as far as Chicago and St. Louis to the West.[22]

Two years before the New York Central had consolidated the lines running parallel to Clinton's canal, the Erie Railroad, which a group of New York merchants had chartered in 1832, completed its connections from east to west. With Daniel Webster riding—at least part of the way

—in a rocking chair fastened to the top of a flatcar, and with President Millard Filmore among the celebrities, the first Erie train made its way from Piermont on the Hudson to Dunkirk on Lake Erie in May 1851. This line, running through New York's Southern Tier, although beset by financial and engineering difficulties, did provide the state with another important direct route between New York City and the West.[23]

By the Civil War the United States had over 30,000 miles of railroad tracks, over 3000 of which crisscrossed New York State. It was then possible to travel from New York to Chicago to St. Louis or Memphis and back to New York. In the late 'fifties New York railroads were hauling nearly 3.5 million tons of freight yearly.[24] Freight rates, although slightly higher than water transportation, had been reduced to less than two cents per ton mile. More than any other innovation in the nation's history the railroad gave this country a national economy, completing the demise of self-sufficient farming and household manufacturing.

In 1860 the writer of a New York gazetteer, J. H. French, commented on the impact of the railroad on industrial production; "the lines of internal communication through the State," he wrote, "have greatly facilitated the spread of manufactures; and now flourishing establishments are found in nearly every part of the State." [25]

The railroads' creation of an interdependent national economy had given rise to larger firms and greater regional specialization. New York's manufacturing remained highly diversified; however, certain localities became noted for particular products. The Albany-Troy region emerged as the nation's leading center for the production of iron goods such as stoves, nails, horseshoes, railroad spikes, bells, railroad cars, and coaches and carriages. Iron ore was mined in the southern highlands, chiefly in Orange County, and in the Adirondack and Lake Champlain area of New York, but by the 'forties a great deal of iron ore was being brought in from out-of-state via the Erie Canal. In 1850 the yearly net value of New York State's metal products, including machinery, was nearly $28 million.[26]

To the north of the Albany-Troy complex was the state's valuable lumber industry. Northern river towns on the fringe of the Adirondack forests such as Glens Falls, Watertown, Ticonderoga, Mechanicville, and Schuylerville became great lumber producing centers. Lumbering was also extensive in the western part of the state. New York led all other states up through the Civil War period in the manufacture of wood articles such as furniture, cabinets, and kitchen utensils. The total net value of New York's wood products was approximately $14.5 million in 1850.[27]

Another important industry was the manufacture of leather and leather goods. With the possible exception of textile manufacturing, the leather industry employed more persons than any other in the state. Tanneries were found throughout New York, but particularly in the Catskill Mountain region, where use was made of the vast hemlock forests in the tanning process. New York City was the center for the manufacture of finished leather products. Goods produced ranged from leather undergarments—"much more conductive [sic] to health as well as more pleasant to wear than flannel"—to saddles, shoes, shirts, and gloves. The 1850 valuation for leather and leather products was over $11.6 million.[28]

In New York's western cities, manufacturing remained more diversified.[29] Yet here too specialization was apparent. Both Rochester and Buffalo were the nation's flour-grinding centers until surpassed by cities farther to the West in the mid-'fifties.[30]

The chief manufacturing center of the state was, of course, the mushrooming metropolis, New York City.[31] In Gotham, industrialists made everything from ships to socks. Dilapidated sweatshops along Chatham Street between the Battery and City Hall Park were the center of New York's numerous ready-made clothing shops. After the perfection of the sewing machine by Elias Howe in 1846, this industry flourished, turning out much of the clothing for the country. Along the East and North rivers bordering on lower Manhattan were located the various shipbuilding and marine-supply establishments. It was here that many of America's ante-bellum sailing ships were constructed, including the famous clipper ships. Other important city industries included such things as furniture-making, sugar-refining, distilling, shoe-making, textile production, and the making of precision implements and musical instruments.[32]

Thomas Cochran recently wrote that "the nation's business in 1855 was nearly as intersectional as in 1870. . . . By the late 1850's the United States was a rapidly maturing industrial state with its major cities connected by rail, its major industries selling in a national market, and blessed or cursed with financiers, security flotations, stock markets, and all the other appurtenances of industrial capitalism." [33] For New York State this was unquestionably the case. By the mid-century period the factory system had superseded handicraft and domestic production. New York has passed through the most fundamental stages of the industrial revolution.

III

The changes wrought by the economic transformation which took place between 1830 and 1860 had a profound effect on American society. Tocqueville had speculated in the early 'thirties on what long-range consequences factory production might have on American society. He deprecated the trend toward greater specialization of labor. "What," he asked, "can be expected of a man who has spent twenty years of his life in making heads for pins?" His answer was that the more labor was subdivided, the weaker the individual laborer would become. On the other hand, he predicted that as manufacturing expanded, wealthy capitalists would emerge who would take a broad view of the entire business and not see just one aspect. The difference between owners and workers would increase with factory production. "Each of them fills the station which is made for him, and out of which he does not get: the one is continually, closely, and necessarily dependent upon the other, and seems as born to obey as the other is to command. What is this but aristocracy?" [34]

Native Americans witnessing the early changes caused by industrialization expressed similar fears. A labor paper, the *Mechanics' Free Press* (Philadelphia), August 9, 1828, was alarmed by the thought that the United States "shall soon add one more to the catalogue of nations, whom aristocracy has blasted, and whom inequality of wealth, has precipitated from a comparatively prosperous situation to the lowest grade of degradation and misery." A few years later Ralph Waldo Emerson confessed in his *Journal* the fear that the increasing power of the rising industrialists would "upset the balance of man, and establish a new, universal monarchy more tyrannical than Babylon or Rome." [35]

By the mid-'forties it seemed to many Americans that these earlier forebodings had become realities. The most obvious aspect of the industrial revolution was the physical change in production methods—the use of water power and steam-driven machines, and the new factory system. But an equally important aspect of this revolution was what one historian has termed the less dramatic "social revolution in which sovereignty in economic affairs passed from the community as a whole into the keeping of a special class." [36] Two new classes emerged—capitalists and workers—and, just as Tocqueville had foreseen, the gap between these classes was accentuated. In the factories, no longer did a master-owner work by the side of his journeymen and apprentices.

In the major manufacturing enterprises ownership was widely removed from the workers. This was particularly true of corporations, a form of business organization which multiplied in the two decades before the Civil War. Corporations easily withstood the strong sentiment against them in the Jacksonian period. Laws of general incorporation which helped separate the corporation from politics and special privilege were adopted in most states by the 'forties. In 1846 New York State revised its corporation law of 1811 to allow any company to incorporate regardless of capital. This law also provided for limited liability to stockholders. The advantages of conducting business under this method of organization were many. The corporation with transferable shares was the best method of raising large capital, and it had longevity, something which proprietorships and partnerships lacked. Because of these features many of New York's major enterprises were incorporated.[37]

The incorporated factory was an impersonal entity in which the actual owners seldom had a direct role in supervising the labor force. In the 'forties and 'fifties corporation directors were learning how to control great fortunes and use them to gain personal profits, with little risk involved and with no concern about laboring conditions. Railroad corporations led the way in this development. It was in this period that financiers such as Daniel Drew, Edward Crane, Robert Schuyler, and Cornelius Vanderbilt started their railroad empires. Although the railroad multi-millionaires were a postwar phenomenon, the way was certainly cleared for these rail kings, and by the 'fifties railroads like the Erie were the playthings of Wall Street.[38]

The industrial production of the 'seventies and 'eighties makes that of the 'forties and 'fifties seem small scale; but this is misleading. The rate of industrial growth in terms of the value added by manufactures was greater in the two decades from 1839 to 1859 than during any other twenty-year period of the nineteenth century.[39] But quite apart from economic statistics is the fact that the generation of the 'forties and 'fifties was the first to experience fully the effects of the industrial revolution. This experience must have been a greater shock than anything felt by Americans of the late nineteenth century, since it marked such a radical departure from the agrarian past. Virtually all of the major industrial problems associated with the Gilded Age—from urban slums to a grossly unequal division of wealth—were experienced first by Americans of the generation immediately preceding the Civil War.

Industry produced more wealth than had hitherto existed in America, while at the same time the distribution of wealth became more and more ill-balanced. Mrs. Lydia Child, an American writer of juvenile fiction, described the visibility of New York City's growing inequality of fortunes in the mid-'forties. "A few moments' walk from salons superbly furnished in the style of Louis XIV, brings us to Loafers' Hall, a dreary desolate apartment where shivering urchins pay a cent apiece, for the privilege of keeping out of the watchmen's hands, by sleeping on boards ranged in tiers." In the early 'sixties a Scottish artisan living in New York wrote:

> The independent, equal, and familiar relation which masters and men were wont to bear to each other is daily assuming a more exclusive character; the moneyed men will not be content with the mere value in labour for their cash; they must have that respect, or outward show of it which their wealth demands. . . . Men value money for two things: in the first place, it ministers to their creature comforts, and in the second, it gives them power, both socially and morally.[40]

In 1820 there were only 102 men in New York City whose personal property had an assessed value of over $20,000. Twenty-five years later when Moses Yale Beach issued his fifth edition of *Wealth and Biography*, comprising brief sketches of New Yorkers worth over $100,000, there were 950 persons in this category, including twenty-one "millionaires"—a term that first came into vogue in the early 'forties.[41]

Not all this wealth, of course, was a direct result of industrialization. Along with its pre-eminent position as a manufacturing center, New York State retained its commercial leadership. In 1851 New York's commerce accounted for 41 per cent of the nation's export trade and 61 per cent of the import trade. Many of the state's richest men were in the traditional commercial professions of shipping, auctioneering, importing or exporting, and banking.[42]

Two of the country's richest men by the late 'forties were Alexander T. Stewart and Horace B. Claflin, rival dry goods merchants in New York City. Stewart, a Scots-Irish immigrant, had opened a small shop on Broadway in the mid-'twenties. By the late 'thirties he was doing the largest retail and wholesale dry goods business in the country. His marble store on Broadway between Reade and Chambers Street was America's first modern department store. Stewart was one of the earliest businessmen to realize the value of selling great quantities of goods at a small profit, making money through the high volume of sales. In this manner he made millions, and by the 1850's was the second richest man in America.[43]

Claflin, his chief competitor, was a New Englander who did not enter the New York dry goods business until 1843, after a successful merchandising career in Massachusetts. Like Stewart, he soon built up a nation-wide wholesale business as well as a large retail trade through his Broadway store. By the time of the Civil War his wealth was conservatively estimated at $10 million.[44]

Others made great fortunes from urban real estate. If one was fortunate or farsighted enough to own land in or around an expanding city, it was almost a mathematical certainty that this land would increase in value. City real estate was not subject to the extreme fluctuations that affected rural landholdings. This was particularly true of land in New York City. When Henry Brevoort died at the age of ninety-four in 1848, his estate was valued at about one million dollars. Most of this wealth came from the ownership of eleven acres of land in the heart of the city.

Formerly a dairy and vegetable farm to the north of the city in Greenwich Village, the growth of New York placed the Brevoort farm running from 8th Street and Fourth Avenue to 13th Street and Sixth Avenue nearly in the city's center.[45] Other New York City families such as the Schermerhorns, Rhinelanders, Goelets, and Lorillards owed their wealth chiefly to landholdings in Manhattan.[46]

New York's greatest landlord and the country's richest man was John Jacob Astor. While amassing his fur fortune in the early nineteenth century, Astor, visualizing the phenomenal growth of New York, invested an average of $35,000 annually in city real estate between 1800 and 1819. He bought such property as the Medeef Eden farm, which ran from the future site of 42nd Street to 46th and from Broadway to the Hudson. By the time of his death in 1848 the Astor landholdings were worth over $20 million.[47]

Conventionally, historians in speaking of New York society of the pre-Civil War generation have made a distinction between mercantile and landholding families on the one hand and rising capitalist-industrialists on the other, implying that these groups—representing an "old" and a "new" aristocracy—were somehow diametrically opposed to one another.[48] This division is highly misleading. For one thing there was no such clear-cut split between types of wealth. Virtually every New Yorker of fortune had money tied up in more than one enterprise, and most were quick to support new enterprises in the fields of industry and transportation. For example, Robert Schuyler, scion of the Hudson Valley gentry, was one of the leading pre-Civil War railroad magnates and president of the New York and New Haven Railroad.[49]

William Aspinwall, a wealthy and highly respected merchant who, together with William Howland, headed New York's largest importing and exporting firm, retired from this field in 1851 to devote his full time to railroad development. He and his associates financed the building of the lucrative trans-Panama railroad, which provided the fastest transportation to California. By 1859 the railroad alone netted a profit of over $6 million, and Aspinwall became one of New York's richest citizens. Another well-to-do importer, John Jay Phelps, also became a prominent railway promoter.[50]

Examples of this sort could be multiplied endlessly, but the point is that there was not such a sharp division between an "old" and a "new" wealth. The common meeting ground of all New York men of fortune was the Stock Exchange. Here could be found wealthy industrialists such as Peter Cooper and William Colgate talking familiarly with an Astor or a Goelet on the latest price of Hudson River Railway. By the 'forties and 'fifties the stock market on Wall Street was a well-organized and highly developed institution, largely serving the rich. Investors, whether merchants, landholders, or industrialists, were chiefly concerned with making a profit. In this period the instrument of profit-making became the corporation, which skilled financiers learned to control and to manipulate on the stock market for private gain.[51]

Stock manipulation was common, and certainly no bar to respectability. "The greatest gambling in the Republic," wrote a New Yorker, "is going on, and the deepest dishonesty is concealed by the garb of commercial honor. No one asks nor expects favors. All stratagems are deemed fair in Wall Street." [52] "Bulls" would purchase shares at a low price and then spread rumors of government grants or large dividends to raise the price. "Bears" gossiped to send prices tumbling and then bought low. Out of all this great profits were made by insiders, while the small investor was fleeced.

There was also wide selling of unauthorized or forged stocks. Robert Schuyler in his position as president of the New York and New Haven Railroad in 1854 sold 20,000 hypothecated shares in his own company for a personal profit of over $2 million. As the diarist George Templeton Strong noted, this swindle was committed "by no nameless money-making speculator, but by one of our 'first' people in descent and social position and supposed wealth. . . ." Schuyler fled with the money and was never brought to justice. That same year Alexander Kyle of the Harlem Railroad sold $300,000 worth of forged stock for his own profit. Two years later, Charles B. Huntington, a Wall Street broker and well-known figure in New York society, was apprehended after forging some $300,000 worth of stock certificates. Though occasionally criminal activity of this sort was discovered and condemned, many dishonest stock market manipulations were dismissed or even praised because of their success.[53]

Heirs of patroons and the first Grace Church pew purchasers and newer Episcopalians alike were capable of formulating and following together a new Wall Street ethic. G. G. Foster, a prolific New York author, described the financial magnate of the 1850's as follows:

The engines and instruments by which this man works are numerous and characteristic. Sometimes he forestalls the market of a certain kind of product and then when his carefully concealed operations are completed, gradually expands the price in accordance with the increasing demand, until he thus gathers his thousands from the absolute necessities of the community. Sometimes he organizes a company to kindly supply the people with money, or to dig coal, or copper, or zinc, or lead, from fabulous mines, drawn carefully out on paper maps, and situated in some inaccessible Sahara amid the wild regions of New

Jersey. Then he sells the stock out upon a fictitious valuation got up by incessant puffs in the leading commercial papers, and so makes a fortune, and the scheme explodes. Sometimes he discovers that the interests and honor of the nation require a railroad from Frogtown to Tadpolopolis, and a similar operation lines his pocket at the cost of a few hundred green victims; or perhaps the commercial prosperity of the Empire State demands that a line of steamships should be established to break down all opposition and prove that some things can be done as well as others. Straightway the newspaper pumps are put in operation, and the books of subscription opened, and flaming appeals made to the patriotism of Congress for a small appropriation of a million or two, just by way of experiment, and to sustain the honor of the country. Of course the stock is subscribed and paid for by the victims, while the appropriation goes into the pockets of the shrewd capitalist, and he becomes more magnificent, more haughty and insolent than ever. Arrived at the station of millionaire . . . he has forgotten himself and all the incidents that might embarrass or humiliate him in his present position.[54]

The industrial revolution, in conjunction with gains in commercial wealth and urban land values, created a powerful and prestigious class of financial magnates. Although all barriers between the so-called "old" family rich and "new" were not entirely broken down so far as the drawing room was concerned, it was no longer meaningful to speak of these precise divisions by the 1850's. The old Knickerbocker elite of the 'thirties who retained both wealth and position in the 'forties and 'fifties generally did so by amalgamating with the new moneyed class. Together they acquired wealth, social recognition, and a good deal of control over the nation's manufacturing, transportation, and commercial facilities.

6

———◆◆◆◆———

THE WIDENING GAP: LABOR
IN THE 'FORTIES AND 'FIFTIES

Money is the be-all and the end-all in the States. With it
you are everything, without it nothing. The working man is
as much hemmed in the iron circle of his class as with us
[in England]; the petty storekeeper even looks down on him,
and "the dignity of labour" is both disbelieved in and ridiculed. *I assert that in no country in the world are social distinctions more rigidly enforced.*

—*London* v. *New York* (1859)

THE depression of 1837, which lasted through the early
'forties, marked a major turning point in the history of
labor in America. Previously, working conditions had
been harsh, but a vigorous labor movement had buoyed
up the position of the skilled workers throughout the
Jacksonian period. In the 'thirties the factory system was
not yet dominant, and immigration was only beginning to
be in substantial numbers. After 1837, however, both
skilled and unskilled workers were left without effective
organizations at a time when industrial expansion and
mass immigration were depressing the entire wage-earning class and widening the gap between classes.

The depression itself nipped the emerging labor movement in the bud and ushered in several years of severe

hardship. In his *Recollections,* Horace Greeley wrote of the early effects of the depression in New York City, that "the winter of 1837–38, though happily mild and open till far into January, was one of pervading destitution and suffering in our city, from paralysis of business and consequent dearth of employment. The liberality of those who could give was heavily taxed to save from famishing the tens of thousands who, being needy and unable to find employment, first ran into debt so far as they could, and thenceforth must be helped or starve." One source estimated that by January 1838, some 50,000 persons were unemployed in New York City. Another 200,000, it was said, were living "in utter and hopeless distress with no means of surviving the winter but those provided by charity." [1]

Labor suffered not only from widespread unemployment but also from reduced wages for those with jobs. Work was so scarce that thousands were willing to work for almost nothing. In August 1837, five hundred had turned up in answer to an advertisement for twenty spade laborers to work for $4 a month with board. Obviously, under these circumstances striking to maintain wages or jobs was out of the question. Employers took full advantage of the opportunity to crush the labor movement. One New York newspaper recommended that businessmen "employ no men who do not forever abjure unions." It further advised that "the rules of unions as to hours, pay, and everything else, ought to be thoroughly broken up." [2]

General economic distress caused a growing class consciousness on the part of New York workers, while at the same time respectable persons feared the possibility of class warfare. Late in 1837 angry Manhattan workers, incensed by high food prices, had attacked a flour warehouse on Washington Street and ransacked it after driving off the mayor and the police. That following spring a magazine writer observed growing signs of unrest. From everywhere, he wrote, "comes rumor after rumor of riot, insurrection, and tumult." Hordes of beggars crowded New York streets. The rich held concerts and balls to raise funds for poor relief, but these were insufficient. The problem of conducting large-scale public relief was relatively new in America and it was handled haphazardly. Perturbation continued; a New York observer in 1841 saw a growing restlessness of the "noisy and tumultuous masses—shouting for change, reform, and progress." [3]

Poverty and unemployment such as people experienced during this first major industrial depression were hard for Americans to understand. The traditional notion was that destitution stemmed from individual indolence or ineptitude, and that any honest and willing worker could find employment at a decent wage. A few humanitarians such as Horace Greeley could sympathize with the poor mechanic "whose cry was, not for the bread and fuel of charity, but for Work!" [4] But most Americans were contented to let things take their course in the optimistic belief that improvement was inevitable.

By 1843 the depression had run its course, and business once more picked up. But for the laborer prosperity did not return. "How is it," asked a New York workingman in the early 'forties, "that a country as rich as ours is yet pinched for the common necessaries of life?" [5] Workers' wage cuts ranged from 30 to 50 per cent during the depression years. In the 'forties increased industrialization in conjunction with large-scale immigration worked to keep wages low. John Finch, an English Owenite, made the following comparison of wages in Britain and in the United States in 1844:

It is much easier to obtain employment, at present, in the United States than in England; but in this respect they [American workers] are getting into worse and worse condition. The manufacturers, in the East, have introduced all our improvement in machinery, (and the effects are the same as in this country) they are making very large quantities of goods; competition is increasing, prices are very much reduced, and the wages of labour, generally, throughout the States and Canada, have been reduced from thirty to fifty per cent within the last four years . . . and, if competition continue, no parties can prevent wages from falling as low there as they are in England, and this within a comparatively short period. Wages in America are not much higher, even now, than they are with us.[6]

To the skilled artisan industrialization came as a threat. In industry after industry he felt himself challenged by new methods which required little skill or training. By the 'forties, factories had made the skill of cordwainers, coopers, and ironsmiths nearly obsolete. Printers, challenged by revolutionary new presses and steam power, found their wages, status, and independence declining. "Machinery has taken almost entire possession of the manufacture of cloth," complained Thomas Devyr, an associate of George Henry Evans on *The Working Man's Advocate;* "it is making steady—we might say rapid—advances upon all branches of iron manufacture; the newly invented machine saws, working in curves as well as straight lines, the planing and grooving machines, and the tenon and mortise machine, clearly admonish us that its empire is destined to extend itself over all our manufactures of wood; while some of our handicrafts are already extinct, there is not one of them but has foretasted the overwhelming competition of this occult power." [7]

Among the trades generally, the introduction of machinery and the use of cheaper immigrant labor caused insecurity and a drop in wages. The pay of journeymen hatters fell from an average of twelve dollars a week in 1835 to about eight dollars a week in 1845. New York cabinetmakers, facing stiff competition from factories mass-producing furniture with the aid of cheap German labor, were compelled to work longer and longer hours to earn as much as five dollars per week. A group of mechanics seeing the trend in wages asked in 1845: "How much can a mechanic lay up for sickness and old age—and what comforts the mechanic in New York can enjoy from his wages, in comparison with those engaged in some sort of business, are questions which we should like some of the brethren in New York to answer." [8]

While wages decreased or at best stayed the same in the 1840's and 1850's, the cost of living was rising. This was particularly true of New York City, where the growing population made land values soar and rents rise correspondingly. "The high price of living in New-York," wrote a resident of that city, "has borne so heavily upon the poor that it has crowded them into tenement houses, and compelled them to subsist in the most unnatural manner." [9]

Americans at the time were quick to blame the thousands of foreigners coming to this country yearly for many of the social ills of the day, especially unemployment and low wages. Yet as one historian has stated: "If the economic pattern of the time had involved a fair return for the great contribution of the immigrant, the number of foreign-born paupers would have been negligible." [10]

In November 1853 a writer for the *New York Times* drew up a budget for a working-class family of four "living moderately." The yearly budget ran as follows: [11]

Item	Amount
Groceries	$273
Rent	100
Clothing, bedding, etc.	132
Furnishings	20
Fuel	18
Lights	10
Taxes, Water, Commutation, etc.	5
Physicians' and druggists' charges	10
Travelling	12
Newspapers, postage, and library fees	10
Church, Charity, etc.	10
Total	$600

Two years earlier Horace Greeley in the *New York Tribune* had estimated a similar workingman's budget, and although Greeley allowed less for such things as traveling, newspapers, and library fees, the totals were about the same. Both sources figured the weekly income necessary for a workingman to sustain a family was approximately eleven dollars per week. But except for the workers in certain skilled trades, notably building, few received weekly wages anywhere near this sum. Factory operatives and common laborers in the early 'fifties averaged less than five dollars a week. Skilled mechanics and craftsmen earned anywhere from $1.25 to $2.00 daily. Women needle-workers, probably the lowest paid employees, seldom earned as much as two dollars weekly.[12]

These low wages created a situation where thousands of urban working-class families were living on the level of barest subsistence with no ability to save funds for any emergency. "In the city of New York," remarked a humanitarian minister in the late 'forties, "there are multitudes who earn by their daily labour just enough to maintain themselves and those dependent on them; and if sickness lays its hand on the head of the family, or one of the members, the income ceases altogether, or is inadequate to the increased expense, and aid must be obtained from abroad, or there is instant suffering for want of it." [13]

Charles Brace, organizer of the Children's Aid Society in 1853, described a New York laboring family at about that date. The husband worked in an iron foundry, but when Brace visited the family the husband had been ill for several weeks. To survive, the mother had sent her ten-year-old child out to beg in the streets. "You know how it is sir with working people," she told Brace. "If a man falls out of work for a day, the family feels it for a week after. We can hardly make the two ends meet when he's well, and the moment he is sick it comes hard upon us. Many's the morning he's gone down to the foundry without his breakfast. . . ." [14]

Working-class living conditions reflected the low wage-scales. In 1845, nearly half a century before Jacob Riis called attention to New York's poverty in *How the Other Half Lives,* Dr. John H. Griscom, a tireless worker on behalf of the poor, described in language strikingly similar to that of Riis *"the system of tenantage* to which large numbers of the poor are subject." Dr. Griscom painted a grim picture of these tenements:

> Every corner of the room, of the cupboards, of the entries and stairways, is piled up with dirt. The walls and ceilings, with the plaster broken off in many places, exposing the lath and beams, and leaving openings for the escape from within of the effluvia of vermin, dead and alive, are smeared with the blood of unmentionable insects, and dirt of indescribable colours. [15]

The actual date of the first house built expressly for multi-family dwelling in New York City is uncertain. One source speaks of a seven-story tenement at 65 Mott Street in use as early as 1825, but probably this was a converted warehouse.[16] In October 1833, James P. Allaire, a wealthy engine manufacturer, built a four-story apartment house on Water Street, which one writer claimed was "the first house constructed proper or exclusively for tenants. . . ." [17] While such a dwelling was still unique in the early 1830's, a decade later habitations of this sort had become commonplace. New York City's population far outstripped the rate of house construction. Consequently, more and more persons were forced to occupy less and less space. Landlords erected cheap apartment houses or converted into apartments the mansions abandoned by the well-to-do in their exodus to more fashionable uptown areas. Tenement houses were generally double buildings, with two apartments on each floor in the front and a similar arrangement in the rear reached by an alley. Most rooms were small, dark, and poorly ventilated. Tenants seldom had running water and almost never had indoor toilets. Rents were high, anywhere from four to ten dollars per month in the late 'forties for two rooms.[18]

New York's tenement house population spread like an endemic and infectious disease. By the Civil War over half of the city's population, nearly 500,000 persons, lived in some 18,000 tenements. New York became the most densely populated city in the Western world.[19]

The Sixth Ward, bounded by fashionable Broadway to the west, Chatham Street to the south, the Bowery to the east, and Canal Street to the north, was the most notorious slum in the country. Here was an area of overwhelming poverty, infamous for its concomitant ills of crime, vice, filth, and disease. At the center of this ward was the foul Five Points section, formed by the intersection of Orange, Cross, and Anthony Streets. It was here in 1842 that Charles Dickens, protected by two policemen, descended into the "narrow ways, diverging to right and left, and reeking everywhere with dirt and filth." [20] Here one could find drunks, sickly begging children, bedraggled women, and other figures who might have just stepped out of Hogarth's Gin Lane. A New York minister gave the following description of the housing conditions:

> Lodging-rooms above ground are numerous in the narrow lanes, and in the dark dangerous alleys that surround the Five Points. Rooms are rented from two to ten dollars a month, into which no human being would put a dog,—attics, dark as midnight at noonday, without window or door they can shut, without chimney or stove, and crowded with men, women, and little children. Children are born in sorrow, and raised in reeking vice and bestiality, that no heathen degradation can exceed.[21]

New York landlords put all available space to use in housing the urban poor. The most offensive of all places for residence, according to Griscom's report, were cellars. By 1850 about 29,000 persons, largely immigrants, lived underground. Many of these dwellings were below sea-level, and flooding was a major problem. Others were filled with stagnant water, rotting garbage, or worse wastes. "In many cases," wrote an observer, "the vaults of privies are situated on the same or a higher level, and the contents frequently ooze through walls into the occupied apartments." Griscom described one cellar at 50 Pike Street that housed two families—ten persons in all—in a room 10 feet by 10 feet. The Reverend George Hatt, an inspector for Dr. Griscom, reported a tiny cellar on Washington Street housing thirteen persons, four adults and nine children. "At times the tide came in; it was always damp, and there was a woman sick with Pleurisy." Writers invariably picture cellar dwellings as dark, damp, smelly, and small, but because they rented for slightly less than rooms above ground they were rarely vacant.[22]

Many wealthy New Yorkers viewed the tenement house system as a lucrative investment. Profits often ran as high as 20 per cent in a single year. In 1864 a city sanitary inspector gave the following report on the exploitation of tenants by owners:

> The houses are in many instances owned by large capitalists by whom they are farmed out to a class of factors, who make this their especial business. These men pay to the owners of the property a sum which is considered a fair return on the capital invested, and rely for their profits (which are often enormous) on the additional amount which they can extort from the wretched tenants whose homes frequently become untenantable for want of repairs, which the "agent" deems it his interest to withhold. These men contrive to absorb most of the scanty surplus which remains to the tenants after paying for their miserable food, shelter, and raiment. They are, in many instances, *proprietors of low groceries, liquor stores, and "policy shops" connected with such premises,* —the same individual often being the actual owner of a large number. *Many of the wretched population are held by these men in a state of abject dependence and vassalage little short of actual slavery.*[23]

The chief owner of slum real estate in the 'fifties was William B. Astor—"the landlord of New York"—who had a reputation of being stern with agents and of doing nothing to improve the dilapidated condition of the buildings he owned.[24]

While the rich profited from this tenantage system, it was the cause of untold suffering to working-class persons. Humanitarians such as Dr. Griscom noticed the close connections between slum dwelling and ill health. He found that almost without exception tenements had insufficient ventilation. "The smell," he wrote, "becomes intolerable, and its atmosphere productive to the most malignant diseases." Epidemics frequently swept through the heavily populated sections of the city. "Cholera is in town, and pretty active," noted the diarist George Templeton Strong in June 1854. "Fifty odd deaths last week. . . . All are thus far confined to the lowest and filthiest classes, whose existence from one day to another in their atmosphere of morphic influences is a triumph of vital organization and illustrates the vigorous tenacity of life (under deadliest conditions) bestowed on the human species." [25]

In the slums of lower Manhattan dirt and garbage were often piled up several feet above the sidewalk, spilling into the roadway. On Centre Street, for example, a journalist reported "the dirt hills rise to a height of three or four feet; and as no ash-carts have visited this neighborhood for several weeks past, and will not probably for some weeks to come, the prospect of the poor residents is most deplorable." [26]

Living in these overcrowded, ill-ventilated tenements, working when employed at low paying, menial tasks, men soon lost their will to succeed. Physical energy became sapped, the mind dulled. In this state it was a short step to heavy drinking or crime.[27]

Deplorable living conditions were undoubtedly all the more galling to workingmen, since wealth was so visibly present in a city such as New York. Horace Greeley found it ironic that the laborers who built the city's sumptuous mansions more often than not lived "in a squalid lodging which the builders of palaces in the fifteenth century can hardly have dwelt in more wretched. . . ." [28] A *New York Times* article of February 6, 1858, referred to New York as a "Babel of marble palaces and wretched dens of shame and of want. . . ." "Nothing ever moves me more," wrote the Reverend Samuel Prime, "than this almost union of extremes in the city: I have seen a poor blind beggar leaning against the wall of the house where gorgeous magnificence was displaying itself in a luxurious banquet, the wine of which would cost more money than it would take to make that beggar comfortable for a life time." [29]

Witnessing the sharp contrasts between wealth and poverty, Parke Godwin, a New York newspaperman and Fourier socialist, came to the conclusion that "our modern world of industry is a veritable HELL" in which "the few rich are becoming more and more rich," while "the un-numbered many are becoming poorer." "Was the penalty of Sisyphus," he asked, "condemned to roll his stone to a summit from which it was forever falling, more poignant than that of many fathers of families, among the poorer classes, who, after laboring to exhaustion during their whole lives, to amass somewhat for their old age or for their children, see it swallowed up in one of those periodical crises of failure and ruin which are the inevitable attendants of our methods of loose competition?" [30] By the 1850's this would not have seemed a bad question to many New York laborers. Thousands of workingmen, native-born and foreign alike, were living in an environment in which equality of opportunity in the American race for riches was clearly lacking.

II

Naturally laborers did not accept their declining position in society without attempting once again to organize
and better their lot. However, the same factors that were
making wages lower and workers less independent—industrialization and the mounting tide of immigration—
hindered any significant large-scale organization of labor.
After the collapse of the labor movement following the
panic of 1837, workers found it difficult to revive the
flourishing trade-union activity of the 'thirties. The atmosphere of the 1840's was different for labor from what it had
been in the preceding decade. Heavy immigration created
a labor surplus, making it nearly impossible to unionize
effectively; while at the same time the traditional crafts
were being replaced or greatly modified by mechanical
processes. Under these circumstances the leadership of the
labor movement temporarily passed into the hands of
humanitarian reformers, usually middle-class idealists who
believed strongly in a single panacea to end the ills of
industrialization.[31]

Associationism, Fourierism, agrarianism, socialism, and
communitarianism vied with one another to win the support of the workingman and transform the chaotic, capital-
istic industrial society into a co-operative Utopia. In New
York the concepts of Fourier socialism were widely prop-
agated. Charles Fourier, a French commercial employee,
assumed—as had Robert Owen and other communitarian
reformers—that men were basically good, and that if they
abandoned the competitive system and joined in "phalanxes," or co-operative communities, they could transform the world into a paradise. Fourier believed that the

difficulty with modern society was that men's natural abilities were misused. In his communities talents would be fully utilized and harmony would prevail.[32]

Fourier, who never visited America, had waited ten years for a wealthy patron to finance his project. When he died in 1837 he had not found any rich backers. However, his ideas had reached Albert Brisbane, a young man from western New York, who had become familiar with Fourier's work while a student in France. In the depression year of 1840 Brisbane published *Social Destiny of Man,* a detailed exposition of Fourier's ideas. Brisbane won the support of Horace Greeley for his schemes, and Greeley contributed both money and newspaper space to support "industrial association," as they called the Fourier system.[33]

Supporters of Associationism were successful in establishing Fourier societies in many eastern states. In New York, societies existed in the City, in Rochester, Buffalo, Albany, and many other towns. Brisbane, early in 1843, reported in the *Tribune* after a tour of New York State that "in all the principal towns and many of the smaller ones the people are taking up the subject with the greatest enthusiasm and energy—forming societies for the dissemination of the doctrines and organizing small associations." [34]

During the 'forties more than forty different Fourier phalanxes were established, with perhaps 8000 members. These communities attracted persons from all ranks of society, including many skilled mechanics who saw in Associationism a chance to overcome the evils of industrialization. The first community was founded in western Pennsylvania in 1843 by a group of skilled craftsmen from Albany and New York City. It failed the following year. In the next ten years virtually all the other phalanxes similarly failed, including the transcendental haven of

Brook Farm and Brisbane's own community, the North American Phalanx.

Communitarian societies such as the Fourier phalanxes may have had some value as social laboratories, but they did not help to alleviate the problems of the working class. Their chief flaw undoubtedly lay in the fact that they were a quixotic attempt to escape from industrialization, not to come to grips with it. Besides this, most of these communities were marked by internal bickerings, poor planning, lack of capital, and external hostility.

Greeley and a number of other reformers turned from Associationism in the late 'forties to encourage laborers within industrial towns and cities to form both consumers' and producers' co-operatives. For a time, craftsmen in a number of trades were successful in establishing worker-owned shops. In New York City in the spring of 1850 groups of coopers, hat finishers, shade painters, German cabinetmakers, and tailors reportedly had organized co-operatives. Similar consumers' co-operatives were established to sell goods at wholesale prices to members. But these ventures were in the long run no more successful than the phalanxes. Few survived beyond the mid-'fifties, and their over-all effect on working conditions was negligible.[35]

Well before the final demise of the communitarian and co-operative movements a new panacea, land reform, had gained wide support. This was undoubtedly the most practical of all the cure-alls offered by middle-class reformers. The high priest of the land reform movement was George Henry Evans, the former publisher of *The Working Man's Advocate*. Evans revived the *Advocate* in 1844, and sought to rally workers behind a plan to secure national legislation providing for a division of the public domain

into free 160 acre homesteads. To gain greater support
for his scheme, Evans founded the National Reform Association in 1845. That year the walls of New York were
plastered with handbills headed "Vote Yourself a Farm."
"Are you tired of slavery," the handbill asked, "of drudging
for others—of poverty and its attendent miseries? Then,
Vote yourself a farm." [36]

Viewing the working situation in the industrial towns
of the East, a committee of the National Reform Association found "a much larger number of laboring people
. . . than can find constant and profitable employment."
The committee also reported that "we find in our cities,
and Factory Stations, an increasing population, the great
majority of whom depend for a subsistence on Mechanical
labor; and . . . we find the new born power of machinery
throwing itself into the labor-market, with the most as-
tounding effects—withering up all human competition
with a sudden decisiveness that leaves no hope for the
future." The committee's solution was "at once simple,
satisfactory, and conclusive. . . . Let an outlet be formed
that will carry off our superabundant labor to the salu-
brious and fertile West. In those regions thousands, and
tens of thousands, who are now languishing in hopeless
poverty, will find a certain and a speedy independence.
The labor market will be thus eased of the present dis-
tressing competition, and those who remain, as well as
those who emigrate, will have the opportunity of realizing
a comfortable living." [37]

Although not all laborers were taken up with land reform, many skilled mechanics rallied strongly to the National Reform Association and the free land program. For
example, the first central committee included four printers,
two cordwainers, a chairmaker, a bookbinder, a black-

smith, a picture-frame maker, a carpenter, a machinist, and a clothier. Several of these men had been active in labor in the 'thirties. Labor journals, immigrant guidebooks, Greeley's *Tribune,* and reform publications generally supported the land reform movement. Up until the passage of the Homestead Act in 1862 strong pressure was put on politicians through the National Reform Association and other agencies to pass such legislation. In New York, particularly as poverty and working conditions worsened, support for free land became very general. Not only the *Tribune* but also the *Times* and the *Sun* advocated this policy in the 1850's. Convinced that charity within the city was a waste, the *Sun* recommended in 1855 that instead of "soup houses we ought to send the unemployed where they can obtain work and good wages." [38]

While the movement initiated by Evans helped lead to the passage of the Homestead Act, its benefit to New York workers in the 'forties and 'fifties seems to have been inconsequential. Historians have shown that relatively few wage earners and artisans from New York or other eastern cities became western farmers.[39] The same factors which made it difficult for newly arrived immigrants to extricate themselves from east coast cities also affected native-born laborers. Aside from many workers' preference for urban life, in general they lacked funds to travel, buy land, and begin a successful farm. An English traveler visiting America in 1843 asked a group of obviously exploited factory workers why they did not leave the mill and go to the land. They are purported to have replied:

> We should want money to travel, then money would be wanted to buy land, to buy agricultural implements, to buy seed, and then we should want more to support us till we could dispose of part of our crops, and we have no

money at all. But, suppose we had all these means, we know nothing about cultivation of land—we have all our lives worked in a factory, and know no other employment, and how is it likely that we should succeed? besides which, we have always been used to live in a town, where we can get what little things we want if we have money, and it is only those who have lived in the wilderness, who know what the horrors of a wilderness-life are.[40]

Money was least available for an urban exodus during times of depression, with the result that people went West chiefly during prosperous times and not when this movement would do the most to relieve unemployment and low wages in the cities.[41]

Throughout the period from 1830 to 1860, as transportation improved, the trans-Appalachian lands were increasingly used to raise staple crops. The days of the squatters were passing, and in their place came a new class of more substantial farmers. Unlike the earlier pioneers, the successful farmers of this era were those who bought improved lands at good prices. In order to compete with this group one needed fertile land, costly machinery, and labor. There was some opportunity for an eastern laborer to find employment as a farm hand, but even this was precarious. As Mathew Carey remarked in the early 'thirties:

It is frequently said, as a panacea for the distresses of those people—"let them go into the country; there they will find employment enough." To say nothing of the utter unfitness of most of those persons for country labour, this is taking for granted what remains to be proved. The country rarely affords employment for extra hands, except for a few weeks in harvest time. Farmers are generally supplied with steady hands at all other

> seasons. But . . . take the case of a man of a delicate
> constitution, with a wife and three or four small chil-
> dren; what a miserable chance would he stand of sup-
> port by country labor! [42]

In New York throughout this period western settlement
lagged behind urban growth due to the great influx of
immigrants and the movement of native Americans from
the country to the city. The result was a lowering of the
living standards of the industrial population in spite of
the existence of the frontier.[43]

Workers were coming to realize by the late 'forties that
industrialization could not be stopped or society radically
altered through any of the simple solutions offered by the
numerous utopian reformers. But at the same time, organizing a genuine labor movement to work for such practical measures as shorter hours and better wages proved
exceedingly difficult. During the 'forties, however, there
was renewed agitation for a ten-hour workday. This
movement took the form of pressuring state legislatures to
pass laws limiting the hours in private industry. In New
York, Evans's National Reform Association and other
workingmen's organizations took up this cause. Tammany
Democrats, hoping to win worker support, introduced a
ten-hour bill in 1847, but the measure was never voted on.
Several other attempts to pass ten-hour legislation succeed-
ed in the Assembly, only to be defeated in the more conservative Senate. In 1853, a ten-hour law was passed for labor employed on public works. However, this was only in
the absence of contracts and thus proved virtually mean-
ingless. No further legislation on the question of shorter
hours was brought up in New York until 1859. Long working hours were also the rule in other states, and the
American average workday throughout the 'forties and

'fifties remained well over the ten-hour goal, although there seems to have been a slight reduction in the average daily hours during the period.[44]

Unions had been slow to reorganize during the 'forties, but after 1850, a sharp rise in living costs, due largely to the California gold discoveries together with renewed prosperity, turned skilled workers back to union activity. Between 1850 and 1854 most of the craft trades in New York unionized, and nationally organized trade unions such as the National Typographical Union were also established during this period. At this time labor made a conscious effort to extricate itself from the humanitarianism of the 'forties. The pioneer labor historian J. R. Commons has called this period the beginning of modern trade-unionism. "There is," he writes, "an impressive difference between the 'pure and simple' unionism of the middle of the decade and the unionism of the 'thirties, the 'forties, and the beginning of this decade. Stripped of universal and glowing ideals, without establishing a single labour paper to carry an appeal to the country, the skilled trades settled down to the cold business of getting more pay for themselves by means of permanent and exclusive organizations. Here begins that separation from common labour which eventually was to raise the pay of the skilled mechanic far above the level of immigrant competition and to distinguish American unionism from that of any other country." [45]

Skilled labor organized much more clearly along class lines, excluding both common laborers and middle-class reformers. There was a distinct recognition that their struggle against employers would be far more effective if they demanded limited "bread and butter" objectives such as higher pay, a minimum wage, maintenance of appren-

ticeship rules, collective bargaining, the closed shop, and
shorter hours. This entailed an acceptance of inequality in
that these workers, by forming tightly organized craft
unions, were claiming that their interests were not the
general interests of society. Workers now realized, as one
union declared, that under existing conditions "there
exists a perpetual antagonism between Labor and Capital
. . . one striving to sell their labor for as much, and the
other striving to buy it for as little as they can." [46]

The chief weapon of these newly organized unions was
the strike. In 1850 New York carpenters, cordwainers,
bootmakers, bricklayers, painters, printers, and certain
common laborers struck, chiefly for higher wages. In 1853
and 1854 the number of strikes increased markedly. "Each
spring," reported the *Tribune*, "witnesses a new struggle
for enhanced wages in some if not most of the trades of
this and other cities." On occasion, as many as twenty-five
or thirty strikes were cited in one issue of the *Tribune* or
Times. These strikes were partially successful in raising
the wages of skilled mechanics. Times were prosperous and
labor was in demand. In certain trades wages rose as much
as 37½ per cent from 1850 to 1854. However, prices were
rising even more rapidly, and, except in a few trades,
wages did not keep pace. Employers took every opportunity to weaken the unions, and were often successful during slack seasons in driving down newly won wage increases.[47]

Just as in the 'thirties, the labor organizations of the
'fifties proved to be precarious institutions, dependent on
general prosperity for their very existence. The sharp recession during the winter of 1854–55 seriously hurt organized labor. Skilled mechanics were laid off in large
numbers in the fall and early winter of 1854. In December

less than one-fifth of the building workers in New York City were employed. By mid-winter over one-half of the nation's skilled laborers were out of work. Unable to maintain wage gains or keep workers employed, the trade-union movement collapsed.[48]

Business picked up again in the summer of 1855, and the few unions that had survived led in an attempt to rebuild the movement. By the summer of 1856 unions had revived somewhat, and were again able to force better terms from their employers.

Before these reorganized unions had made any significant gains, however, the depression of 1857 destroyed the movement even more completely than had been the case in 1854–55. By October 1857, at least 200,000 were unemployed. Immigrant laborers crowded the New York docks begging for the opportunity of working their way back to Europe. On November 2, 1857, some 12,000 unemployed New York City workers met in Tompkins Square to take "prompt, vigorous and decisive action to prevent our families from starving." [49]

Three days later, on November 5, 1857, a meeting 15,000 strong again gathered at Tompkins Square. A parade was formed and thousands of unemployed workers marched down Wall Street chanting: "We want work." Later, desperate New York workers broke into the shops of flour merchants and stole goods to keep their families alive. Some public relief as well as public works projects were established to aid the large number of jobless. Workers were employed in grading Central Park and in pulling down an old almshouse on Chambers Street. However, unemployment and low wages remained a problem in the years just before the Civil War. Unions did begin to revive by 1859 and 1860, but their impact was slight. Generally,

working conditions were as bad if not worse in the late
'fifties than they had been at the beginning of the decade.[50]

III

An old New York cartman, one of those human haulers
who transported much of the city's goods before the ad-
vent of motorized trucks, made the following comparison
of working conditions in the late 'fifties with those of the
'thirties:

> There is one thing . . . that is quite certain. With all her
> glitter of prosperity, and her rapid increase of wealth and
> population, New York is not now the place for a poor
> man that it was when I first took up my residence there.
> *Then* there was plenty of work for all; wages were high,
> and all the necessaries of life were low in price and better
> in quality than they are at present; *now* wages are low,
> work scarce, and all the necessaries of life poor and high
> in price. *Then* you could hire good, comfortable apart-
> ments for $75 a year; *now* the same accommodations will
> cost you twice that amount for the same space. . . .
> *Then* the farmers brought their own produce to market,
> and you could go down to the wharves and purchase *at
> retail* anything you wanted from first hands; *now* you
> cannot purchase anything from first hands at all, but have
> to pay two or three commissions upon every article you
> obtain from the markets. . . . *Then* the workingman was
> looked upon and treated as a human being; *now* he is
> looked upon and treated more like a brute than like a
> man and brother. Verily, verily, I say unto you, that New
> York has been growing *great,* without growing *good.*[51]

Obviously this nostalgic reminiscence paints an exaggerated picture of the changes that had taken place in laboring conditions between the Jacksonian period and the

Civil War. But there exists ample evidence to show that the laborer's situation had declined over these three decades. Horace Greeley, reflecting on the changes in New York between the early 1830's and 1850, stated that while the city's population and wealth had more than doubled, the conditions of labor had not improved, and in fact had worsened, since rents and living expenses had greatly increased while wages remained the same. Greeley was particularly struck by the close connection of low wages to vice, poverty, and destitution. Ten thousand poor women, he maintained, "because they cannot acquire by any sort of honest industry" more than two dollars per week, were driven into infamy. "Thousands of poor children are daily driven forth from the cellars and wretched rookeries of this Christian emporium to gain by thieving or the most horrid pollutions the means of their own and their parents' subsistence." [52]

Signs of poverty multiplied yearly in New York, reflecting low wages, unemployment, and worsening labor conditions. In the mid-'forties there were seventy-six pawnshops in the City; by 1860 they numbered in the hundreds. As might be expected, the pawnbroker never located in the fashionable neighborhoods; rather his three gold balls gleamed out of the city's slums.[53]

Begging in the streets greatly increased during the period. In the 'thirties it was rare to see a beggar, but by the Civil War there were several thousand. Greeley termed the New York of the 'fifties "the metropolis of beggary," while a Londoner of the same period found little difference between the begging in his native city and that in the greatest city of the New World. Even a class of professional beggars practiced their art along with those who were truly destitute.[54]

LIBRARY - Allegheny Campus

Immigration, industrialization, and the growth of urban areas greatly enlarged the number of persons classified as "paupers" in New York State. In 1823 only 22,111 received poor relief out of a population of 1,500,000; in 1855 the state census listed over 204,000 paupers on relief out of a total population approximating 3,400,000. The suffering of these paupers was severe. "The truth is," wrote G. G. Foster in 1850, "that the condition, both moral and physical, in which such a city as New York permits its poor to exist, is utterly disgraceful—not to the poor, for they deserve only our deepest pity, but to the community—the powerful, enlightened, wealthy community—which permits its unfortunate children who know nothing but how to work, to become thus horribly degraded." [55]

During periods of panic and depression, of course, poverty was far more widespread than usual. In November 1858, when the unemployed numbered well over 50,000 in New York City alone, some cruel joker advertised a dole of bread and meat to all the poor people present at noon in Union Square on Thanksgiving Day. Several thousand lean, weary people came and waited for hours in vain.[56]

Not all of labor's hardships were the result of low wages and periodic unemployment. Norman Ware, the leading authority on American labor conditions in the two decades before the Civil War, maintains that "the losses of the industrial worker in the first half of the century were not comfort losses solely, but losses, as he conceived it, of status and independence." Skilled mechanics, as has been shown, yearly found their independence lessening and their skills declining in value. In industry after industry artisans felt themselves challenged by new methods which required little skill or training. "Boys do the work which men are wanting," complained a group of New York printers, "and at half, or less than half, men's wages." Another group complained that "the capitalists have taken to bossing all the mechanical trades, while the practical mechanic has become a journeyman, subject to be discharged at every pretended 'miff' of his purse-proud employer." [57]

Even when skilled workers were able to win such benefits as higher wages and shorter hours, their sense of loss was not offset. Shorter hours were often accompanied by a speed-up of production which entailed a tightening of discipline over workers and a further loss of independence. Higher wages in most instances were eradicated by rising living costs. Even the best paid employees found themselves falling behind in the American quest for the Almighty Dollar.

With the triumph of mechanization and the replacement of the craft shop by the factory, the artisan lost his earlier position in the community. Instead of selling his product he was selling his labor; he no longer owned the tools of production. As more and more workers became mere wage-earners, the general dignity of labor diminished. The great use of cheap immigrant labor also made laboring less respectable than it had been. Mechanics employed in factories began to consider themselves as "wage slaves" in a very real sense.

There was little that the worker could do to escape the system. No longer did apprentices and journeymen have much hope of one day becoming independent, shop-owning masters. During this time, in cities and factory towns, workers were yearly more divorced from their former rural agricultural ties. A large class of laborers became completely dependent on the industrial system. For the majority of workers, whether native or foreign-born, this brought great hardships, often entailing long hours spent at tedious routine work. Lacking capital reserve, and working for wages that were seldom above a subsistence level, the laborer had little opportunity to better his position. By the outbreak of the Civil War there existed a sizable pauperized proletariat.

7

THE NEW ARISTOCRACY

Rapid approximation to the European style of living is more and more observable in this city. The number of servants in livery visibly increases every season. Foreign artistic upholsterers assert that there will soon be more houses in New York furnished according to the fortune and taste of noblemen, than there are either in Paris or London; and this prophecy may well be believed, when the fact is considered that it is already not very uncommon to order furniture for a single room, at the cost of ten thousand dollars.

—L. M. Child,
Letters From New York (1845)

There is an untitled aristocracy both in New York and the other great cities of the Union, more haughty and exclusive than any within the region of Belgravia.

—James D. Burn,
*Three Years Among the Working Classes
in the United States* (1865)

POLITICS overshadowed all other concerns in 1860, with the antagonism between North and South moving rapidly toward an open breach. However, in New York, among the best society the greatest excitement was not occasioned by the election of Lincoln in November, but by the social event of the season, the visit of the Prince of Wales, the future Edward VII, who arrived in New York on October 11.[1]

New York's elite pondered for months how to make a good impression on the nineteen-year-old Prince. A committee of some fifty leading citizens headed by General Winfield Scott, William B. Astor, and Peter Cooper planned a great ball and reception for the British heir on his arrival in the city. For weeks before his coming the newspapers played up the preparations being made to receive royalty. On the day of the Prince's arrival the New York diarist George Templeton Strong, who was a member of the planning committee, wrote: "Everybody has talked of nothing but His Royal Highness for the last week. . . . I fear we are a city of snobs." [2]

More than 200,000 New Yorkers crowded Broadway on October 11 to witness the parade and, hopefully to glimpse the Prince being pulled in a six-horse barouche. Baron Salomon de Rothschild, residing in New York at the time, gave the following description of the event:

> Try to imagine all the ships in the port and in the bay decorated with flags; the army and the whole militia under arms, passing in review, and following along, the Prince's coach; and a population of a million people sticking their heads out of the windows and jamming into all the streets along his route. These poor people waited without a murmur from ten or eleven o'clock in the morning to seven at night, the military review having delayed the royal cortège considerably. When it finally arrived, it was already dark; it was impossible to see anything, but you should have heard the frenzied "hurrahs" of these good republicans, who greeted the royal scion with more enthusiasm than they would have shown for a liberator of their own country.[3]

The parade was for the many; the grand ball on the following night was for the few. The *New York Times* felt it incongruous that only the "aristocracy" had been invited to this affair, excluding even the city Alderman. But it was evident that the great interest taken in the Prince's reception by the upper class resulted from the fact that the guest list for the ball indicated who was "in society" and who was not. New York's "best society" crowded into the Academy of Music to be present with royalty. Lesser nobles were forgotten; when Baron Rothschild arrived an hour before the Prince, "his coming," according to the *Times*, "created no sensation." [4]

At ten in the evening the Prince was led in by the reception committee, headed by the wealthy and aristocratic Hamilton Fish and followed by the iron and glue magnate Peter Cooper, looking, in Strong's words, "like one of Gulliver's Yahoos caught and cleaned and dressed up." Unfortunately, as people crowded in to watch the first *quadrille d'honneur,* part of the temporary dance floor collapsed. However, order was quickly restored, and soon the dancing was resumed. Even the worldly Baron Rothschild remarked on the brilliance of the occasion: "There were dresses of an elegance and sumptuousness without compare, magnificently beautiful jewelry; but what ought particularly to have struck the young Prince . . . was the immense number of pretty women who were present. As a matter of fact I have never in my life seen such a collection." [5]

The dinner prepared by Delmonico's was as unrepublican as possible, running from *consommé de volaille* through dozens of courses, concluding with *glaces à la vanille* and *charlottes russes.* In the supper room "stood an army of servants, elbow to elbow, all in livery," waiting to serve the guests. Tired but contented, New York fashionables having feted a prince finally returned to their mansions as day was dawning.[6]

A few days later the Prince left New York, continuing

his journey to West Point and Boston and then England. In reflecting on the visit, Strong drew the following conclusions:

> (1) No community worships hereditary rank and station like a democracy. (2) The biggest and finest specimens of flunkeyism occur in the most recently elevated strata of society, as for example, Cooper: the "self-made millionaire glue-boiler," [Charles] Leary: the fashionable hatter's son, and others. (3) Under all this folly and tuft-hunting there is a deep and almost universal feeling of respect and regard for Great Britain and Her Britannic Majesty.[7]

New York's high society in 1860, of which George Strong was both a member and a critic, was far removed from the staid Knickerbocker elite of the early 'thirties. In the intervening years, a wealthy plutocracy had emerged which included self-made millionaire glue-boilers as well as opulent old-family patricians. New Yorkers were, as Strong had concluded, very status-conscious, probably more so than persons living in the traditionally aristocratic societies of Europe. The absence of legitimate aristocratic tradition—one in which social rankings were unquestioned—made all Americans emphasize status. And since claim to higher status ran counter to the basic belief that all are socially equal, those claiming a higher station felt compelled continually to assert it. Thus, to be present as one of the select guests at a reception for royalty was a means of affirming social position.

More than ever, wealth was the distinguishing factor characterizing New York's best society. Nearly ten years before the Prince's ball, Strong had noted the tendency of the aristocracy to assert their position by means of conspicuous consumption. "It is terrific to see," wrote Strong, "the strides extravagance and luxury are making in these days: [Woodbury] Langdon's arrangements for his ball tonight remind one of the fact. Though I thought a few years ago that I was or might be hereafter tolerably well off, I'm satisfied from the way the style of living grows and amplifies that I am to be always poor, relatively speaking, and perhaps some day an absolute pauper, unable to live in New York." [8]

Other New Yorkers ridiculed the spending of the city's socialites. The journalist G. G. Foster called the "aristocracy of the New World—a race of beings who . . . have never been equaled on the face of this earth, in all that is pompous without dignity, gaudy without magnificence, lavish without taste, and aristocratic without good manners." The essayist George William Curtis in his highly popular *Potiphar Papers* of 1854 wittily satirized the showiest, wealthiest New Yorkers. His fictional characters —the pushy, *nouveau riche* Mrs. Potiphar, the smug Reverend Cream Cheese, and the gossipy Minerva Tattle— each had a hundred likenesses in the New York of the 'fifties. Curtis began his satire with the following picture of Gotham's social display:

> If gilt were only gold, or sugar-candy common sense, what a fine thing our society would be! If to lavish money upon *objets de vertu,* to wear costly dresses, and always to have them cut in the height of the fashion; to build houses thirty feet broad, as if they were palaces; to furnish them with all the luxurious devices of Parisian genius; to give superb banquets at which your guests laugh, and which make you miserable; to drive a fine carriage and ape European liveries, and crests, and coats-of-arms; . . . to talk much of "old families" and of your aristocratic foreign friends; to despise labour; to prate of "good society";

to travesty and parody, in every conceivable way, a society which we know only in books and by superficial observation of foreign travel; . . . if all this were fine, what
a prodigiously fine society would ours be! [9]

The growth of conspicuous and extravagant living was
reflected in New York's architecture. The brick and
wooden structures of Knickerbocker New York gave way
to the dreary but costly brown sandstone and the more
tasteful and still more expensive marble. Wealthy persons
who weathered the depression of 1837 generally emerged
in the early 'forties richer than ever, while new fortunes
continued to be made. The 950 names that Moses Beach
published in 1845, "of persons estimated to be worth
$100,000 and upwards," give some indication of this. These
persons continued to push the fashionable section of the
city further to the north. As Strong wrote in 1847 when
contemplating a move uptown to Gramercy Park: "a street
of emigrant boarding houses and dirty drinking shops is
not a pleasant place to live." [10]

New mansions built around Stuyvesant and Union
Squares, Gramercy Park, Fourteenth, and Twenty-third
streets, and upper Broadway rivaled one another in gaudi-
ness. When the Hungarian liberals Francis and Theresa
Pulszky, touring America as guests of the country with
the celebrated Louis Kossuth, arrived in New York in
1851, they were surprised at the numerous substantial
dwellings, many with elegant marble façades. Mrs. Pulszky
described one especially lavish house belonging to Dr. Benjamin Haight, an eminent Episcopalian minister. Haight's
mansion had "an Italian winter garden, playing fountains,
large saloons in the Parisian fashion, a drawingroom in the
style of the Taj Mahal at Agra, a splendid library, etc." [11]

By the early 'fifties Fifth Avenue had become the most sumptuous residential street in America. One source relates that three Fifth Avenue dwellings built in the year 1851 had each cost over $50,000. At the end of the 'fifties, Fifth Avenue from Washington Square to the beginning of Central Park was an almost unbroken line of mansions. Some of the most impressive homes along *the* Avenue were those of the Brevoorts, Parishes, Astors, Roberts, Rhinelanders, and Minturns.[12]

The interior furnishings of these nabob palaces often cost more than the dwellings themselves. Massive and ornate furniture became a reflection of wealth and status. Elaborately draped beds were popular; so too were heavy imported silk or satin draperies, usually in floral patterns. Mahogany was the favored wood in this age of oppressive taste. Also popular were rosewood and satinwood. Furniture made abundant use of marble and gilt. Strong, while making the traditional fashionable New Year's Day calls in 1846, was struck by the interior display at the home of William Aspinwall. "One can't make a satisfactory guess at the amount he's invested in rosewood and satin, mirrors, cabinets, and vertu. . . . [Woodbury] Langdon, William B. Astor, [James F.] Penniman go beyond him in display and costliness. . . . Langdon's arrangements are said to have cost not much less than eighty thousand dollars." Another New Yorker described the interior of a $100,000 mansion on the corner of Fifteenth Street and Fifth Avenue. The lady's bedroom was palatial. The bed was inlaid with pearls and draped with satin and lace; the roof was of glass, framed in arabesque tracery-work. One part of the dwelling was a greenhouse, containing exotic flowers, birds, and a large fountain. Other rooms were walled with mirrors and fine paintings.[13]

Wealthy families in the 'forties and 'fifties frequently had extensive private libraries and art collections. Both Philip Hone and George Templeton Strong, the two diarists, had excellent collections of American and European art works as well as fine libraries. Probably the best art collection in the city was that of John Taylor Johnson, the first president of the Metropolitan Museum of Art after its founding in 1869. Johnson's marble mansion on the southeast corner of Eighth Street and Fifth Avenue, which was completed in 1855, contained a large art gallery at the rear of the house which he opened to the public one day a week. William Aspinwall, August Belmont, William B. Astor, Cornelius Vanderbilt, A. T. Stewart, and others also had substantial collections of pictures. The practice of scouring Europe for art treasures by rich Americans was already well developed by the Civil War.[14]

There were myriad other ways in which wealthy New Yorkers displayed their riches. Private carriages, not very common in the 1830's, became standard possessions of those with social pretensions in the 'forties and 'fifties. Not only did the number of private equipages yearly increase, but it became common to see carriages with heraldic crests and liveried footmen and coachmen. In the late 'fifties the newly opened Central Park became the great display place for fashionable carriages. "On pleasant afternoons," wrote the author of a New York guidebook, "the Park presents a brilliant appearance, and reveals not only the worth and wealth, but the pretension and parvenuism of this aristocratic-democratic city. One would hardly believe he was in a republican country to see the escutcheoned panels of the carriages, the liveried coachmen, and the supercilious air of the occupants of the vehicles, as they go pompously and flaringly by." [15]

The extravagant attire of New York socialites, particularly the ladies, another visible indication of the great increase in wealth, was another symbol of status. A woman complained in 1850 that dress was "running wild, in the direction of expense." [16] The British novelist William Makepeace Thackeray viewed the New York lady's attire more favorably. On his lecture tour of 1852, he was struck by the prodigious luxury in the city. "Surely Solomon in all his glory or the Queen of Sheba when she came to visit him in state was not arrayed so magnificently as these New York damsels. . . . I never saw such luxury and extravagance such tearing polkas such stupendous suppers and fine clothes. I watched one young lady at 4 balls in as many new dresses, and each dress of the most 'stunning' description." [17]

Women generally followed the latest Paris fashions in their dress. As the noted geologist Sir Charles Lyell remarked in the mid-'forties:

> Every fortnight the "Journal des Modes" is received from France, and the ladies conform strictly to Parisian costume. Except at balls and large parties, they wear high dresses, and, as usual in mercantile communities, spare no expense. Embroidered muslin, of the finest and costliest kind, is much worn; and my wife learnt that sixteen guineas were not unfrequently given for a single pocket handkerchief. Extravagantly expensive fans, with ruby or emerald pins, are also common.

In the display of jewelry, according to the French Baron M. de Trobriand, "American ladies rival the sumptuousness of the titled dames of Europe." Numerous shops existed to cater to the whims of the wealthy. Broadway was the center for fashionable stores; it was on that thoroughfare that Tiffany's and Stewart's were located.[18]

European styles were consciously imitated not only in women's attire but also in nearly all aspects of society life. As the wealthy social lioness Mrs. Tiffany says in Anna Mowatt's play *Fashion,* a delightful social satire of the mid-'forties: "You have yet to learn, Mr. Snobson, that the American *ee-light*—the aristocracy—the *how-ton*—as a matter of conscience, scrupulously follow the foreign fashions." American taste relied heavily on the prevailing English modes. But in the decade before the Civil War French fashions became more influential. "The taste of America," wrote the novelist Anthony Trollope in 1862, "is becoming French in its conversation, French in its comforts and French in its discomforts, French in its eating, and French in its dress, French in its manners, and will become French in its art." [19]

Even more than in the 1830's, New York fashionables doted on nobility. Their reception of the Prince of Wales was a good example of this. Not only did aspiring Americans cultivate the acquaintance of princes, dukes, and barons, but also a number of marriages between wealthy daughters of American plutocrats and European noblemen took place. One of the most famous of these marriages occurred on October 13, 1859, when Miss Frances Amelia Bartlett, daughter of wealthy New York parents, married a Spanish nobleman, Don Estaban Santa Cruz de Oviedo, at St. Patrick's Cathedral. Described as "the Diamond Wedding," it highlighted New York's social season. The bridegroom, in addition to being titled, was a very wealthy Cuban, owning several large plantations. Many dignitaries were present. The wedding presents were said to be valued at anywhere from $50,000 to $100,000, and included a great necklace of diamonds from Tiffany's.[20]

For those unable to marry into nobility there was always

the hope of searching back into one's genealogy and turning up a stray duke. On Broadway there existed an office of heraldry, where for a fee the socially ambitious and prosperous would be informed of their noble lineage. In the early 'fifties, according to Nathaniel Willis, a tome entitled *American Hand Book of Heraldry* was published by Gwilt Mapleson, containing the pedigrees and coats-of-arms of some of New York's leading families, along with "directions for crests, mottoes and liveries." Included in the book were pictures of the family crests of such families as the Allens, Christies, Doanes, Emburys, Grays, Grymes, Haggertys, Hones, Livingstons, McVickars, Mounts, Porters, Schermerhorns, Taylors, and Wards. This book reportedly sold "like hot cakes" among the pretentious aristocrats of New York.[21]

Social affairs among New York fashionables in the Jacksonian period, although quite exclusive, were neither too costly nor frequent to be beyond the means of the average upper-middle-class New Yorker. A decade later this was not the case. As in the earlier period, social life consisted chiefly of exclusive balls, dinners, and parties. But both in frequency and lavishness the affairs of the 'forties and 'fifties far surpassed those earlier.

The tone that High Society was to adopt was clearly indicated as early as 1840. In that year several balls were staged, the likes of which had not been seen previously. The most elaborate was the Brevoort Costume Ball given on February 27 at the Brevoort mansion on the corner of Fifth Avenue and Ninth Street. "Never before," according to Philip Hone, "has New York witnessed a fancy ball so splendidly gotten up, in better taste, or more successfully carried through." According to the *New York Herald,* the first paper to perfect the art of society-page coverage, nearly six hundred of the *"elites* of this country were there." People came as Hamlets, Othellos, Romeos, Caesars, Sultans, Queen Victoria, and sundry other personages. One dress, the *Herald* reported, cost more than $2500. The ball lasted from eight in the evening to five the next morning. Servants, and excellent food and wines were found in abundance. The *Herald* devoted its entire first page to the affair, describing it in characteristically overexuberant terms as having "created a greater sensation in the fashionable world than any thing of the kind since the creation of the world, or the fall of beauteous woman, or the frolic of old Noah, after he left the ark and took to wine and drinking." [22]

From the time of the Brevoort Ball in 1840 to the reception for the Prince of Wales in 1860, fashionable soirees yearly became more extravagant and elaborate. By 1850 it was not unusual for $3000 or $4000 to be spent on a single party. A contemporary satirized the extremes to which those in society went to outdo one another: "If Mrs. A. had a thousand dollars' worth of flowers in her rooms, Mrs. B. will strain every nerve to have twice or three times as many, though all the greenhouses within 10 miles of the city must be stripped to obtain them. If Mrs. C. bought all the game in market for her supper, Mrs. D.'s anxiety is to send to the prairies for hers,—and so on in other matters. Mrs. E. had the *prima donna* to sing at her soiree, and Mrs. F. at once engages the whole opera troupe." [23]

The Episcopal Church continued to be the church of the aristocracy. One indication of this was the fact that the unofficial ruler of New York's High Society was Isaac H. Brown, the famed sexton of Grace Church. In 1846 the congregation of Grace Church moved from its downtown

location on Rector Street to the beautiful marble structure designed by James Renwick on Broadway at Tenth
Street. This new site, central to the recherché uptown residences, made Grace more than ever the most fashionable
church in New York. Thousands of dollars were paid for
the yearly rent of a single pew. Brown stood at the entry
way to the best society. He knew the antecedents and the
fortunes of all the leading families in the city. It was to
Brown that persons of social standing entrusted the invita-
tions for any important occasion. As a contemporary noted:
"He gets up parties, engineers bridals, and conducts funerals, more genteelly than any other man." Another
writer called Brown "a kind of master of ceremonies and
general referee in aristocratic society." [24]

In addition to the rounds of balls and parties, New
York's elite frequented certain theaters and the opera. The
latter was particularly fashionable, and opera companies
were patronized almost exclusively by High Society. In
1847 the Astor Place Opera Theatre opened. "Never perhaps," wrote New Yorker Charles Haswell, "was any theatre built that afforded a better opportunity for the display
of dress." When a new Italian opera company opened on
November 2, 1849, the *Tribune* reported that the "elite
of New York aristocracy" were present, "about a thousand
of the most brilliantly-dressed and expensively-bred ladies
and gentlemen in New York. . . ." As with Grace Church,
people spent thousands for choice season seats. "The Italian
Opera," wrote a journalist in the early 'fifties, "has become one of the established and most conspicuous of our
glorious institutions, and not to be familiar with its organization, its characteristics, its beauties and general atmosphere, marks one as very low down in the scale of refinement, elegance and social distinction." [25]

Palatial mansions, lavish furnishings, collections of European art, regal equipages, real or feigned titles, costly parties, and various other forms of display were indicative of a class of persons attempting to assert their superiority in an ostensibly democratic society. Well before Mark Twain and Charles Dudley Warner's phrase "The Gilded Age" became the most lasting epithet describing post-Civil War business civilization, New York had a "gilded" society. An Englishman remarked in the late 'fifties: "There is perhaps, more of what is called 'living for appearances' in New York than in any other American city. . . . The tasteless ostentation of vulgar wealth is by no means wanting. . . ." "We live on the sidewalks," wrote a New Yorker, "we dine, dress, talk, and make society in public; we marry for money and live for appearance. . . ." [26]

Some persons lamented that the spectacle of lavish spending in the 'forties and 'fifties marked the end of the true aristocracy in New York. The Episcopal Bishop William Kip complained that the growing facilities for making fortunes had ushered in "the age of gaudy wealth." "Wealth came in and created social distinction which took the place of family, and thus society became vulgarized." [27]

Great wealth was a factor in society which a person like the reminiscing Bishop Kip did not fully understand. It did, as he fretted, create garishness and vulgarity, but enjoying luxurious goods and services was not the chief reason persons sought to accumulate large fortunes. These were secondary concerns. Of primary importance was the fact that wealth conferred both power and honor on its possessors. Even the old Knickerbocker families whom Kip apparently saw as the true aristocracy generally followed the same pattern as the parvenu in the 'forties and 'fifties. Thus, the numerous mansions of Fifth Avenue were built not only by the *nouveaux riches* but also by such respectable old families as the Brevoorts, Rhinelanders, Howlands, Grinnells, Griswolds, Lenoxes, Lorillards, and others.[28]

Power and distinction, two of the most important attributes of aristocracy, were substantially augmented by the great increase in fortunes. The real change which did take place between the 'thirties and the mid-'forties and 'fifties was the maturing of "High Society"—a society-page class partially dependent on conspicuous consumption to gain social notoriety. The way of life of this wealthy set distinguished them from the rest of society far more pronouncedly than did the less ostentatious life of the earlier Knickerbocker elite.

It was in this period of lavish spending that the term the "Upper Ten Thousand" came into vogue as descriptive of New York's best society. The phrase was originated by Nathaniel Willis in the magazine of New York society, the *Home Journal*.[29] In 1852, Charles Astor Bristed, who was John Jacob Astor's grandson and Henry Brevoort's son-in-law, published a book entitled *The Upper Ten Thousand,* sketching New York society life. In the London edition of this work Bristed felt compelled to explain that America was not "wild, savage, and frightful." He wrote:

> You will be surprised when, in presenting you in American society, I introduce you among a set of exquisites,— daintily-arrayed men, who spend half their income on their persons, and shrink from the touch of a woollen glove,—who are curious in wines and liquors, and would order dinner against the oldest frequenter of the Trois Frères; delicate and lovely women, who wear the finest

furs and roll in the most stylish equipages,—who are well up in the latest French dances and the newest French millinery,—who talk much such English as you do yourself, and three or four continental languages into the bargain.[30]

As the term "Upper Ten Thousand" implies, no small set dominated New York's High Society, although there were a number of restricted coteries. "No society in the world," claimed the New York journalist Junius Browne, "has more divisions and subdivisions than ours—more ramifications and inter-ramifications—more circles within circles—more segments and parts of segments." Browne maintained that there were three basic divisions among the aristocracy—the Knickerbockers, the newly rich, and the social adventurers.[31] These categories have some merit, but are much too clear-cut. Although family, education, and manners continued to be important as a basis for high social standing, the common denominator of New York's elite was wealth. Without wealth even the oldest families tended to sink into social obscurity; with it, one sooner or later acquired enough of the trappings of education, culture, and manners to become respectable.

That wealth gave one status was basic to the American dream. It was this factor that gave men the incentive to amass fortunes well beyond their actual needs. Americans generally were proud of the speed with which they could accomplish anything; this included the development of an aristocracy. "An Englishman," according to Nathaniel Willis, "must have a grandfather, to be a gentleman, while an American needs but a father." [32] Some individuals did not even need fathers, as the careers of such persons as John Jacob Astor, Cornelius Vanderbilt, Ezra Cornell, Alexander Stewart, and a host of others indicate.

Etiquette books of the time were designed to transform persons of wealth into ladies and gentlemen. As the well-born authoress Catherine M. Sedgwick wrote: "I have seen it gravely stated by some writers on manners that 'it takes three generations to make a gentleman.' This is too slow a process in these days of accelerated movement. . . . You have it in your power to fit yourselves by cultivation of your minds and the refinement of your manners for inter-course, on equal terms, with the best society in our land." Numerous books on etiquette were written during the period from 1830 to 1860. Arthur Schlesinger records the publication of twenty-eight books on social decorum in the 'thirties, thirty-six in the 'forties, and thirty-eight in the 'fifties.[33]

The great majority of these etiquette books aimed not only at teaching manners, but also at instilling class distinctions and appealing to social snobbery. The popular-ity of the Earl of Chesterfield's maxims on behavior is a good example. Lord Chesterfield's work with its chivalric ethic of courtly self-gratification went through many Amer-ican editions. *The American Chesterfield,* a condensed manual with what American editors considered impro-prieties expurgated, became the most popular etiquette book in this country, teaching a highly aristocratic moral code. American writers on manners, though usually more moralistic than the English Earl, also assumed and en-couraged a class-structured society. Mrs. James Parton (known to her readers as Fanny Fern) gave such ironical advice in her "Rules for Ladies" as: "Always keep callers waiting, till they have had time to notice the outlay of money in your parlors"; or "Always whisper and laugh at concerts, by way of compliment to the performers, and to show your neighbors a sovereign contempt for their com-

fort." In addition to etiquette books, the fashionable maga-
zines such as *Godey's Lady's Book* and the *Home Journal*
were filled with didactic essays on breeding and ill-breed-
ing as well as sentimental stories depicting heroes and
heroines of great gentility and servants who knew their
place and served happily.[34]

Naturally, a society based primarily on wealth fluctuated
with the rise and fall of fortunes. There were individuals
with some means or some credit who would live pre-
tentiously for as long as their money, credit, or wits would
allow. Such persons often blazed resplendently across the
social scene only to burn out and disappear. One such
individual was Dr. Samuel "Sarsaparilla" Townsend, who
had made a small fortune from that beverage. In the late
'fifties, Townsend built the largest mansion in the city,
occupying three lots on the corner of Fifth Avenue and
Thirty-fourth Street. According to a contemporary, Townsend's palace was "large enough for a hotel, and showy
enough for a prince. It was burnished with gold and silver,
and elaborately ornamented with costly painting." This
mansion was the nine days' wonder of the city. Men and
women crowded to see it at twenty-five cents a head. But in
less than three years Townsend went bankrupt, and the
house passed out of his hands. Eventually A. T. Stewart
bought the property, razed the dwelling, and just after the
Civil War built a million-dollar white-marble mansion
which then was the most splendid in America.[35]

The "Sarsaparilla" Townsends were the exceptions, not
the rule. The great majority of New York's elite were far
more permanent both in their wealth and social status.
Great fortunes began to tell, and by the 1850's newly rich
industrial families such as the Havemeyers, Stuarts, Col-
gates, Coopers, Allaires, and Hoes were accepted as social

equals by the Livingstons, Schuylers, Fishes, Van Cortlandts, and others.[36]

Marriage alliances between wealthy families were common. It has been said that Beach's *Biography of Wealth*
served as a marriage guide for mercenary mothers looking
for a good match. It was not unusual for marriages to be
arranged between families. Often rich but not old families
would actually buy brides or grooms by offering large
sums to respectable families. Junius Browne termed these
marriages "coldblooded calculations, determinations for
vulgar display, meretricious shows from beginning to end.
There is slender opportunity or desire for election in
them. They are . . . managed, directed, and accomplished
by and through ambitious mothers and their thoroughly
disciplined daughters." Despite occasional moral condem-
nations of this type of mercenary mating, arranged marriages between upper-class families grew in frequency
during the 'forties and 'fifties. At the other extreme,
genuine love matches between persons of different class
produced a general shock in society. In 1857, wrote Charles
Haswell, "the public was much surprised and interested
in reading the announcement of the marriage of Miss Mary
Ann Baker, daughter of a very much esteemed citizen, to
John Dean, her father's coachman. So distasteful was the
marriage to her father that he essayed to remove her from
the country, and also to have her declared a lunatic. . . ." [37]

Marriage plans were often cemented, sometimes by
chance and sometimes by arrangement, at the various elegant summer spas and resorts frequented by persons of
fashion. Watering spots such as Saratoga Springs and Ball-
ston Spa in New York or Berkeley Springs and White
Sulpher Springs in Virginia were developed in the late
eighteenth century chiefly for the sickly. At that time the

mania for useful work was so universal in America that the notion of a summer resort in which to spend leisure hours was virtually unheard of. By the Jacksonian period these spas became the first theaters of conspicuous leisure in America. Still in the guise of health resorts, the watering places each year attracted the elite of both North and South. In mid-Victorian America, Saratoga Springs was the nation's most fashionable resort. "All the world is here," wrote Philip Hone from Saratoga in 1839, "politicians and dandies; cabinet ministers and ministers of the gospel; officeholders and office-seekers; humbuggers and humbugged; fortune-hunters and hunters of woodcock; anxious mothers and lovely daughters. . . ." [38]

During the summer of 1838, Hone was staying at the elegant United States Hotel, of which he wrote: "no watering-place in this or any other country can boast of a pleasanter establishment." Present at the time when Hone wrote were President Martin Van Buren, Henry Clay, New York Governor William Seward, Edward P. Livingston, General Winfield Scott, and hundreds of other leading figures. Hone wrote that the Saratoga season united "as in one brilliant focus the talent, intelligence, and civic virtues of the various parts of the country." [39]

Yearly, resorts such as Saratoga became less self-conscious. By the mid-'forties people seldom made the excuse that they were visiting a spa for their health. In 1850 Saratoga introduced horse-racing; shortly after this gambling casinos were added. But above all the spa was the great spot for matchmaking. The Baron Salomon de Rothschild, visiting Saratoga in August 1860, wrote that "every day the young girls put on new dresses in order to attract admirers. When one of them has several around her, she encourages them all until she has made a decision in favor of one of them. I was present several times as a confidant at these intrigues and it is quite diverting, I assure you." [40]

After his stay in Saratoga, Baron Rothschild went on to Newport, Rhode Island, which by the late 'fifties had surpassed Saratoga Springs as the center of fashion. "All of New York society," wrote the Baron, "is gathered here. Boston, Philadelphia, and especially the South have sent a good share of theirs, too." Among the notable New Yorkers residing at Newport that summer were Hamilton Fish, F. W. Rhinelander, Erastus Corning, James Lenox, Henry Van Rensselaer, William Schermerhorn, August Belmont, and Ward McAllister. At Newport there were a number of luxury hotels, but many of the wealthy summer visitors built "cottages," some of which rivaled the most extravagant Fifth Avenue mansions. Ward McAllister, the self-appointed leader of High Society, termed Newport "the most enjoyable and luxurious little island in America." On one occasion McAllister decided to give his cottage ground "an animated look" for the benefit of "a gathering of the brightest and cleverest people in the country." He hired for the day an entire flock of Southdown sheep, two yoke of cattle, and several cows.[41]

So general among the well-to-do did spending summers at fashionable resorts become that not to do so became a mark of social inferiority. Apparently some people even went to the extreme of pretending to be out of town in summer when they were not. G. G. Foster satirized the fashionable summer routine:

> The first week of bright sunshiny weather dismays all these persons, who pack off in hot haste to be roasted at Saratoga, or broiled and bleached at Newport, lest somebody should suspect they are not "fashionable." If, by any sad mischance, one of this class should be obliged to

remain in town, he straightway bars up his front door, offers inducements to spiders to colonize the portico— while members of the household exist in the kitchen and steal out after dark through the back streets for fear some one should recognize them and report them not "fashionable." [42]

Although a small leisure class had developed by the 'fifties, most men of wealth continued to work regardless of the size of their fortunes. This gave them something in common with virtually every other American male. But for the wives and daughters of the well-to-do a way of life developed which was strikingly different from the American norm.

> Very many things are considered unfeminine to be done, [wrote Mrs. Lydia Child] and of those duties which are feminine by universal consent, few are deemed genteel by the upper classes. It is not genteel for mothers to wash and dress their own children, or make their clothing, or teach them, or romp with them in the open air. Thus the most beautiful and blessed of all human relations performs but half its healthy and renovating mission. . . . Some human souls, finding themselves fenced within such narrow limits by false relations, seek fashionable distinction, or the excitement of gossip, flirtation, and perpetual change because they can find no other unforbidden outlets for the irrepressible activity of mind and heart.[43]

These wives and daughters of wealth did lead a life of leisure. They had enough servants to take care of the ordinary domestic duties. It was tacitly assumed in upper-class society that a woman did not work. Perhaps at no other time in American history were women so pampered

as in mid-nineteenth-century America. Mrs. A. J. Graves
in *Women in America,* published in 1855, wrote:

> The tendency to Orientalism is visible . . . in the false
> position in which woman is placed, as a being formed for
> no higher purpose than to be decorated, admired, and
> valued for her personal charm. Do we not see females in
> every fashionable circle who fill no loftier station in social
> life, and who live as idly and as uselessly as the gorgeously
> attired inmates of the harem. . . .

An Englishwoman, Mrs. Barbara Bodichon, wrote in 1859
that "there is in America, a large class of ladies who do
absolutely nothing. . . . In America—in that noble, free,
new country, it is grievous to see the old false snobbish
idea of 'respectability' eating at the heart of society, making
generations of women idle and corrupt, and retarding the
onward progress of the great Republic." [44]
The contrast was very great between the leisurely life
of women of fashion and that of the majority of women,
who were burdened down with domestic duties, or with
outside employment, or both. Mrs. Bodichon noted that
"there are thousands who have to do household work,
bear and nurse children, cook and wash, and live continually indoors, often in badly built, undrained, unhealthy
wooden houses, and suffer terribly. . . . As a pendant to
this, side by side, may be seen a sister, living in the midst
of luxuries, which many an English lady of rank would refuse as superfluous." [45]
Not having domestic duties nor being allowed to follow
a profession or even a serious intellectual pursuit, aristocratic ladies gave an inordinate amount of attention to
fashion. In New York a fashionable woman set aside one
morning each week as a day to receive her friends. On that

given day, according to a writer in the early 'fifties, "you will find her enshrined in all that is grand and costly; her door guarded by servants, whose formal ushering will kill within you all hope of unaffected and kindly intercourse; her parlors glittering with all she can possibly accumulate that is *recherché*, . . . and her own person arrayed with all the solicitude of splendor that morning dress allows, and sometimes something more." [46]

With the great growth of luxurious living the number of persons catering to the whims of wealth and fashion increased noticeably. Nathaniel Willis noted "the many ministers to taste and luxury who follow the garden of refinement on its 'Westward course.'" Those serving the needs of aristocracy included portrait painters, dancing masters, upholsterers, glove fitters, gardeners, hairdressers, carriage makers, milliners, fine chefs, and various other retainers. Many foreigners, particularly Frenchmen, Italians, and Germans, served in these special capacities.[47]

The growing number of servants in New York and other cities was perhaps the clearest index of the rise of an urban aristocracy. As related in an earlier chapter, by the mid-'forties the term "servant" and the wearing of livery were commonplace. Advertisements such as the following from the *New York Tribune,* January 30, 1851, were frequent: "WANTED—Situations for about seventy excellent servants . . ." Mrs. Mowatt in her play *Fashion* has Zeke, the Negro servant of the pretentious Mrs. Tiffany, say of his uniform: "Dere's a coat to take de eyes ob all Broadway! Ah! Missy, it am de fixins dat make de natural *born* gemman. A libery for ever!" [48] Zeke had enough actual counterparts in New York of the 'forties and 'fifties to give this satire a firm basis in reality.

Complaints of bad and insufficient servants continued

to be heard, but not as frequently as in the Jacksonian period. Foreigners no longer found servants so inconveniently democratic. An English woman visiting America at mid-century said: "So far as the observations and enquires of sixteen months could elicit such facts, I have not discovered that the servants in the United States are of a worse description than the same class of persons in England." Evidence seems to indicate that what difficulty in obtaining good servants remained in the 'forties and 'fifties did not stem chiefly from an equalitarian dislike of service, but rather from the fact that servants were poorly paid and forced to work long hours. Strong went so far as to say that slaves "are more kindly dealt with by their owners than servants are by Northern masters." Another writer observed that contempt for servants seemed to be a badge of gentility. The rich showed their superiority by "enforcing caste in our treatments of domestics." [49]

III

The generation before the Civil War witnessed the emergence of a class of wealthy persons set apart quite clearly from the rest of society. This New World aristocracy was urban-centered, New York City being its chief focal point. "The best society in New York," stated an English traveler in 1854, "would not suffer by comparison in any way with the best society in England." Another foreigner residing in New York in the early 'sixties predicted that very soon the different classes in America "will be as marked, if not more so, than in the old regions of titled nobility." [50]

Actually, on the eve of the Civil War there were two distinct types of aristocracy in America. In the North, centering in New York and other cities, there existed a plutocracy of merchants, mill owners, shipping magnates, and speculators in city real estate. In the South, aristocracy had followed a divergent path because of quite different economic and social conditions. There a planter aristocracy controlled the best lands and the slave labor supply. Southern planter magnates had increasingly claimed to be the only true aristocrats in the country. In some respects this claim seemed valid. Like the former feudal nobility of Europe, Southern planters had large land holdings, servants and subservient workers, elegant manors, political power, and various social privileges. However, Southern aristocracy remained dependent on the institution of slavery, and just as slavery was anachronistic in mid-nineteenth-century America, so too was an agrarian-based aristocracy. The future lay with those who controlled the nation's industries, financial institutions, merchandising facilities, and transportation systems.[51]

Even before the Civil War forced the collapse of antebellum Southern society, the triumph of the Northern industrial elite seemed clear. The Civil War strongly reinforced the power of the Northern aristocracy, and gave to the Northern elite a greater degree of national political power than it had hitherto enjoyed. But it could be argued that well before the firing on Fort Sumter the Northern aristocracy was already more powerful and more firmly entrenched than that of the South.

From the point of view of wealth and style of living, certainly the Northern millionaires and lesser magnates far surpassed the Southern planter. Ward McAllister, who had been born on a Georgia plantation and knew the best society of the South intimately, disputed the planters' claim that only Southern gentlemen lived well and "that there was no such thing as good society in New York or other Northern cities; that New Yorkers and Northern people were simply a lot of tradespeople, having no antecedents, springing up like the mushroom." McAllister argued that, on the contrary, no one in America lived more aristocratically than New Yorkers, whom he claimed dined better and had better servants than the slaveholding Southerners.[52]

The question of the actual power wielded by the Northern elite is more difficult to ascertain. In the Jacksonian period most trades were still dominated by independent skilled workers, and only in the South did the aristocracy control a large labor supply. In 1830 there was not a clear economic basis for distinct class lines in the North. Only in the matter of finance was a select group able to effect any widespread control over the economy, and Jackson's attack on the Bank actually weakened this power.

Between the 'thirties and the Civil War this situation was greatly altered. In the North, and particularly in New York, the wealthy classes were beginning to exercise a power and an influence far greater than had ever been possessed by any earlier American elite. Private corporations were able to have great control over such things as banking and the transportation system. The factory system, largely unchecked either by government or by an effectively organized labor force, gave to a few capitalists the virtual control of the destinies of many.

By the 'fifties, unregulated industrial growth had led to the decline of the status of free labor and had created a propertyless urban population dependent on the industrial system for its very existence. At the same time, the emergence of a wealthy plutocracy created far greater extremes between rich and poor than had previously existed. The fact that many of the proletariat consisted of foreign immigrants further widened the social division between capital and labor.

Americans tolerated the stratification of what had once been a fairly homogeneous, middle-class society for a number of reasons. In the first place, those who were most harmfully affected by this development had the least power to do anything about it. Workers were unsuccessful in meeting the challenge of industrialization either through unions or politics. Even if they had possessed political power, which they did not, there was the added difficulty that the government of the United States was highly decentralized both by nature and choice at a time when the economy was becoming more and more centralized, controlled by the new capitalist elite. Under different circumstances, politicians in the 'fifties and 'sixties might have been forced to come to grips with some of the basic social and economic problems stemming from industrialization. However, the slavery crisis, the Civil War, and reconstruction absorbed political attention during these decades, while the rich grew yearly richer and more powerful.

Another factor was the strong American belief in social mobility, a belief which made Americans more tolerant of plutocrats, as well as paupers, than any society in the Western world. Equality meant the ability to get ahead. Thus, the Astors, Stewarts, Vanderbilts, Coopers, and Cornells of society were not hated for their wealth; they were heroes who had triumphantly climbed the American success ladder. It took Americans a long time to realize that the very success of these persons limited future opportunities and lessened social mobility. But as recent studies have shown, the chances of rising from rags to riches became less of a reality with each passing decade.[53]

The rich helped to make their position more acceptable

by using their wealth philanthropically. Many of New York's wealthiest citizens gave away a certain percentage of their yearly incomes to favorite charities. William Colgate, the soap king, gave large sums to Hamilton Literary and Theological Seminary (Colgate University after 1890). The Stuart brothers, Robert and Alexander, owners of the nation's largest sugar refinery located in New York City, donated over a million dollars to Princeton University and several hundred thousand dollars to Presbyterian Hospital of New York. Peter Cooper founded Cooper Union in the late 'fifties as a free school for adults. Both Alexander Stewart and Horace Claflin, the dry-goods princes, practiced extensive philanthropy.[54]

Often philanthropy was highly paternalistic and did little to win friends for the wealthy. During the panic of 1854 when thousands were unemployed, New York's elite held a grand ballet at the Fourteenth Street opera house to help relieve the suffering of the poor. As George Strong wrote:

> To a poverty stricken demagogue, the plan of feasting the aristocracy on boned turkey and *pâté de foie gras* that the democracy may be supplied with pork and beans, and assembling the Upper Ten in brocade and valenciennes that the lower thousand may be helped to flannel and cotton shirting, would furnish a theme most facile and fertile.

Nevertheless, as Strong later wrote: "There has been vast improvement during the last three or four years in the dealings of the 'upper class' with the poor; not merely in the comparative abundance of their bounty, but in the fact that it has become fashionable and creditable and not unusual for people to busy themselves in personal labors for the very poor and in personal intercourses with them." [55]

For these and other reasons, then, Americans generally tolerated the major social and economic changes between 1830 and 1860 without effective protest.

IV

The social and economic changes that brought a wealthy plutocracy to the pinnacle of Northern society in the period before the Civil War were not accepted without resentment. As the rich became richer and the poor more numerous, hostilities and even open class conflicts frequently occurred, particularly in New York City. In the dreary slum-ghettos of Manhattan, immigrant and native workers often expressed unrest and dissatisfaction in the form of brawls, riots, and other violent outbreaks. For example, on Friday, May 10, 1849, the fashionable Astor Place Opera House was the scene of a bloody fracas, when a large mob, chiefly Irish, stormed the theater, where the hated English actor William Charles Macready was playing. Shouting "burn the damn den of aristocracy," the unruly crowd attacked, throwing bricks and abuse, only to be driven back by a round of musket fire from the forewarned militia. The riot that ensued saw sides taken along class lines, with the rich supporting Macready while the mob championed the American actor Edwin Forrest. Before the troops and the police could restore order, some 200 persons were killed or seriously wounded.[56]

Angry outbursts of distraught citizens were reported intermittently for the next decade. During the depression year 1857, New York's debased slum population seemed especially restless. An Independence Day quarrel between two rival gangs, the Dead Rabbits and the Bowery Boys, turned into a major riot. Streets were barricaded as whole sections of the city became a battle ground. Several persons were killed and many others wounded before the police, aided by vigilante groups composed of some of the leading citizens, were able to suppress the rioters. Nor was this the end. A little over a week later on July 13, an angry mob of some 500 persons attacked the police with pistols and bricks. Later that same year, as unemployment multiplied, working-class people on several occasions held large public demonstrations and paraded through the streets demanding bread and work. Shops were sometimes sacked, and on November 10 an angry crowd seized control of part of City Hall. United States Marines were brought in from Governor's Island and posted in front of the Custom House and Treasury Office. Order was once more restored, but periodic violence remained common in the years immediately preceding the Civil War.[57]

The clearest example of major class strife in New York occurred during the war years. The Civil War hurt the laboring classes for, although unemployment was checked, the cost of living soared while wages seldom kept pace. Added to this was a growing fear among immigrant workers, especially the Irish, that a war to free the Southern slave would bring in thousands of Negroes to take over their jobs. These discontents were brought to a head when the conscription of soldiers under the newly passed Draft Act began in New York in July 1863. In the eyes of laborers the law seemed to bear out the familiar adage that this was a rich man's war and a poor man's fight, since for $300 anyone could buy a substitute and avoid the draft.

Hatreds aroused by economic distress, racial antagonism, and class bitterness were vented through burning, pillaging, and general carnage during the terrifying week of July 13, 1863. The draft riots began on Monday morning when an angry mob broke into the registry office on the corner of Third Avenue and Forty-sixth Street, where drafting was in progress.[58] After driving out the officials and burning the building, rioters then beat off a group of soldiers and police. Emboldened by their initial success the mob roamed the city almost at will, attacking Negroes, abolitionists, public officials, and well-dressed gentlemen. Stores and houses were sacked, an orphan asylum for Negro children was burned. Terror gripped the city. Business closed down, public transportation halted, and factories ceased to operate as workers joined the swelling mob. Rich men feared for their lives and property. George Templeton Strong noted in his diary on the evening of the second day of rioting: "At eight to Union League Club. Rumor it's to be attacked tonight. Some say there is to be great mischief tonight and that the rabble is getting the upper hand. Home at ten and sent for Dudley Field, Jr., to confer about an expected attack on his house and his father's. . . ." Two days later on July 16 Strong reported that the rioters "are in full possession of the western and eastern sides of the city, from Tenth Street upward, and of a good many districts beside. I could not walk four blocks eastward from this house this very minute without peril." [59]

The rioters numbered well over ten thousand. Many were, as one contemporary noted, "the scum of the city"; others were, as Strong contemptuously observed, "the lowest Irish day laborers." Yet it would be a great falsification to blame these riots simply on the poorest foreign immigrants. From first to last the rioters' ranks were swelled with respectable working-class citizens, many of whom were native Americans. As a recent student of immigrant life in New York City has concluded: "the draft riots were a manifestation, not of immigrant feeling, but of genuine working-class discontent, augmented by fierce racial antipathies characteristic of the war years." [60]

Order was restored only after a series of pitched battles reminiscent of the bloodiest days of the Paris Commune. In all over 1000 persons were killed, some 8000 wounded, and more than a hundred buildings destroyed before the combined efforts of the police, militia, army veterans, and private citizens could suppress the rioters.

Thus, well before the turbulent industrial disputes of the late nineteenth century, violence had come to characterize urban-industrial America. The favored minority maintained their superior position, but did so only at the social cost of increasingly alienating the lower classes. These industrial aristocrats were not entirely at ease in their eminence. They lacked the mutual bonds between themselves and the working classes that had tied the feudal lord to his serf. Their services to society seldom seemed indispensable. Nor did they help the masses toward greater social and economic equality. The vast sums they spent in conspicuous display, though sometimes admired by the less opulent majority, in the long run only increased the odium which the masses felt for the flashy rich. Furthermore, in republican America these aristocrats were clearly out of touch with the democratic ideals of the age.

In 1840 Tocqueville had warned that "the manufacturing aristocracy which is growing up under our eyes is one of the harshest which ever existed in the world. . . . If ever a permanent inequality of conditions and aristocracy again penetrate into the world, it may be predicted that this is the gate by which they will enter." [61] Two decades later this prediction was realized in the state of New York. The generally democratic and agrarian society of farmers, craftsmen, and merchants of the Jacksonian period had given way to a hierarchical urban-industrial society dominated by an aristocracy of wealth. Clearly, the foundations for the plutocracy of the Gilded Age had been laid, and democracy itself stood challenged.

Americans of the Jacksonian era associated freedom and equality with their republican institutions. As a people they sensed a special destiny. "Providence," President Jackson told them, "has showered on this favored land blessings without number and has chosen you as the guardians of freedom to preserve it for the benefit of the human race." [62] To realize this prophecy, all that was believed to be necessary was for the genius of the people—the majority —to express itself through this nation's democratic institutions. Monarchy, oligarchy, or any form of special privilege was to be avoided.

Economic rewards were to go to the honest toiler. "The planter, the farmer, the mechanic, and the laborer," asserted Jackson in his Farewell Address, "all know that their success depends upon their own industry and economy and that they must not expect to become suddenly rich by the fruits of their toil." "Let us," proclaimed a supporter of Old Hickory, "avoid luxury as the greatest bane to liberty." [63] These were the ideals of exuberant and optimistic young America.

Yet within a decade after Jackson retired from the political scene, this democratic faith stood distinctly challenged. In the years before the Civil War, special privilege became a far more pronounced feature of New York society than in the days of Jackson's struggle to end such exclusive rights through his war on the Bank. Honest toil in the Jacksonian sense, though still rewarding the patient per-

son with modest ambitions, had decidedly not proved
to be the way to wealth, power, and recognition. Above all,
luxury, "the greatest bane to liberty," had become a salient
feature of life.

Clearly, the vague notion that the anti-democratic ills
affecting American society in the late nineteenth century
were exclusively the result of the Civil War and postwar
industrialization, is highly questionable. All the problems associated with that later period had already afflicted
New York society in reputedly republican mid-nineteenth-
century America.

NOTES

PREFACE

1. Benson, *The Concept of Jacksonian Democracy* (New York, 1964 ed.), pp. 5, 329–38.
2. *Ibid.*, p. 336.
3. John William Ward, "The Age of the Common Man," in John Higham, ed., *The Reconstruction of American History* (New York, 1962), p. 82; for a recent critical evaluation of Fish's *The Rise of the Common Man* see: Marcus Cunliffe, *The Nation Takes Shape, 1789–1837* (Chicago, 1959), pp. 150–57.
4. Quoted in Joseph L. Blau, ed., *Social Theories of Jacksonian Democracy* (New York, 1954), pp. 185, 290.

CHAPTER 1 EQUALITY

1. Colton, *Manual for Emigrants to America* (London, 1832), p. 62. For a discussion of the origins and development of the American philosophy of equality prior to the Jacksonian era see: Jane Frances Ferguson, *The Philosophy of Equality* (Washington, D.C., 1943), pp. 20–28; Robert John O'Connor, "An Analysis of the Bases for the Concept of Equality" (unpublished doctoral dissertation, University of Southern California, 1960), pp. 39–41.
2. Tocqueville, *Democracy in America*, trans. Henry Reeve (2 vols., New York, 1961), I, lxvii; Chevalier, *Society, Manners, and Politics in the United States*, John William Ward, ed. (Garden City, New York, 1961), pp. 182–3.
3. Francis J. Grund, *Aristocracy in America* (New York, 1959), pp. 29–30; Thomas Cather, *Voyage to America* (New York, 1961), p. 103; James Stuart, *Three Years in North America* (2nd ed., 2 vols., Edinburgh, 1833), II, 182; Frances Trollope, *Domestic Manners of the Americans*, Donald Smalley, ed. (New York, 1960), pp. 392–5; James Fenimore Cooper, *The American Democrat* (New York, 1956), p. 154.
4. *The Picture of New-York and Stranger's Guide to the Commercial Metropolis of the United States* (New York, 1828), pp. 364–5.
5. Francis J. Grund, *The Americans in Their Moral, Social, and Political Relations* (2 vols., London, 1837), II, 13; William Cobbett, *A Year's*

Residence in the United States (3 vols., New York, 1818), I, 201. There is no recent study of domestic service in this period. The best general work on the subject is the older study by Lucy Maynard Salmon, *Domestic Service* (New York, 1897).

6. John Fowler, *Journal of a Tour in the State of New York in the Year 1830* (London, 1831), p. 218; Basil Hall, *Travels in North America in the Years 1827 and 1828* (3 vols., Edinburgh, 1829), I, 142, II, 156–7; *The Laws of Etiquette* (Philadelphia, 1836), p. 89.

7. Harriet Martineau, *Society in America* (2 vols., London, 1837), II, 63.

8. H. E. Scudder, ed., *Recollections of Samuel Breck* (Philadelphia, 1877), pp. 275–6.

9. A good account of the spread and triumph of evangelical religion in New York is Whitney R. Cross, *The Burned-Over District* (Ithaca, 1950); see also: Bernard A. Weisberger, *They Gathered at the River* (Boston, 1958), pp. 14, 81–2, 96–9, 105–9, 135.

10. Grund, *Aristocracy*, pp. 25–6.

11. Quoted in William Cobbett, *The Emigrant's Guide* (London, 1830), p. 91.

12. *Aristocracy*, p. 30.

13. F. B. Hough, *Census of Electors of the State of New York* (Albany, 1857), p. x; see also Chilton Williamson, *American Suffrage: From Property to Democracy, 1760–1860* (Princeton, 1960), p. 197.

14. Williamson, *American Suffrage*, p. 195.

15. N. H. Carter, W. L. Stone, and M. T. C. Gould, *Reports of the Proceedings and Debates of the Convention of 1821* (Albany, 1821), pp. 219–22; the best account of Kent's role in the convention is found in John Theodore Horton, *James Kent: a Study in Conservatism* (New York, 1939), pp. 243–63.

16. Quoted in David M. Ellis, *et al.*, *A Short History of New York State* (Ithaca, 1957), p. 147.

17. The best account of the New York Constitutional Convention is still Dixon Ryan Fox's *The Decline of Aristocracy in the Politics of New York* (New York, 1919), pp. 229–70.

18. Allan Nevins, ed., *The Diary of Philip Hone, 1828–1851* (New York, 1936), pp. 235–6.

19. *American Quarterly Review*, XX (September 1836), 208.

20. The English visitor Charles Mackay made this observation in the 1850's in his book *Life and Liberty in America* (New York, 1859), p. 304; see also: Williamson, *American Suffrage*, pp. 281–2; Lee Benson, *The Concept of Jacksonian Democracy: New York as a Test Case* (Princeton, 1961), p. 10.

21. Quoted in Robert G. Gunderson, *The Log-Cabin Campaign* (Lexing-

ton, 1957), p. 107; see also: Dixon Wector, *The Saga of American Society* (New York, 1937), pp. 95–6.

22. *Saga of American Society*, pp. 92–4.

23. Tocqueville, *Democracy in America*, I, 202; Grund, *Aristocracy*, pp. 171, 264.

24. Potter, *People of Plenty* (Chicago, 1954), pp. 114–16; Hall, *Travels in North America*, II, 136–7.

25. *Democracy in America*, II, 290.

26. Collins, *Emigrant's Guide*, p. 94; Ellis, *et al.*, *Short History of New York*, pp. 150–62.

27. Alexander C. Flick, ed., *History of the State of New York* (10 vols., New York, 1933–37), V, 162–72.

28. *Democracy in America*, II, 184–5.

29. *Reminiscences* (New York, 1852), p. 219.

30. Rev. Isaac Fidler, *Observations on Professions, Literature, Manners, and Emigration in the United States and Canada* (New York, 1832), p. 159.

31. *Democracy in America*, II, 162.

32. *How To Behave* (New York, 1856), p. 124.

33. *Society and Manners*, pp. 261–2.

34. Thomas L. Nichols, *Forty Years of American Life, 1821–1861* (New York, 1937), p. 195.

35. *Democracy in America*, I, 230, II, 164–5; an excellent study of Tocqueville's analysis of Jacksonian society is Marvin Meyers, *The Jacksonian Persuasion* (New York, 1960), pp. 33–56; indispensable in using Tocqueville as a source is the work by George W. Pierson, *Tocqueville and Beaumont in America* (New York, 1938).

36. Alexis de Tocqueville, *Journey to America*, J. P. Mayer, ed. (New Haven, 1960), pp. 69, 157, 217, 260; B. F. Tefft, *Inequality in the Condition of Man Inevitable* (Greencastle, Ind., 1845), pp. 3–4; Thomas Hamilton, *Men and Manners in America* (2 vols., Edinburgh, 1833), I, 109.

CHAPTER 2   LABOR IN JACKSONIAN NEW YORK

1. Michael Chevalier, *Society, Manners, and Politics in the United States* (Garden City, 1961 ed.), pp. 267–8; Alexis de Tocqueville, *Democracy in America* (2 vols., New York, 1945), II, 182–3; Abram C. Dayton, *Last Days of Knickerbocker Life in New York* (New York, 1897), p. 194.

2. *The Emigrant's Guide to the United States of America* (London, 1830), p. 58; on actual wages in the 1830's see: John R. Commons and others, *History of Labour in the United States* (4 vols., New York, 1918–35), I, 415–16; Philip S. Foner, *History of the Labor Movement in the United States* (2 vols., New York, 1947), I, 98–101.

3. Chevalier, *Society, Manners, and Politics in the United States*, pp. 330–32.

4. Parks, quoted in William Cobbett, *The Emigrant's Guide* (London, 1830), pp. 65–6; Thomas Cather, *Voyage to America* (New York, 1961), p. 102.

5. *America, Historical, Statistical, and Descriptive* (3 vols., London, 1841), II, 414–15.

6. Quoted in Cobbett, *Emigrant's Guide*, p. 92.

7. [New York] *Evening Journal*, January 9, 1830; [New York] *The Working Man's Advocate*, March 6, 1830; Walter Hugins, *Jacksonian Democracy and the Working Class: A Study of the New York Workingmen's Movement, 1829–37*, Stanford Studies in History, Economics, and Political Science, XIX (Stanford, Calif., 1960), pp. 51–3; Carl R. Fish, *The Rise of the Common Man, 1830–1850* (New York, 1927), pp. 88–9.

8. John R. Commons and others, eds., *A Documentary History of American Industrial Society* (10 vols., Cleveland, 1910), V, 23.

9. Foster Rhea Dulles, *Labor in America* (New York, 1960 ed.), pp. 20–24; Commons and others, *History of Labour*, I, 34–61.

10. Alexander C. Flick, ed., *History of the State of New York* (10 vols., New York, 1933–37), V, 346–56.

11. The role of the merchant-capitalist is discussed in: Fred M. Jones, *Middlemen in the Domestic Trade of the United States, 1800–1860*, Illinois Studies in Social Sciences, XXI (Urbana, Ill., 1937).

12. Quoted in *New York Panorama* (New York, 1938), p. 382.

13. *Working Man's Advocate*, March 13, 1830.

14. *Evening Journal*, October 17, 1829.

15. Commons and others, *History of Labour*, I, 153–7; Joseph G. Rayback, *A History of Labor* (New York, 1959), pp. 58–9.

16. [New York] *The Man*, May 13, 1835; Commons and others, *History of Labour*, I, 171–5.

17. *Working Man's Advocate*, October 31, 1829, January 6, February 27, 1830.

18. *The Picture of New York and Stranger's Guide to the Commercial Metropolis of the United States* (New York, 1828), p. 333; Commons and others, *History of Labour*, I, 181.

19. Quoted in *The Working Man's Advocate*, March 13, 1830.

20. Commons and others, eds., *Documentary History of American Industrial Society*, V, 157–8.

21. Quoted in *The Working Man's Advocate*, January 30, 1830.

22. [New York] *The Union*, April 30, 1836.

23. *Working Man's Advocate*, January 3, 1835.

24. Dulles, *Labor in America*, pp. 29–31; Commons and others, *History of Labour*, I, 162–5.

25. Skidmore's economic thought is treated in: Joseph Dorfman, *The Economic Mind in American Civilization* (3 vols., New York, 1946–49), II, 641–5.

26. Commons and others, eds., *Documentary History of American Industrial Society*, V, 155–6; *Working Man's Advocate*, November 7, 1829.

27. Commons and others, *History of Labour*, I, 260–65.

28. *Ibid.*, I, 242–60; Commons and others, eds., *Documentary History of American Industrial Society*, V, 157–77.

29. *Jacksonian Democracy*, p. 110.

30. [New York] *Sentinel and Working Man's Advocate*, June 23, 1830.

31. Flick, ed., *History of the State of New York*, VI, 68; Alice Felt Tyler, *Freedom's Ferment* (New York, 1962), p. 285; Dulles, *Labor in America*, pp. 49–50; Commons and others, *History of Labour*, I, 329–30; Rayback, *A History of American Labor*, pp. 89–90.

32. Commons and others, *History of Labour*, I, 234–5; Rayback, *A History of American Labor*, pp. 59–60, 77.

33. Commons and others, eds., *Documentary History of American Industrial Society*, V, 212.

34. *The Union*, April 30, 1836.

35. Commons and others, *History of Labour*, I, 350–56; Dulles, *Labor in America*, pp. 54–8.

36. Commons and others, *History of Labour*, I, 365–9; Dulles, *Labor in America*, pp. 58–9; Rayback, *A History of American Labor*, pp. 78–81.

37. Foner, *History of the Labor Movement in the United States*, I, 108; Dulles, *Labor in America*, p. 71.

38. Quoted in Dulles, *Labor in America*, p. 64.

39. Commons and others, *History of Labour*, I, 405–7.

40. *Ibid.*, I, 409–11; Dulles, *Labor in America*, p. 65; Commons and others, eds., *Documentary History of American Industrial Society*, V, 314–22; for a contemporary account by a conservative see: Allan Nevins, ed., *The Diary of Philip Hone* (New York, 1936), pp. 211–12.

41. Commons and others, *History of Labour*, I, 454–8.

42. *Appeal to the Wealthy of the Land, Ladies as Well as Gentlemen, on the Character, Conduct, Situation, and Prospects of Those Whose Sole Dependence for Subsistence Is on the Labour of Their Hands* (Philadelphia, 1833), p. 5.

43. *Ibid.*, pp. 11, 16–17.

44. *Ibid.*, pp. 3–5, 8–10.

45. Richard Henry Dana, Jr.'s classic *Two Years Before the Mast* (1840) is the best contemporary account of the common seaman's life in the 1830's.

46. *Appeal to the Wealthy*, p. 3.

47. *Ibid.*, pp. 15–16, Dr. Rensselaer to M. Carey.

48. *Recollections of a Busy Life* (New York, 1868), p. 144.

49. Contemporary accounts on the effects of the cholera epidemic on New York City's working people are: Nevins, ed., *The Diary of Philip Hone*, pp. 73–4; Greeley, *Recollections*, pp. 88–9.

CHAPTER 3 MANORS AND COUNTING HOUSES

1. Tocqueville, *Democracy in America* (2 vols., New York, 1945), I, 51; James Fenimore Cooper, *The American Democrat* (New York, 1956), pp. 40–43, Hubbard, *Autobiography of N. T. Hubbard with Personal Reminiscences of New York City from 1798 to 1875* (New York, 1875, pp. 89–90; Charles H. Haswell, *Reminiscences of an Octogenarian of the City of New York* (New York, 1896), pp. 181–2.

2. S. H. Collins, *The Emigrant's Guide to the United States of America* (London, 1830), p. 49; Francis J. Grund, *Aristocracy in America* (New York, 1959), p. 83; Edwin Harrison Cady, *The Gentleman in America* (Syracuse, 1949), pp. 6, 20–1.

3. Hubbard, *Autobiography*, pp. 160–61; [Joseph A. Scoville], *The Old Merchants of New York*, 5 vols. (New York, 1863–66), I, 14–15.

4. Cooper, *The American Democrat*, pp. 78–80.

5. Grund, *Aristocracy in America*, pp. 10, 52, 170.

6. See: *The Working Man's Advocate*, March 13, 1830.

7. *Aristocracy in America*, p. 145.

8. Hall quoted in Clayton Mau, *The Development of Central and Western New York* (Rochester, 1944), p. 266; Murray, *Travels in North America During the Years 1834, 1835, and 1836* (2 vols., New York, 1839), I, 65.

9. James Arthur Frost, *Life on the Upper Susquehanna, 1783–1860* (New York, 1951), p. 123.

10. Henry Christman, *Tin Horns and Calico* (New York, 1961), p. 21.

11. *Ibid.*, p. 24; David M. Ellis, *et al.*, *A Short History of New York State* (Ithaca, 1957), pp. 21–2, 71–5.

12. Alexander C. Flick, ed., *History of the State of New York* (10 vols., New York, 1933–37), VI, 292–3.

13. David M. Ellis, *Landlords and Farmers in the Hudson-Mohawk Region, 1790–1850* (Ithaca, 1946), pp. 16–65; Edward P. Cheyney, *The Anti-Rent Agitation in the State of New York, 1839–1846* (Philadelphia, 1887), p. 19.

14. William B. Fink, "Stephen Van Rensselaer, the Last Patroon" (unpublished doctoral dissertation, Columbia University, New York, 1950), pp. 2–14.

15. Cheyney, *The Anti-Rent Agitation*, pp. 19–20; Christman, *Tin Horns and Calico*, pp. 25–9; Fink, "Stephen Van Rensselaer," pp. 247–51, 253; Ellis, *Landlords and Farmers*, pp. 232–3.

16. Fink, "Stephen Van Rensselaer," pp. 251–4; Ellis, *Landlords and Farmers*, pp. 233–4.

17. Quoted in Christman, *Tin Horns and Calico*, p. 40; see also: John Bach McMaster, *A History of the People of the United States from the Revolution to the Civil War* (8 vols., New York, 1883–1913), VI, 521.

18. Cheyney, *The Anti-Rent Agitation*, pp. 31–5; McMaster, *History of the People of the United States*, VI, 522–3.

19. From "The Helderberg War," an Anti-Rent ballad quoted in Christman, *Tin Horns and Calico*, p. 345.

20. *Ibid.*, pp. 129–42, 190–95.

21. Ellis, *Landlords and Farmers*, pp. 272–5; Flick, ed., *History of the State of New York*, VI, 313–18.

22. Christman, *Tin Horns and Calico*, pp. 278–87, 292, 301.

23. Cheyney, *The Anti-Rent Agitation*, pp. 48–50; Ellis, *Landlords and Farmers*, pp. 306–10; Christman, *Tin Horns and Calico*, pp. 302–3.

24. Cooper, *The American Democrat*, pp. 92–102, 133–9; Cady, *Gentleman in America*, pp. 103–26; Cooper wrote three novels in which the doctrines of the Anti-Renters are denounced; these are: *Satanstoe* (1845), *The Chainbearer* (1845), and *The Redskins* (1846).

25. This phrase was coined by Washington Irving during the Jacksonian era. See: Van Wyck Brooks, *The World of Washington Irving* (New York, 1944), p. 314.

26. *The Picture of New York and Stranger's Guide to the Commercial Metropolis of the United States* (New York, 1828), pp. 153–7; I. N. Phelps Stokes, *New York, Past and Present* (New York, 1939), p. 78.

27. Chevalier, *Lettres sur l'Amerique du Nord* (2 vols., Brussels, 1837), II, 36; Frances Trollope, *Domestic Manners of the Americans* (New York, 1960), pp. 336–7.

28. James Hardie, *The Description of the City of New York* (New York, 1827), pp. 146–7; *The Picture of New York and Stranger's Guide*, pp. 139–57.

29. Mrs. Anne Royall quoted in W. S. Tryon, ed., *My Native Land* (Chicago, 1952), p. 54; Abram C. Dayton, *Last Days of Knickerbocker Life in New York* (New York, 1897), p. 154.

30. Charles Dickens, *American Notes for General Circulation* (New York, 1942), pp. 393–5, 397–8; Trollope, *Domestic Manners of the Americans*, p. 337.

31. Trollope, *Domestic Manners of the Americans*, p. 339; [Scoville], *The Old Merchants of New York*, I, 14.

32. By 1830 the term Knickerbocker was loosely applied to persons

comprising New York's best society and not exclusively to those of Dutch descent. See: [Scoville], *The Old Merchants of New York*, I, 10–15.

33. *Last Days of Knickerbocker Life in New York*, p. 196.

34. [Scoville], *The Old Merchants of New York*, I, 9, 12.

35. Dayton, *Last Days of Knickerbocker Life*, pp. 313–16.

36. [Theodore Dwight], *The Northern Traveller* (New York, 1826), p. 22; Isaac S. Lyon, *Recollections of an Old Cartman* (Newark, 1872), pp. 6–8; Dayton, *Last Days of Knickerbocker Life*, pp. 30–38, 97; Charles H. Haswell, *Reminiscences of an Octogenarian of the City of New York* (New York, 1896), p. 315.

37. Trollope, *Domestic Manners of the Americans*, pp. 338–9; Dayton, *Last Days of Knickerbocker Life*, pp. xxviii–xxx.

38. *New York Panorama* (New York, 1938), pp. 429–30; Haswell, *Reminiscences*, p. 332.

39. Haswell, *Reminiscences*, p. 243; Trollope, *Domestic Manners*, p. 338, note 3.

40. Thomas Low Nichols, *Forty Years of American Life, 1821–1861* (New York, 1937), p. 166; Phelps Stokes, *New York Past and Present*, p. 78; Allan Nevins, ed., *The Diary of Philip Hone* (2 vols., New York, 1927), I, 202; Allan Nevins and Milton Thomas, eds., *The Diary of George Templeton Strong* (4 vols., New York, 1953), I, 262.

41. Dayton, *Last Days of Knickerbocker Life*, pp. 103–5.

42. Dixon Ryan Fox, *The Decline of Aristocracy in the Politics of New York* (New York, 1919), pp. 29–30.

43. Haswell, *Reminiscences*, p. 317; Allan Nevins, ed., *The Diary of Philip Hone* (New York, 1936), pp. 214, 263.

44. Nevins, ed., *The Diary of Philip Hone* (1936 ed.), pp. 110–11.

45. Grund, *Aristocracy in America*, pp. 10, 55–9, 81, 87, 115, 159; *The New York Journal of Commerce*, March 27, 1830.

46. Grund, *Aristocracy in America*, pp. 131, 107.

47. Francis and Theresa Pulszky, *White, Red and Black* (2 vols., London, 1853), I, 11.

48. Grund, *Aristocracy in America*, pp. 29, 92, 124–8.

49. Quoted in Tryon, ed., *My Native Land*, p. 66.

50. Grund, *Aristocracy in America*, p. 85.

CHAPTER 4   TO THE NEW WORLD

1. Marcus Lee Hansen, *The Atlantic Migration, 1607–1860* (New York, 1961), p. 280; Maldwyn Allen Jones, *American Immigration* (Chicago, 1960), pp. 92–4.

2. Carl Wittke, *We Who Built America* (Cleveland, 1957), p. 101;

Carl R. Fish, *The Rise of the Common Man, 1830–1850* (New York, 1927), p. 109; Jones, *American Immigration*, p. 93.

3. William J. Bromwell, *History of Immigration to the United States* (New York, 1856), p. 15; Wittke, *We Who Built America*, pp. 130–31; Hansen, *The Atlantic Migration*, pp. 107–19.

4. William F. Adams, *Ireland and Irish Emigration to the New World From 1815 to the Famine* (New Haven, 1932), p. 353.

5. Gilman Ostrander, *The Rights of Man in America, 1606–1861* (Columbia, Mo., 1960), pp. 156–8.

6. Hansen, *The Atlantic Migration*, pp. 120–21; John R. Commons and others, *History of Labour in the United States* (4 vols., New York, 1918–35), I, 412–13; Jones, *American Immigration*, p. 93.

7. Jones, *American Immigration*, p. 96; Robert Ernst, *Immigrant Life in New York City, 1825–1863* (New York, 1949), pp. 2–3.

8. Ernst, *Immigrant Life*, pp. 3–6; David M. Ellis *et al.*, *A Short History of New York State* (Ithaca, 1957), p. 282.

9. Jesse Chickering, *Immigration into the United States* (Boston, 1848), p. 59; Jones, *American Immigration*, pp. 95–6; Hansen, *The Atlantic Migration*, pp. 17–24, 199–200, 242–8; Wittke, *We Who Built America*, pp. 129–31; Thomas D'Arcy McGee, *A History of the Irish Settlers in North American* (Boston, 1852), pp. 135–6; Hibernicus [pseudo.], "What Brings so many Irish to America?" (Pamphlet, New York, 1845), pp. 6–34; Oscar Handlin, ed., *Immigration as a Factor in American History* (Englewood Cliffs, N.J., 1959), p. 22; Adams, *Ireland and Irish Emigration*, p. 391.

10. Hansen, *The Atlantic Migration*, pp. 284–94; Wittke, *We Who Built America*, pp. 187–99; John A. Hawgood, *The Tragedy of German-America* (New York, 1940), p. 57.

11. *New York Daily Tribune*, February 19, 1851, September 23, 1850; Horace Greeley wrote a series of scathing editorials on immigrant ship conditions: see *New York Daily Tribune*, November 19, 22, 26, and December 3, 1853.

12. Stephen Byrne, *Irish Emigration to the United States* (New York, 1873), p. 20; one of the most vivid accounts of immigrant ship horrors is William Smith, *An Emigrant's Narrative; or a Voice from the Steerage* (New York, 1850); see also: John Francis Maguire, *The Irish in America* (London, 1868), pp. 134–45, 179–83; Edith Abbott, ed., *Immigration: Select Documents and Case Records* (Chicago, 1924), pp. 13–42.

13. Alexander C. Flick, ed., *History of the State of New York* (10 vols., New York, 1933–37), VII, 42–3, 55–8.

14. Ellis *et al.*, *Short History of New York State*, pp. 281–4; Chickering, *Immigration into the United States*, pp. 5–10, 35–6.

15. Thomas Butler Gunn, *The Physiology of New York Boarding-Houses* (New York, 1857), p. 266.

16. *Ibid.*, pp. 263–70; Ernst, *Immigrant Life*, pp. 27–9, 37.

17. Wittke, *We Who Built America*, pp. 125–6; Flick, ed., *History of the State of New York*, VII, 53; for a contemporary account of the working of the Board of Commissioners of Emigration see: Thomas Mooney, *Nine Years in America* (Dublin, 1850), p. 79.

18. Ernst, *Immigrant Life*, p. 31; Wittke, *We Who Built America*, pp. 126–7; James D. Burn, *Three Years among the Working-Classes in the United States during the War* (London, 1865), pp. 284–5.

19. Calvin Colton, *Manual for Emigrants to America* (London, 1832), p. 55; [George Nettle], *A Practical Guide for Emigrants to North America* (London, 1850), p. 24; Maguire, *The Irish in America*, p. 214.

20. *Annual Report of the Alms House Commissioner For the Year 1848* (New York, 1849), p. 4; Mooney, *Nine Years in America*, p. 39.

21. Maguire, *The Irish in America*, p. 215.

22. Bayrd Still, ed., *Mirror for Gotham* (New York, 1956), p. 129; Ellis *et al.*, *Short History of New York State*, p. 283.

23. United States Census, 1860, *Population* (Washington, D. C., 1864), p. xxxii; Still, ed., *Mirror for Gotham*, pp. 160–63; Wittke, *We Who Built America*, pp. 187, 198–9.

24. Matthew Hale Smith, *Sunshine and Shadow in New York* (Hartford, 1868), p. 205.

25. Charles Loring Brace, *The Dangerous Classes of New York and Twenty Years' Work among Them* (New York, 1872), pp. 194–7.

26. Gunn, *The Physiology of New York Boarding-Houses*, pp. 270–76.

27. D. W. Mitchell, *Ten Years in the United States* (London, 1862), pp. 147–8.

28. Colton, *Manual for Emigrants*, p. 64; "A Few Weeks in New York," by a returned immigrant, *The New Monthly Magazine and Humorist*, XLVIII, pt. 3 (1836), 358.

29. *American Notes for General Circulation* (New York, 1942), p. 394.

30. Mooney, *Nine Years in America*, p. 86; Charles Mackay, *Life and Liberty in America* (New York, 1859), p. 21; Thomas L. Nichols, *Forty Years of American Life, 1821–1861* (New York, 1937), p. 255; Ernst, *Immigrant Life*, pp. 66–9.

31. *The Dangerous Classes of New York*, p. 147.

32. *Irish Emigration*, p. 12.

33. *Annual Report of the Alms House Commissioner for 1847*, p. 7; S. H. Collins, *Emigrant's Guide to the United States of America* (London, 1830), p. 68; Maguire, *The Irish in America*, pp. 217–18; *Annual Report of the Alms House Commissioner for 1848*, p. 44.

34. The New York report is cited in Mitchell, *Ten Years in the United States*, pp. 151–5.

35. *Ibid.*, pp. 156–7.

36. Ernst, *Immigrant Life*, p. 187; William Hancock, *An Emigrant's Five Years in the Free States* (London, 1860), p. 204.

37. Mooney, *Nine Years in America*, p. 100.

38. James Frost, *Life on the Upper Susquehanna, 1783–1860* (New York, 1951), pp. 13–16, 90–91.

39. Adams, *Ireland and Irish Emigration*, p. 341.

40. Hawgood, *The Tragedy of German-America*, pp. 22–34; Marcus Lee Hansen, *The Immigrant in American History* (Cambridge, Mass., 1940), pp. 60–76; Flick, ed., *History of the State of New York*, VII, 33–7; Wittke, *We Who Built America*, pp. 208–10; Thomas Dudgeon, *A Nine Years Residence in the States of New York and Pennsylvania, For the Use of Labourers, Farmers, and Emigrants* (Edinburgh, 1841), p. 21.

41. Flick, ed., *History of the State of New York*, VII, 31–41, 5, 166.

42. Ellis *et al.*, *Short History of New York State*, p. 284; Wittke, *We Who Built America*, pp. 198–9; Flick, ed., *History of the State of New York*, VII, 33–7.

43. Handlin, *Immigration as a Factor in American History*, pp. 2–3; see also: Handlin, *Race and Nationality in American Life* (Boston, 1957), pp. 188–207; David M. Potter, *People of Plenty* (Chicago, 1954), pp. 94–5.

44. Adams, *Ireland and the Irish Emigration*, p. 355; Brinley Thomas, *Migration and Economic Growth* (Cambridge, Eng., 1954), pp. 25, 153–4.

45. [Nettle], *A Practical Guide for Emigrants*, pp. 28–9.

46. Quoted in: Ray Allen Billington, *The Protestant Crusade, 1800–1860* (New York, 1938), p. 200; Jones, *American Immigration*, pp. 131–2; Fish, *The Rise of the Common Man*, pp. 113–14; Adams, *Ireland and Irish Emigration*, pp. 340–41, 354–5.

47. Harry Jerome, *Migration and Business Cycles* (New York, 1926), p. 242; Adams, *Ireland and the Irish Emigration*, p. 359.

48. Norman Ware, *The Industrial Worker, 1840–1860* (Boston, 1924), pp. 10, 12; Adams, *Ireland and Irish Emigration*, p. 355; Foster R. Dulles, *Labor in America* (New York, 1960), pp. 78–9.

49. Francis Wyse, *America, Its Realities and Resources* (3 vols., London, 1846), I, 51.

50. Mooney, *Nine Years in America*, pp. 87–8.

51. See Chapter I, pp. 5–7.

52. Lucy M. Salmon, *Domestic Service* (New York, 1897), pp. 62–5, 70–72; Fish, *The Rise of the Common Man*, p. 113; Nichols, *Forty Years of American Life*, p. 255.

53. Wyse, *America*, III, 31; see also Chickering, *Immigration*, p. 64; Hawgood, *The Tragedy of German-America*, p. 258.

54. Rowland T. Berthoff, ed., "Life in America: A Disillusioned Welshman in New York," *New York History*, XXXVII (January 1956), pp. 80–84.

55. *America*, I, 40–41.

56. Ernst, *Immigrant Life in New York City*, pp. 220–21.

57. Thomas, *Migration and Economic Growth*, pp. 152–3.

CHAPTER 5 FACTORIES AND FORTUNES

1. Quoted in Thomas C. Cochran and William Miller, *The Age of Enterprise* (New York, 1942), p. 6.

2. Alexander C. Flick, ed., *History of the State of New York* (10 vols., New York, 1933–37), V, 344–9.

3. Quoted in Richard Hofstadter, William Miller, and Daniel Aaron, *The United States* (Englewood Cliffs, N. J., 1957), p. 182.

4. August Beer Gold, "A History of Manufacturing in New York City, 1825–1840" (unpublished M. A. thesis, Columbia University, 1932), pp. 17–18.

5. Flick, ed., *History of the State of New York*, V, 350–51.

6. Victor S. Clark, *History of Manufactures in the United States: 1607–1860* (Washington, D. C., 1916), pp. 274–308; Gold, "A History of Manufacturing in New York City," pp. 18–21; Flick, ed., *History of the State of New York*, V, 352–4.

7. Nathan Miller, *The Enterprise of a Free People* (Ithaca, 1962), pp. 12–14; Don C. Sowers, *The Financial History of New York State from 1789–1912* (New York, 1914), pp. 263–5.

8. For example the New York Manufacturing Company was capitalized at $1,200,000; Flick, ed., *History of the State of New York*, V, 354–5; Miller, *Enterprise of a Free People*, p. 14.

9. Clark, *History of Manufactures*, pp. 347–8; Carter Goodrich, *Government Promotion of American Canals and Railroads, 1800–1890* (New York, 1960), pp. 279–80; Noble E. Whitford, *History of the Canal System of the State of New York* (2 vols., Albany, 1906), II, 808–907.

10. James Hardie, *The Description of the City of New York* (New York, 1827), p. 329; Calvin Colton, *Manual for Emigrants to America* (London, 1832), p. 61.

11. Cochran and Miller, *The Age of Enterprise*, p. 13; Allen Johnson and Dumas Malone, eds., *Dictionary of American Biography* (22 vols., New York, 1928–44), IX, 192.

12. Walter Hugins, *Jacksonian Democracy and the Working Class* (Stanford, 1960), pp. 79–80.

13. *New York: A Guide to the Empire State* (New York, 1940), pp. 94–5; Flick, ed., *History of the State of New York*, VI, 194–6; Albert S. Bolles, *Industrial History of the United States* (Norwich, Conn., 1879), pp. 412–13.

14. For example in Dutchess, the leading wool producing county, the number of fulling mills declined from 117 in 1821 to 15 in 1840; Flick, ed., *History of the State of New York*, VI, 196–8.

15. According to the New York State Census of 1825, the total household manufacture of textiles amounted to approximately 16.5 million yards annually, which was nearly 9 yards per capita. Ten years later the census reported that less than 9 million yards were produced in the home, slightly more than 4 yards per person. By 1855 less than 930,000 yards of homespun were reported as having been produced; this represented about a fourth of a yard per person. These statistics give a good indication of what happened as the factory came to dominate a particular industry. Rolla Milton Tryon, *Household Manufactures in the United States, 1640–1860* (Chicago, 1917), pp. 303–7, 315–17, 370–76; Arthur Harrison Cole, *The American Wool Manufacture* (Cambridge, Mass., 1926), p. 280.

16. Clark, *History of Manufactures*, p. 465.

17. A random sampling of information on New York towns from an 1842 gazetteer gives a good indication of this. The town of Factoryville on the north shore of Staten Island had a population of 600; there were 100 houses, 1 Episcopal chapel, 4 taverns, 5 stores, 1 grist mill, and the New York Dyeing and Printing Company, "one of the largest works of the kind in the Union; it is owned by a chartered company, with a capital of $200,000—giving employment to about 300 workers." Pleasant Valley in Dutchess County with a population of 650 boasted 100 houses, 3 churches, 2 public houses, 5 stores, 1 saw mill, and a cotton factory containing 3000 spindles and 72 power looms. In western New York, Batavia in Genesee County, a town of 2000 inhabitants, was listed as having 5 churches, a female seminary "in flourishing condition," 2 banks, 7 hotels and taverns, 30 stores, shops and groceries, 1 flour mill, 2 furnaces, 1 tannery, 3 printing offices, "besides several other kinds of mechanics' shops." J. Disturnell, *A Gazetteer of the State of New York* (Albany, 1842), pp. 161, 327, 74, 347.

18. Adna F. Weber, *The Growth of Industry in New York* (Albany, 1904), p. 25; Flick, ed., *History of the State of New York*, VI, 193; Disturnell, *Gazetteer*, pp. 474–5.

19. Peter d'A. Jones, *America's Wealth* (New York, 1963), pp. 60–83; see also: Goodrich, *Government Promotion*, pp. 265–97. In 1850 the yearly value of manufactured goods was listed as $1,055,500,000; agricultural products that year were valued at $900,000,000. Ten years later industrial output had nearly doubled in value, reaching $1,885,861,000. However, agricultural output had regained the lead in market value of product (for the last time), reaching an estimated value of $1,910,000,000.

20. According to the 1850 Census, New York possessed one-seventh of the true valuation of property in the entire country; the state's manufactured products equaled 23 per cent of all goods produced in America. *New York: A Guide to the Empire State*, pp. 69, 97; David M. Ellis, *et al.*, *Short History of New York State* (Ithaca, 1957), p. 264.

21. Flick, ed., *History of the State of New York*, VI, 127–52; J. H. French

Gazetteer of the State of New York (Syracuse, 1860), pp. 66–9; Disturnell, *Gazetteer*, p. 48; U. S. Bureau of the Census, *Historical Statistics of the United States, 1789–1945* (Washington, D. C., 1949), p. 200.

22. Flick, ed., *History of the State of New York*, VI, 152–3; Goodrich, *Government Promotion*, p. 60; Lee Benson, *Merchants, Farmers, and Railroads* (Cambridge, Mass., 1955), pp. 9–16.

23. Flick, ed., *History of the State of New York*, VI, 161–72; for a detailed description of the route of the Erie see: *Harper's New York and Erie Rail-Road Guide Book* (New York, 1851).

24. French, *Gazetteer*, pp. 70–79.

25. *Gazetteer*, pp. 109–10.

26. *New York: A Guide to the Empire State*, p. 95; Bolles, *Industrial History of the United States*, pp. 277–80, 556; Flick, ed., *History of the State of New York*, VI, 205–10; Weber, *The Growth of Industry in New York*, pp. 34–5.

27. Flick, ed., *History of the State of New York*, VI, 218–20; *New York: A Guide to the Empire State*, p. 96; Weber, *The Growth of Industry in New York*, pp. 34–5.

28. Flick, ed., *History of the State of New York*, VI, 215–18; Bolles, *Industrial History of the United States*, pp. 451–4; *New York: A Guide to the Empire State*, pp. 95–6; Weber, *The Growth of Industry in New York*, pp. 34–5.

29. An 1860 gazetteer, for example, listed the following manufacturing establishments in Rochester: 24 flour mills, 41 flour barrel factories, 8 forges, 1 safe factory, 2 cotton factories, 17 breweries, 15 boat yards, 8 coach and carriage makers, 5 boot and shoe factories, 8 cabinet shops, 2 chair factories, 1 carpet factory, and 1 paper mill as well as several saw mills, soap makers, and tanneries. This same source relates that Buffalo in 1847 had over 400 manufactures. Prominent were flour mills, ship builders, leather makers, machine shops, stove factories, distilleries, and piano makers. French, *Gazetteer*, pp. 402, 286.

30. In the late 'thirties Rochester's 21 flour mills, utilizing the power of the Genesee River, were turning out nearly 500,000 barrels of flour annually. By the 1850's Rochester's mills produced over 800,000 barrels annually, a production figure that was nearly equaled by Buffalo and was surpassed by Oswego. Blake McKelvey, *Rochester the Water-Power City, 1812–1854* (Cambridge, Mass., 1945), p. 209; Blake McKelvey, *Rochester the Flower City, 1855–1890* (Cambridge, Mass., 1949), pp. 13–14; Flick, ed., *History of the State of New York*, VI, 232–3; French, *Gazetteer*, p. 402.

31. The Census of 1860 revealed that 20 per cent of the state's manufacturing establishments were located within the city limits, and that these produced 40 per cent of the total product. Clark, *History of Manufactures*, p. 465.

32. Bolles, *Industrial History of the United States*, pp. 399–400; Flick,

ed., *History of the State of New York*, VI, 220–31; Clark, *History of Manufactures*, p. 470; Gold, "History of Manufacturing in New York City."

33. "Did the Civil War Retard Industrialization?", *The Mississippi Valley Historical Review*, XLVIII (Sept. 1961), 209.

34. *Democracy in America* (1961 ed.), II, 190–94.

35. Quoted in Dixon Wecter, *The Saga of American Society* (New York, 1937), p. 103.

36. Norman Ware, *The Industrial Worker, 1840–1860* (Boston, 1924), p. xi.

37. Proprietorships and partnerships continued to be the leading form of business organization in New York State down to the Civil War in terms of numbers, but not in terms of wealth. See: Jones, *American Wealth*, pp. 98–101; Flick, ed., *History of the State of New York*, VI, 349–50; French, *Gazetteer*, p. 80.

38. Cochran and Miller, *The Age of Enterprise*, pp. 67–70; Benson, *Merchants, Farmers and Railroads*, pp. 58, 129–31, 136–7.

39. Cochran, "Did the Civil War Retard Industrialization?", p. 199; *Historical Statistics of the United States, 1789–1945* (Washington, 1949), pp. 176–87.

40. Child, *Letters From New York*, Second Series (New York, 1845), pp. 279–80; James D. Burn, *Three Years among the Working-Classes in the United States during the War* (London, 1865), p. 20.

41. Flick, ed., *History of the State of New York*, VI, 351; Beach's 5th edition of *Wealth and Biography* is reprinted in *The New York Herald*, January 11, 1845; see also: William Miller, "The Realm of Wealth," pp. 137–8 in John Higham, ed., *The Reconstruction of American History* (New York, 1962).

42. Flick, ed., *History of the State of New York*, VI, 343–6.

43. Johnson and Malone, eds., *Dictionary of American Biography*, XVIII, 3–5; Matthew H. Smith, *Sunshine and Shadow in New York* (Hartford, 1868), pp. 52–62; Junius H. Browne, *The Great Metropolis, A Mirror of New York* (Hartford, 1869), pp. 289–94.

44. Johnson and Malone, eds., *Dictionary of American Biography*, IV, 110; Browne, *The Great Metropolis*, pp. 667–8.

45. Allan Nevins, ed., *Diary of Philip Hone* (New York, 1936), p. 556.

46. Hone in his diary gives an indication of how valuable New York real estate could be. In 1832 a lot at the corner of Broadway and Park Place, 25 feet by 120 feet, sold for $37,000. In the prosperous year of 1835, a lot 30 feet by 75 feet on William Street between Pine and Wall sold for $51,000. That same year, following a disastrous fire, twenty burned downtown lots sold at auction for $765,100. Hone sold his own house at 235 Broadway for $60,000 in 1836. Nevins, ed., *Diary of Philip Hone*, pp. 54, 156, 199, 201.

47. The Astor fortune is treated unsympathetically but fully in: Gustavus Myers, *History of the Great American Fortunes* (New York, 1937), pp. 93–138. See also: Wector, *The Saga of American Soectiy*, pp. 113–15.

48. Flick, ed., *History of the State of New York*, VI, 241–2; Robert Ernst, *Immigrant Life in New York City* (New York, 1949), pp. 15–17.

49. Allan Nevins and Milton H. Thomas, eds., *The Diary of George Templeton Strong* (4 vols., New York, 1953), II, 178–9.

50. Johnson and Malone, eds., *Dictionary of American Biography*, I, 396, XIV, 533.

51. Goodrich, *Government Promotion*, pp. 292–3; Cochran and Miller, *The Age of Enterprise*, p. 67.

52. Browne, *The Great Metropolis*, pp. 43–4.

53. Nevins and Thomas, eds., *The Diary of George Templeton Strong*, II, 178–9, 313–15; C. H. Haswell, *Reminiscences of an Octogenarian*, p. 293; Cochran and Miller, *The Age of Enterprise*, pp. 74–5; Benson, *Merchants, Farmers, and Railroads*, pp. 7–58, 135–7.

54. *Fifteen Minutes Around New York* (New York, 1853), pp. 18–19.

CHAPTER 6   THE WIDENING GAP: LABOR IN THE 'FORTIES AND 'FIFTIES

1. Greeley, *Recollections of a Busy Life* (New York, 1868), p. 144; *The New Yorker*, January 20, 1838; for other accounts of the suffering during the depression see: Frederick Marryat, *A Diary in America* (Paris, 1839), p. 17; Levi Beardsley, *Reminiscences* (New York, 1852), p. 328.

2. *The New Yorker*, July 24, 1841; Samuel Rezneck, "The Social History of an American Depression, 1837–1843," *American Historical Review*, XL (July 1935), 664.

3. *The Knickerbocker*, IX (May 1838), 488; *Arcturus*, I (February 1841), 133; Rezneck, "The Social History of an American Depression," pp. 665–76.

4. Quoted in Rezneck "The Social History of an American Depression," p. 666; see also: Robert H. Bremner, *From the Depths: the Discovery of Poverty in the United States* (New York, 1956), pp. 13–15.

5. Quoted in Greeley, *Recollections*, p. 145.

6. John R. Commons and others, eds., *A Documentary History of American Industrial Society* (10 vols., Cleveland, 1910), VII, 47–8; Foster Rhea Dulles, *Labor in America* (New York, 1960 ed.), pp. 77–8; Philip S. Foner, *History of the Labor Movement in the United States* (2 vols., New York, 1947), I, 168.

7. *Working Man's Advocate*, March 30, 1844.

8. Commons and others, *Documentary History*, VII, 217–18.

9. Junius H. Browne, *The Great Metropolis* (Hartford, 1869), p. 548; Thomas Mooney, *Nine Years in America* (Dublin, 1850), p. 82.

10. David M. Schneider, *The History of Public Welfare in New York State, 1609–1866* (Chicago, 1938), pp. 296–7.

11. *New York Times*, November 8, 1853.

12. *New York Daily Tribune*, March 27, 1851; Mooney, *Nine Years in America*, p. 22; Foner, *History of the Labor Movement*, I, 220; John R. Commons and others, *History of Labour in the United States* (4 vols., New York, 1918–35), I, 487–8.

13. Samuel I. Prime, *Life in New York* (New York, 1847), p. 95.

14. *The Dangerous Classes of New York and Twenty Years' Work Among Them* (New York, 1872), pp. 168–70.

15. *The Sanitary Condition of the Laboring Population of New York* (New York, 1845), pp. 6–7.

16. *New York Panorama* (New York, 1938), p. 429.

17. Charles H. Haswell, *Reminiscences of an Octogenarian of the City of New York* (New York, 1896), p. 332.

18. Descriptions of New York City's tenements abound in the literature of the period. See: Matthew H. Smith, *Sunshine and Shadow in New York* (Hartford, 1868), p. 365; Peter Stryker, *The Lower Depths of the Great American Metropolis* (New York, 1866), p. 10; James D. Burn, *Three Years Among the Working Classes in the United States During the War* (London, 1865), p. 8; Griscom, *Sanitary Conditions*, pp. 6–15; D. W. Mitchell, *Ten Years in the United States* (London, 1862), pp. 145, 156–7.

19. For example in the early 1860's London's highest rate of population was in East London where it reached as high as 175,816 persons per square mile. In comparison parts of New York's Fourth Ward in 1864 was "packed in at the rate of about 290,000 inhabitants to the square mile." John F. Maguire, *The Irish in America* (London, 1868), p. 221; Brace, *The Dangerous Classes of New York*, pp. 53–6.

20. Dickens, *American Notes for General Circulation* (New York, 1942), pp. 399–402.

21. Smith, *Sunshine and Shadow*, pp. 205–6; for other descriptions of the Five Points area see: *Putnam's Monthly Magazine*, I (May 1853), 510–11; Adolph B. Benson, ed., *America in the Fifties: Letters of Fredrika Bremer* (New York, 1924), pp. 325–6; W. S. Tryon, ed., *My Native Land* (Chicago, 1952), p. 116.

22. Griscom, *The Sanitary Condition*, pp. 8–10, 26; Robert Ernst, *Immigrant Life in New York City, 1825–1863* (New York, 1949), p. 49; Maguire, *Irish in America*, pp. 225–6; Stryker, *The Lower Depths*, pp. 3–4; Smith, *Sunshine and Shadow*, pp. 2–5.

23. Quoted in Maguire, *Irish in America*, p. 227; see also: Griscom, *The Sanitary Condition*, p. 6.

24. Allen Johnson and Dumas Malone, eds., *Dictionary of American Biography* (22 vols., New York, 1928–44), I, 401.

25. Griscom, *The Sanitary Condition*, pp. 7–8, 46–7; Allan Nevins and Milton H. Thomas, eds., *The Diary of George Templeton Strong* (4 vols., New York, 1953), II, 177.

26. Mitchell, *Ten Years in the United States*, pp. 146–7. Mitchell found the sanitary conditions of New York far inferior to those of London.

27. Maguire, *Irish in America*, p. 229; Brace, *The Dangerous Classes*, pp. 25–9, 57.

28. *New York Daily Tribune*, February 9, 1850.

29. *Life in New York*, p. 91.

30. Parke Godwin, *Democracy, Constructive and Pacific* (1844) in Merle Curti, Willard Thorp, and Carlos Baker, eds., *American Issues: The Social Record* (Philadelphia, 1960), pp. 412–4.

31. Commons and others, *History of Labour*, I, 493–6; Alice Felt Tyler, *Freedom's Ferment* (New York, 1962), p. 196.

32. Edmund Wilson, *To the Finland Station* (Garden City, 1955), pp. 86–91; Commons and others, *History of Labour*, I, 496–7.

33. Wilson, *To the Finland Station*, p. 91; Foner, *History of the Labor Movement*, I, 174–5.

34. Quoted in Foner, *History of the Labor Movement*, I, 176; Commons and others, eds., *Documentary History of American Industrial Society*, VII, 185–7.

35. *New York Daily Tribune*, August 12, 13, 15, 1850; Commons and others, *History of Labour*, I, 506–10; Foner, *History of the Labor Movement*, I, 178–83.

36. Commons and others, eds., *Documentary History of American Industrial Society*, VII, 305–7.

37. *Ibid.*, VII, 294–305.

38. *New York Sun*, January 13, February 21, 1855; *New York Times*, July 25, 1853; Commons and others, *History of Labour*, I, 531–2.

39. Carl N. Degler, "The West as a Solution to Urban Unemployment," *New York History*, LIII (April 1955), 63–84; David M. Ellis *et al.*, *Short History of New York State* (Ithaca, 1957), p. 291.

40. Commons and others, *Documentary History of American Industrial Society*, VII, 54–5.

41. James A. Frost, *Life on the Upper Susquehanna* (New York, 1951), pp. 121–2; Degler, "The West as a Solution to Urban Unemployment," pp. 78–9.

42. *Appeal to the Wealthy of the Land* (Philadelphia, 1833), p. 8.

43. Norman Ware, *The Industrial Worker, 1840–1860* (Boston, 1924), pp. xx, 1.

44. Commons and others, *History of Labour*, I, 542–3; Joseph G. Ray-

back, *A History of American Labor* (New York, 1959), pp. 96–7; Foner, *History of the Labor Movement,* I, 218. Both Foner and Rayback, using the same statistics, maintain that the general tendency was toward shorter hours. However, this inference is based on the reported hours of a very limited number of establishments.

45. *History of Labour,* I, 575–6.

46. Quoted in Dulles, *Labor in America,* p. 89.

47. *New York Daily Tribune,* April 20, 1854; Commons and others, *History of Labour,* I, 576, 597, 607–13.

48. Commons and others, *History of Labour,* I, 613–4; Rayback, *A History of American Labor,* p. 105.

49. *New York Herald,* November 2, 1857; *New York Times,* October 16, 1857.

50. *New York Daily Tribune,* November 6, 1857; Leah H. Feder, *Unemployment Relief in Periods of Depression* (New York, 1936), pp. 21, 34; Haswell, *Reminiscences,* p. 505; Commons and others, *History of Labour,* II, 5–12; Foner, *History of the Labor Movement,* I, 240.

51. Isaac S. Lyon, *Recollections of an Old Cartman* (Newark, 1872), pp. 8–9.

52. *New York Daily Tribune,* January 18, February 9, 1850.

53. Prime, *Life in New York,* pp. 221–3; Browne, *The Great Metropolis,* p. 474.

54. Browne, *The Great Metropolis,* pp. 456–65; Greeley, *Recollections,* pp. 192–3; William Hancock, *An Emigrant's Five Years in the Free States of America* (London, 1860), p. 185; Lyon, *Recollections of an Old Cartman,* pp. 27–33.

55. Foster, *New York by Gas-Light* (New York, 1850), p. 123; Ellis *et al., Short History of New York State,* p. 315.

56. Nevins and Thomas, eds., *The Diary of George Templeton Strong,* II, 422.

57. Ware, *Industrial Worker,* pp. x-xiv; Commons and others, *Documentary History of American Industrial Society,* VII, 110; *State Mechanic* [New York], September 10, 1842.

CHAPTER 7   THE NEW ARISTOCRACY

1. Allan Nevins and Milton H. Thomas, eds., *The Diary of George Templeton Strong* (4 vols., New York, 1953), III, 32; Charles H. Haswell, *Reminiscences of an Octogenarian of the City of New York* (New York, 1896), pp. 526–30.

2. Nevins and Thomas, eds., *The Diary of George Templeton Strong,* III, 39, 40, 42–5.

3. Sigmund Diamond, ed., *A Casual View of America: The Home Letters of Salomon de Rothschild* (Stanford, Calif., 1961), pp. 78–9.

4. *New York Times*, September 10, October 13, 14, 1860; Ward McAllister, *Society As I Have Found It* (New York, 1890), p. 129; Nevins and Thomas, eds., *The Diary of George Templeton Strong*, III, 32.

5. Diamond, ed., *A Casual View of America*, pp. 79–80; Nevins and Thomas, eds., *The Diary of George Templeton Strong*, III, 46–9; *New York Herald*, October 13, 15, 1860.

6. *New York Herald*, October 12, 13, 15, 1860; McAllister, *Society As I Have Found It*, pp. 130–33.

7. Nevins and Thomas, eds., *The Diary of George Templeton Strong*, III, 52.

8. *Ibid.*, II, 37–8.

9. Foster, *Fifteen Minutes Around New York* (New York, 1853), p. 19; Curtis, *The Potiphar Papers* (New York, 1854), pp. 1–2.

10. Nevins and Thomas, eds., *The Diary of George Templeton Strong*, I, 294.

11. *White, Red, and Black: Sketches of American Society in the United States During the Visit of Their Guests* (2 vols., London, 1853), I, 71.

12. N. Parker Willis, *The Rag-Bag* (New York, 1855), p. 221; Henry Collins Brown, *Fifth Avenue—Old and New* (New York, 1924), pp. 24–43; Junius H. Browne, *The Great Metropolis* (Hartford, 1869), pp. 221–2; Henry Collins Brown, *Brownstone Fronts and Saratoga Trunks* (New York, 1935), p. 59.

13. Nevins and Thomas, eds., *The Diary of George Templeton Strong*, I, 272–3; Willis, *The Rag-Bag*, pp. 268–9.

14. Brown, *Fifth Avenue*, pp. 30–31; Willis, *Rag-Bag*, pp. 114–15; William Hancock, *An Emigrant's Five Years in the Free States of America* (London, 1860), pp. 68–9.

15. Charles Mackay, *Life and Liberty in America* (New York, 1859), p. 20; Willis, *Rag-Bag*, pp. 150–51; *Putnam's Monthly*, I (February 1853), 170; Hancock, *An Emigrant's Five Years in the Free States*, p. 41; Browne, *The Great Metropolis*, p. 124.

16. Mrs. C. M. Kirkland, *The Evening Book* (New York, 1851), pp. 48–9.

17. Quoted in Bayrd Still, ed., *Mirror for Gotham* (New York, 1956), p. 134.

18. *Ibid.*, p. 142; Willis, *Rag-Bag*, p. 41; Mackay, *Life and Liberty*, p. 15; Pulszky, *White, Red, and Black*, I, 66.

19. Mowatt, *Fashion; or Life in New York* (New York, 1849), p. 31; Trollope, *North America* (New York, 1951 ed.), p. 204; Kirkland, *The Evening Book*, pp. 109–10.

20. Details of the wedding are given in *The New York Herald,* October 14, 1859.

21. Willis, *Rag-Bag,* pp. 49–56; Browne, *The Great Metropolis,* p. 596.

22. Allan Nevins, ed., *The Diary of Philip Hone* (New York, 1936), pp. 462–3, 465; *New York Herald,* February 10, 13, 14, March 2, 1840.

23. Kirkland, *The Evening Book,* p. 44; Nevins and Thomas, eds., *The Diary of George Templeton Strong,* II, 3; *New York Daily Tribune,* January 18, 1850.

24. Haswell, *Reminiscences,* pp. 426–7; Matthew H. Smith, *Sunshine and Shadow in New York* (Hartford, 1868), pp. 38–9; Browne, *The Great Metropolis,* pp. 521–2; Hancock, *An Emigrant's Five Years in the Free States,* pp. 109–10.

25. Haswell, *Reminiscences,* p. 439; *New York Daily Tribune,* November 3, 1849; Foster, *Fifteen Minutes Around New York,* p. 71; see also: Willis, *Rag-Bag,* pp. 89–90; Nevins and Thomas, eds., *The Diary of George Templeton Strong,* I, 332.

26. Hancock, *An Emigrant's Five Years in the Free States,* pp. 85–6; Foster, *Fifteen Minutes Around New York,* p. 23.

27. Kip, "New York Society in the Olden Time," *Putnam's Magazine,* VI (September 1870), 252–4.

28. Brown, *Fifth Avenue,* pp. 22–92.

29. Willis, *Rag-Bag,* pp. 256–7.

30. *The Upper Ten Thousand: Sketches of American Society* (New York, 1852), pp. 5–6.

31. *The Great Metropolis,* pp. 32–7.

32. *Rag-Bag,* p. 275.

33. Sedgwick, *Means and Ends* (Boston, 1839), pp. 15–16, 150; Schlesinger, *Learning How To Behave* (New York, 1946), p. 18.

34. Lord Chesterfield, *The American Chesterfield* (Philadelphia, 1833); Schlesinger, *Learning How To Behave,* pp. 12–14, 17–18; Dixon Wecter, *The Saga of American Society* (New York, 1937), pp. 157–95.

35. Browne, *The Great Metropolis,* pp. 36–7; Smith, *Sunshine and Shadow,* pp. 60–62; Brown, *Fifth Avenue,* pp. 78–9.

36. Alexander C. Flick, ed., *History of the State of New York* (10 vols., New York, 1933–37), VI, 240–41.

37. William Miller, "The Realm of Wealth" in John Higham, ed., *The Reconstruction of American History* (New York, 1962), p. 138; Smith, *Sunshine and Shadow,* pp. 76–7; Browne, *The Great Metropolis,* p. 517; Arthur W. Calhoun, *A Social History of the American Family* (2 vols., New York, 1960 ed.), II, 29, 221; Haswell, *Reminiscences,* p. 514.

38. Nevins, ed., *The Diary of Philip Hone,* p. 415.

39. *Ibid.,* pp. 405–14.

40. Diamond, ed., *A Casual View of America,* p. 66.

41. *Ibid.*, pp. 67–9; Trollope, *North America*, pp. 23–9; McAllister, *Society As I Have Found It*, pp. 110–19.

42. *Celio: or, New York Above-Ground and Under-Ground* (New York, 1850), p. 41.

43. *Letters from New York:* Second Series (New York, 1845), pp. 280–81.

44. Graves and Bodichon quoted in Calhoun, *A Social History of the American Family*, II, 227–9.

45. *Ibid.*

46. Kirkland, *The Evening Book*, pp. 41–2; Pulszky, *White, Red, and Black*, I, 66–7; Calhoun, *A Social History of the American Family*, II, 231–4.

47. Willis, *Rag-Bag*, pp. 45–8; Robert Ernst, *Immigrant Life in New York City, 1825–1863* (New York, 1949), p. 70.

48. *Fashion*, p. 1.

49. Calhoun, *A Social History of the American Family*, II, 147–8, 233; Ernst, *Immigrant Life*, p. 67; Nevins and Thomas, eds., *The Diary of George Templeton Strong*, II, 22; Kirkland, *The Evening Book*, pp. 159–64, 166, 168.

50. Still, ed., *Mirror for Gotham*, p. 158; James D. Burn, *Three Years among the Working-Classes in the United States during the War* (London, 1865), p. 21.

51. Wecter, *The Saga of American Society*, pp. 103–4; W. J. Cash, *The Mind of the South* (New York, 1941), pp. 3–12, 61–81.

52. *Society As I Have Found It*, pp. 98–100.

53. See: William Miller, ed., *Men in Business: Essays in the History of Entrepreneurship* (Cambridge, Mass., 1952); Thomas C. Cochran, *Railroad Leaders, 1845–1890* (Cambridge, Mass., 1953).

54. Flick, ed., *History of the State of New York*, VI, 241; Allen Johnson and Dumas Malone, eds., *Dictionary of American Biography* (22 vols., New York, 1928–44), IV, 299, XVIII, 176–7, IV, 409–10, XVIII, 3–5, IV, 110; Robert H. Bremner, *From the Depths: The Discovery of Poverty in the United States* (New York, 1956), pp. 31–45.

55. Nevins and Thomas, eds., *The Diary of George Templeton Strong*, II, 203–4, 209.

56. *Ibid.*, I, 351–3; I. N. Phelps Stokes, *New York Past and Present* (New York, 1939), p. 80; Wecter, *The Saga of American Society*, pp. 462–3.

57. Nevins and Thomas eds., *The Diary of George Templeton Strong*, II, 346–50, 369–71, 373; Phelps Stokes, *New York Past and Present*, p. 80; Ernst, *Immigrant Life*, pp. 106–7.

58. Nevins and Thomas, eds., *The Diary of George Templeton Strong*, III, 332–43; James Ford Rhodes, *History of the United States from the Compromise of 1850 to the End of the Roosevelt Administration* (9 vols., New York, 1928), IV, 320–28; Paul M. Angle and Earl Schenck Miers, eds.,

Tragic Years, 1860–1865 (2 vols., New York, 1960), II, 679–83; Ernst, *Immigrant Life*, pp. 172–4; Anna E. Dickinson, *What Answer?* (Boston, 1868), pp. 243–57.

59. Nevins and Thomas, eds., *The Diary of George Templeton Strong*, III, 338, 341.

60. Dickinson, *What Answer?*, pp. 243–4; Nevins and Thomas, eds., *The Diary of George Templeton Strong*, III, 335; Ernst, *Immigrant Life*, p. 174.

61. *Democracy in America*, ed. Richard D. Heffner (New York, 1956), p. 220.

62. Quoted in Joseph L. Blau, ed., *Social Theories of Jacksonian Democracy* (New York, 1954), p. 20.

63. *Ibid.*, pp. 17, 61.

BIBLIOGRAPHY

NEWSPAPERS

Albany Argus, 1830–45.
[New York] *Evening Post,* 1830–60.
New York Herald, 1835–63.
[New York] *Journal of Commerce,* 1827–60.
[New York] *The Man,* 1834–35.
[New York] *Morning Courier and Enquirer,* 1829–60.
New York Times, 1851–63.
New York Tribune, 1841–63.
[New York] *The Union,* 1836.
[New York] *The Working Man's Advocate,* 1830–36, 1844–47.
The New Yorker, 1836–41.

MAGAZINES

Gleason's Pictorial Drawing-Room Companion. New York, 1851–54.
Godey's Lady's Book. Philadelphia, 1830–60.
Home Journal. New York, 1846–60.
Knickerbocker Magazine. New York, 1833–60.
Peterson's Ladies' National Magazine. Philadelphia, 1850–60.
Putnam's Monthly Magazine. . . . New York, 1853–60.

DIARIES, AUTOBIOGRAPHIES, AND REMINISCENCES

Beardsley, Levi. *Reminiscences.* New York, 1852.
Breck, Samuel. *Recollections of Samuel Breck,* ed. H. E. Scudder. Philadelphia, 1877.
Dayton, Abram C. *Last Days of Knickerbocker Life in New York.* New York, 1897.
Dodge, William Earl. "A Great Merchant's Recollections of Old New York, 1818–1880," *Valentine's Manual of Old New York,* Vol. V (1921), 149–82.
Floy, Michael, Jr. *The Diary of Michael Floy, Jr.: Bowery Village 1833–1837,* ed. Richard A. E. Brooks. New Haven, 1941.
Greeley, Horace. *Recollections of a Busy Life.* New York, 1868.

Haswell, Charles H. *Reminiscences of an Octogenarian of the City of New York (1816 to 1860)*. New York, 1896.
Hone, Philip. *The Diary of Philip Hone, 1828–1851*, ed. Allan Nevins. New York, 1936.
Hubbard, N. T. *Autobiography of N. T. Hubbard with Personal Reminiscences of New York City from 1789 to 1875*. New York, 1875.
Kip, Bishop [William I.]. "New York Society in Olden Times," *Putnam's Magazine*, VI (Sept. 1870), 241–55.
Lyon, Isaac S. *Recollections of an Old Cartman*. Newark, 1872.
Nichols, Thomas L. *Forty Years of American Life, 1821–1861*. New York, 1937.
Strong, George Templeton. *The Diary of George Templeton Strong, 1835–1875*, ed. Allan Nevins and M.H. Thomas. 4 vols. New York, 1953.

TRAVELERS' AND IMMIGRANTS' ACCOUNTS

Bremer, Fredrika. *America of the Fifties: The Letters of Fredrika Bremer*, ed. Adolph B. Benson. New York, 1924.
Buckingham, James Silk. *America, Historical, Statistical, and Descriptive*. 3 vols. London, 1841.
Burn, James D. *Three Years among the Working-Classes in the United States during the War*. London, 1865.
Cather, Thomas. *Voyage to America: The Journals of Thomas Cather*, ed. Thomas Yoseloff. New York, 1961.
Chevalier, Michael. *Society, Manners, and Politics in the United States*, ed. John W. Ward. Garden City, 1961.
Child, Mrs. L. Maria. *Letters from New York, Second Series*. New York, 1845.
Dickens, Charles. *American Notes for General Circulation*. New York, 1942.
[Dwight, Theodore]. *The Northern Traveller*. New York, 1826.
———. *Sketches of Scenery and Manners in the United States*. New York, 1829.
"A Few Weeks in New York by a Returned Immigrant," *The New Monthly Magazine and Humorist*, XLVIII, pt. 3 (1836), 352–9.
Fowler, John. *Journal of a Tour in the State of New York in the Year 1830*. London, 1831.
Grattan, Thomas C. *Civilized America*. London, 1859.
Hall, Basil. *Travels in North America in the Years 1827 and 1828*. 3 vols. Edinburgh, 1829.
Hamilton, Thomas. *Men and Manners in America*. 2 vols. Edinburgh, 1833.

Hancock, William. *An Emigrant's Five Years in the Free States of America.* London, 1860.

"Life in America, A Disillusioned Welshman in New York," *New York History,* XXXVII (Jan. 1956), 80–84.

London v *New York.* London, 1859.

Mackay, Alexander. *Western World; or, Travels in the United States in 1846–47.* 4th ed., 3 vols. London, 1850.

Mackay, Charles. *Life and Liberty in America: or, Sketches of a Tour in the United States and in Canada in 1857–8.* New York, 1859.

Marryat, Frederick. *Diary in America,* ed. Jules Zanger. Bloomington, Ind., 1960.

Martineau, Harriet. *Society in America.* 3 vols. London, 1837.

Mitchell, D. W. *Ten Years in the United States.* London, 1862.

Mooney, Thomas. *Nine Years in America.* Dublin, 1850.

Murray, Charles Augustus. *Travels in North America during the Years 1834, 1835, and 1836.* 2 vols. New York, 1839.

Pulszky, Francis and Theresa. *White, Red, and Black; Sketches of American Society in the United States during the Visit of Their Guests.* 2 vols. Redfield, Eng., 1853.

Rothschild, Salomon de. *The Home Letters of Salomon de Rothschild, 1859–1861,* ed. and trans. Sigmund Diamond. Stanford, 1961.

Stuart, James. *Three Years in North America.* 2nd ed., 2 vols. Edinburgh, 1833.

Tocqueville, Alexis de. *Democracy in America,* ed. Phillips Bradley. 2 vols. New York, 1945.

———. *Journey to America,* ed. J. P. Mayer. New Haven, 1960.

Trollope, Anthony. *North America,* ed. Donald Smalley and B. A. Booth. New York, 1951.

Trollope, Frances. *Domestic Manners of the Americans,* ed. Donald Smalley. New York, 1960.

Twenty-four Letters from Labourers in America to Their Friends in England, ed. [Benjamin Smith]. London, 1829.

Wyse, Francis. *America, Its Realities and Resources.* 3 vols. London, 1846.

GUIDEBOOKS AND GAZETTEERS

Belden, E. Porter. *New York: Past, Present, and Future.* New York, 1849.

Browne, Junius H. *The Great Metropolis; A Mirror of New York.* Hartford, 1869.

Cobbett, William. *The Emigrant's Guide.* London, 1830.

Collins, S. H. *The Emigrant's Guide to the United States of America.* London, 1830.

Colton, Calvin. *Manual For Emigrants to America.* London, 1832.

Davison, G. M. *The Traveller's Guide through the Middle and Northern States and the Provinces of Canada.* 8th ed. Saratoga, 1840.

Disturnell, J. *A Gazetteer of the State of New York.* Albany, 1842.

Dudgeon, Thomas. *A Nine Years Residence in the State of New York and Pennsylvania, for Use of Labourers, Farmers, and Emigrants.* Edinburgh, 1841.

Dyke, Thomas. *Advice to Emigrants.* London, 1832.

The Emigrant's Hand-Book and Guide to the United States; or England and America Contrasted. London, n.d. [ca. 1849].

French, J. H. *Gazetteer of the State of New York.* Syracuse, 1860.

Hardie, James. *The Description of the City of New York.* New York, 1827.

Harper's New York and Erie Rail-Road Guide Book. New York, 1851.

[Nettle, George]. *A Practical Guide for Emigrants to North America.* London, 1850.

The Picture of New-York and Stranger's Guide to the Commercial Metropolis of the United States. New York, 1828.

OTHER WRITINGS OF CONTEMPORARIES

Armstrong, William. *The Aristocracy of New York: Who They Are, and What They Were; Being a Social and Business History of the City for Many Years.* New York, 1848.

Beach, Moses Yale. *Wealth and Biography of the Wealthy Citizens of New York City.* . . . 6th ed. New York, 1845.

Brace, Charles Loring. *The Dangerous Classes of New York and Twenty Years' Work Among Them.* New York, 1872.

Bristed, Charles Astor. *The Upper Ten Thousand: Sketches of American Society.* New York, 1852.

Bromwell, William J. *History of Immigration in the United States.* New York, 1856.

Byrne, Stephen. *Irish Emigration to the United States: What It Has Been, and What It Is.* New York, 1873.

Carey, Mathew. *Appeal to the Wealthy of the Land . . . on the Character, Conduct, Situation, and Prospects of Those Whose Sole Dependence for Subsistence is on the Labour of Their Hands.* Philadelphia, 1833.

Chesterfield, Lord. *The American Chesterfield.* Philadelphia, 1833.

Chickering, Jesse. *Immigration into the United States.* Boston, 1848.

Cooper, James Fenimore. *The American Democrat.* New York, 1956.

[Curry, Daniel]. *New York: A Historical Sketch of the Rise and Progress of the Metropolitan City of America.* New York, 1853.

Curtis, George W. *The Potiphar Papers.* New York, 1854.

Foster, G. G. *Celio: or, New York Above-Ground and Under-Ground.* New York, 1850.

———. *Fifteen Minutes Around New York*. New York, 1853.

———. *New York by Gas-Light*. New York, 1850.

Griscom, John H. *The Sanitary Condition of the Laboring Population of New York*. New York, 1845.

Grund, Francis J. *Aristocracy in America*. New York, 1959.

Gunn, Thomas Butler. *The Physiology of New York Boarding-Houses*. New York, 1857.

Hibernicus [pseudo.]. "What Brings So Many Irish to America?" Pamphlet. New York, 1845.

Hoyle, Edmund. *Hoyle's Games Improved*. New York, 1823.

King, Charles. *Progress of the City of New-York During the Last Fifty Years*. New York, 1852.

Kirkland, Mrs. C. M. *The Evening Book*. New York, 1851.

The Laws of Etiquette. Philadelphia, 1836.

McAllister, Ward. *Society As I Have Found It*. New York, 1890.

McGee, Thomas D'Arcy. *A History of the Irish Settlers in North America From the Earliest Period to the Census of 1850*. Boston, 1852.

Mowatt, Anna Cora. *Fashion; or, Life in New York*. New York, 1849.

Prime, Samuel I. *Life in New York*. New York, 1847.

[Scoville, Joseph A.]. *The Old Merchants of New York*. 5 vols. New York, 1863–66.

Smith, Matthew Hale. *Sunshine and Shadow in New York*. Hartford, 1868.

Stryker, Peter. *The Lower Depths of the Great American Metropolis*. New York, 1866.

Tefft, B. F. *Inequality in the Condition of Men Inevitable*. Greencastle, Ind., 1845.

Willis, N. Parker. *The Rag-Bag, A Collection of Ephemera*. New York, 1855.

SECONDARY SOURCES

Abbott, Edith. *Immigration: Select Documents and Case Records*. Chicago, 1924.

Adams, William F. *Ireland and Irish Emigration to the New World from 1815 to the Famine*. New Haven, 1932.

Albion, Robert G. *The Rise of New York Port, 1815–1860*. New York, 1939.

Benson, Lee. *The Concept of Jacksonian Democracy: New York as a Test Case*. Princeton, 1961.

Berthoff, Rowland T. *British Immigrants in Industrial America*. Cambridge, Mass., 1953.

Bode, Carl. *The Anatomy of American Popular Culture, 1840–1861*. Berkeley, 1959.

Bolles, Albert S. *Industrial History of the United States*. Norwich, Conn., 1879.

Brady, Katherine L. *Quaint Customs of Former New Yorkers*. New York, 1915.

Bremner, Robert H. *American Philanthropy*. Chicago, 1960.

———. *From the Depths. The Discovery of Poverty in the United States*. New York, 1956.

Brooks, Elbridge S. *The Story of New York*. Boston, 1888.

Brown, Henry C. *Brownstone Fronts and Saratoga Trunks*. New York, 1935.

———. *Fifth Avenue—Old and New*. New York, 1924.

Cady, Edwin H. *The Gentleman in America: A Literary Study in American Culture*. Syracuse, 1949.

Calhoun, Arthur W. *A Social History of the American Family*. Vol. II: *From Independence Through the Civil War*. New York, 1960.

Cheyney, Edward P. *The Anti-Rent Agitation in the State of New York, 1839–1846*. Philadelphia, 1887.

Christman, Henry. *Tin Horns and Calico. . . .* New York, 1961.

Clark, Victor S. *History of Manufactures in the United States, 1607–1860*. Washington, D. C., 1916.

Cochran, Thomas C. and Miller, William. *The Age of Enterprise. . . .* New York, 1942.

Cochran, Thomas C. "Did the Civil War Retard Industrialization?" *The Mississippi Valley Historical Review*, XLVIII (Sept. 1961), 197–210.

Commons, John R. and associates, eds. *A Documentary History of American Industrial Society*. 10 vols. Cleveland, 1910–11.

———. *History of Labour in the United States. 4 vols*. New York, 1918–35.

Cross, Whitney R. *The Burned-over District: The Social and Intellectual History of Enthusiastic Religion in Western New York, 1800–1850*. Ithaca, 1950.

Cunliffe, Marcus. *The Nation Takes Shape: 1789–1837*. Chicago, 1959.

Davidson, Marshall B. *Life in America*. 2 vols. Boston, 1951.

Degler, Carl N. "The West as a Solution to Urban Unemployment," *New York History*, LIII (April 1955), 63–84.

Dulles, Foster Rhea. *Labor in America: A History*. New York, 1960.

Ellis, David M. *Landlords and Farmers in the Hudson-Mohawk Region, 1790–1850*. Ithaca, 1946.

Ellis, David M., et al. *A Short History of New York State*. Ithaca, 1957.

Ernst, Robert. *Immigrant Life in New York City, 1825–1863*. New York, 1949.

Ferguson, Jane Frances. *The Philosophy of Equality*. Washington, D. C., 1943.

Fink, William. "Stephen Van Rensselaer: The Last Patroon," unpublished doctoral dissertation, Columbia University, 1950.

Fish, Carl R. *The Rise of the Common Man, 1830–1850.* New York, 1927.

Flick, Alexander C., ed. *History of the State of New York.* 10 vols. New York, 1933–37.

Foner, Philip S. *History of the Labor Movement in the United States.* . . . 2 vols., New York, 1947.

Fox, Dixon Ryan. *The Decline of Aristocracy in the Politics of New York.* New York, 1919.

Frost, James A. *Life on the Upper Susquehanna, 1783–1860.* New York, 1951.

Gold, August B. "A History of Manufacturing in New York City, 1825–1840," unpublished M. A. thesis, Columbia University, 1932.

Goodrich, Carter. *Government Promotion of American Canals and Railroads, 1800–1890.* New York, 1960.

Hansen, Marcus Lee. *The Atlantic Migration, 1607–1860.* New York, 1961.

Harris, Herbert. *American Labor.* New Haven, 1938.

Hawgood, John A. *The Tragedy of German-America.* New York, 1940.

Hugins, Walter. *Jacksonian Democracy and the Working Class: A Study of the New York Workingmen's Movement, 1829–1837.* Stanford, 1960.

Jerome, Harry. *Migration and Business Cycles.* New York, 1926.

Jones, Maldwyn A. *American Immigration.* Chicago, 1960.

Jones, Peter d'a. *America's Wealth: The Economic History of an Open Society.* New York, 1963.

Krout, John A. and Fox, Dixon Ryan. *The Completion of Independence, 1790–1830.* New York, 1944.

Langdon, William C. *Everyday Things in American Life, 1776–1876.* New York, 1941.

McKelvey, Blake. *Rochester, the Water-Power City, 1812–1854.* Cambridge, Mass., 1945.

———. *Rochester, the Flower City, 1855–1890.* Cambridge, Mass., 1949.

McMaster, John Bach. *The Acquisition of Political, Social, and Industrial Rights in America.* New York, 1961.

———. *A History of the People of the United States, from the Revolution to the Civil War.* 8 vols. New York, 1883–1913.

Maguire, John Francis. *The Irish in America.* London, 1868.

Mau, Clayton. *The Development of Central and Western New York.* . . . Rochester, 1944.

Miller, Nathan. *The Enterprise of a Free People: Aspects of Economic Development in New York State During the Canal Period, 1792–1838.* Ithaca, 1962.

New York: A Guide to the Empire State. New York, 1940.

New York Panorama. . . . New York, 1938.

Nye, Russel Blaine. *The Cultural Life of the New Nation, 1776–1830.* New York, 1960.

O'Conner, Robert John. "An Analysis of the Bases for the Concept of Equality," unpublished doctoral dissertation, University of Southern California, 1960.

Ostrander, Gilman. *The Rights of Man in America, 1606–1861.* Columbia, Mo., 1960.

Phelps Stokes, I. N. *Iconography of Manhattan Island, 1498–1909.* 6 vols. New York, 1915–28.

———. *New York Past and Present.* . . . New York, 1939.

Potter, David M. *People of Plenty: Economic Abundance and the American Character.* Chicago, 1954.

Rayback, Joseph G. *A History of Labor.* New York, 1959.

Rezneck, Samuel. "The Rise and Early Development of Industrial Consciousness in the United States, 1760–1830," *Journal of Economic and Business History,* IV (August 1932), 784–811.

———. "The Social History of an American Depression, 1837–1843," *American Historical Review,* XL (July 1935), 662–87.

Riegel, Robert. *Young America, 1830–1840.* Norman, Okla., 1949.

Salmon, Lucy M. *Domestic Service.* New York, 1897.

Schlesinger, Arthur M. *Learning How To Behave: A Historical Study of American Etiquette Books.* New York, 1946.

Schlesinger, Arthur M., Jr. *The Age of Jackson.* Boston, 1945.

Still, Bayrd, ed. *Mirror for Gotham.* . . . New York, 1956.

Taylor, George R. *The Transportation Revolution, 1815–1860.* New York, 1951.

Thomas, Brinley. *Migration and Economic Growth.* . . . Cambridge, Eng., 1954.

Train, Arthur, Jr. *The Story of Everyday Things.* New York, 1941.

Tryon, W. S., ed. *My Native Land, Life in America, 1790–1870.* Chicago, 1952.

Tyler, Alice Felt. *Freedom's Ferment.* New York, 1962.

Ware, Norman. *The Industrial Worker, 1840–1860.* Boston, 1924.

Weber, Adna F. *The Growth of Industry in New York.* Albany, 1904.

Wecter, Dixon. *The Saga of American Society: A Record of Social Aspirations, 1607–1937.* New York, 1937.

Weisberger, Bernard A. *They Gathered at the River.* Boston, 1958.

Wittke, Carl. *We Who Built America.* . . . Cleveland, 1957.

INDEX

A

Adams, John Quincy, 15
Allaire, James P., 135
Alms House Commissioner, N.Y.C.,
96
American Celt, 81
American Society for the Encouragement of Domestic Manufactures, 108
Anglican Church. *See* Episcopal
Church
Anti-Rent movement: organization
of, 66; resorts to violence, 66–7,
69; as political force, 67–8; success
of, 68–9
Architecture, 74–5, 160–61. *See also*
Mansions
Aristocracy: declines in political
power, 11–18; based on family,
58; theoretical concepts of, 58–9;
resentment of, 61, 184–7; compo-
sition of, 61; landed, decline of,
62–9; becomes urban centered,
69–70; of New York City, 72;
style of living, 1830's, 73–4; upheld by certain institutions, 76–7;
social life of, 77, 165–6; apes
European fashions, 78–9, 164;
dotes on nobility, 78–9, 164–5; increase of, Jacksonian era, 80; industrial, 106, 107, 119–20; "old"
and "new," 124–5, 168–9; concern
with Prince of Wales visit, 155–
8; asserted through conspicuous
consumption, 158–64; private carriages of, 162; marriage alliances
of, 164, 173; of wealth, 168–9; described as Upper Ten Thousand,
169–70; speed of development,
170–72; summer resorts of, 173–
5; servants an index of, 178–9;

North and South compared, 179–
82; power of, 181–2; challenges
democratic ideals, 188–9. *See also*
Class distinctions; High society;
Knickerbocker society; Wealth
Artcher, Michael, 66
Art collections, private, 162
Aspinwall, William H., 124, 161,
162
Associationism. *See* Fourier socialism
Astor, John Jacob: wealth of, 23,
73; invests in manufacturing, 111;
urban landholdings of, 124; one-
generation aristocrat, 170; mentioned, 169
Astor, William B.: as slum landlord, 137–8; on committee to welcome Prince of Wales, 156; art
collection of, 162; mentioned, 161
Astor House (hotel), 74
Astor Place Opera House, 167; riot
of, 184

B

Bank of the United States, 38, 44, 45
Baptist Church, 9–10
Bartlett, Frances Amelia, 164
Beach, Moses Yale, 122, 160, 173
Beardsley, Levi, 22
Beggars: lack of, late 1820's, 28; in
N.Y.C., 130; increased number of,
151. *See also* Paupers
Belmont, August, 162, 175
Biddle, Nicholas, 45–6
Bodichon, Mrs. Barbara, 177
Boughton, Smith (Big Thunder), 67
Bowery Boys, 184
Brace, Charles Loring, 95, 134
Brevoort, Henry, 123–4, 169
Brevoort Costume Ball, 1840, 165–6

Brisbane, Albert, 141, 142
Bristed, Charles Astor, 169
Broadway, 27, 71–2, 163
Brook Farm, 142
Brougham, Henry, 108
Brown, Isaac H., 166–7
Browne, Junius, 170
Buckingham, James Silk, 28
Burn, James D., 155
Byrne, Stephen (Reverend), 95–6

C

Carey, Mathew, 51–3, 145–6
Castle Garden, 90
Catholic Church. See Roman Catholic Church
Central Park, 162
Chesterfield, Earl of (Philip Dormer Stanhope), *The American Chesterfield*, 171
Chevalier, Michael: on equality, 4, 24; on prosperous appearance of laborers, 27; praises N.Y.C., 70
Child, Mrs. L. Maria, 122, 155, 176
Chinese, in N.Y.C., 93
Civil War: and immigrants, 104; increased power of Northern aristocracy, 180; mentioned, 182; draft riots of, N.Y.C., 185–7
Claflin, Horace B., 123, 183
Class conflicts, 129–30, 184–7
Class consciousness: in Jacksonian era, 24; increased by immigration, 84, 100, 102; growth of, depression of 1837, 129–30; and social status, 158
Class distinctions: not fixed by law, 56; basis of, 57; precariousness of, 59–60, 79; emphasized by etiquette books, 171–2; clearly discernible, 179. *See also* Social Stratification
Clay, Henry, 174
Clinton, De Witt, 12, 110
Cochran, Thomas, 118
Colgate, William, 125, 183
Collins, S. H., 26–7

Colton, Calvin, 3
Columbia College, 76–7
Commons, John R., 147
Conspicuous consumption, 79, 158–64
Constitutional Convention of 1821, N.Y., 11–13
Cook, Noah, 41
Cooper, James Fenimore: on inequality, 3; on aggressive egalitarianism, 5; on class distinctions, 59; defends landed aristocracy, 69
Cooper, Peter: on committee to welcome Prince of Wales, 156; founds Cooper Union, 183; mentioned, 125, 157, 158
Cornell, Ezra, 170
Corning, Erastus, 115, 175
Corporations: N.Y. laws on, 109–10, 120; growth of, 120–21; manipulation of, 121; power of, 181
Coster, John, 73
Craft shop, 112–13
Crane, Edward, 121
Curtis, George William, *Potiphar Papers*, 159–60

D

Dayton, Abram C., 73–4
Dead Rabbits, 184
Delmonico's (restaurant), 157
Democracy: triumphant in politics, 11–18; challenged by aristocracy, 188–9
Depression, of 1837: effects of, on labor movement, 49–50, 128–30; of 1857: effects of, 149–50; riots during, 184–5
De Tocqueville, Alexis. *See* Tocqueville, Alexis de
Devyr, Thomas, 131
Dickens, Charles, 94–5, 136
Domestic manufacturing, 112–13
Draft riots, N.Y.C., 185–7
Dress: egalitarian aspects of, 7–8; as symbol of status, 163
Drew, Daniel, 121

Dutch Reformed Church, 9
Dutch West India Company, 63

E

Economic opportunity, 19–24
Edwards, Ogden (Judge), 48–9
Ellis Island, 90
Episcopal Church, 9, 76, 166–7
Emigration, Board of Commissioners of, N.Y.C., 90
Episcopal Church, 9, 76, 166–7
Equality: of Jacksonian era, 3; observed by foreign travelers, 3–4; aggressively asserted, 4–5; reflected in accommodations, 5; reflected in opposition to servitude, 5–7; reflected in dress, 7–8; reflected in public transportation, 8–9; furthered by lack of established church, 9–10; infectious, 10–11; reflected in politics, 11–18; shaped by economic abundance, 19; equated with opportunity, 23–4, 182; never fully realized, 24–5; belief in, emphasized achievement, 25, 60; ridiculed, 78; lack of, 139. See also Economic opportunity; Social mobility
Erie Canal, 20, 22, 110–11
Erie Railroad, 115–16, 121
Etiquette books, 171–2
Evans, George Henry: supports state boarding schools, 41; and land reform, 142–4; supports ten-hour day, 146; mentioned, 36, 131. See also National Reform Association; *Working Man's Advocate, The*
Evening Journal, 34, 35

F

Farming, 21–2, 145. See also Labor
Field, Dudley, Jr., 186
Fifth Avenue, 161, 169, 172
Filmore, Millard, 116
Finch, John, 130–31
Fish, Hamilton, 157, 175

Ford, Ebenezer, 40
Forrest, Edwin, 184
Foster, G. G.: describes financial manipulation, 126–7; on treatment of poor, 152; ridicules lavish spending, 159; satirizes fashionable summer routine, 175–6
Fourier, Charles, 140–41
Fourier socialism: expounded by Fourier, 140–41; growth of, 141; collapse of, 141–2
French, J. H., 116

G

Genealogy, interest in, 79, 165
General Trades' Union, 46–7
German Emigrant Society, 90
Germans: immigration of, 86–7; in urban areas, 92, 95, 99; in farming, 98; reduce wages, 100; as servants, 102–3; second generation, 104. See also Immigrants; Immigration
Gilded Age, the: compared with pre-Civil War society, 121, 168, 188, 189; mentioned, 18
Godey's Lady's Book, 172
Godwin, Parke, 139
Grace Church, 76, 166–7
Graves, Mrs. A. J., 177
Greeley, Horace: on bad working conditions, 54; on depression of 1837, 129; sympathy for poor, 130; working-class family budget of, 133; on visible inequality, N.Y.C., 139; and Fourier socialism, 141; supports co-operatives, 142; on deteriorating working conditions, 151; on beggars, 151
Griscom, John H. (Dr.), 134, 136–7, 138
Grund, Francis: favors equality, 10–11; on aristocracy, 61; on American aristocrats' disdain of America, 78; on rudeness of aristocracy, 79–80
Guyon, Henry G., 41

H

Haight, Benjamin, 160
Hall, Basil, 19, 62
Handlin, Oscar, 99–100
Hardie, James, 111
Harrison, William Henry, 17
Haswell, Charles, 167, 173
Hatt, George (Reverend), 136–7
High society: rise of, 1830's, 79; of
    1860 compared with 1830's, 158;
    elaborate entertainments of, 165–
    6; ruler of, 166; and the opera,
    167; dependence on conspicuous
    consumption, 169; divisions of,
    170; mentioned, 175
Holland Land Company, 20–21
Home Journal, 169, 172
Hone, Philip: on N.Y.C. democracy,
    14–15; private carriage of, 74;
    moves uptown, 76; describes
    fashionable party, 77; invests in
    manufacturing, 111; art collec-
    tion and library of, 162; describes
    Brevoort Costume Ball, 165; de-
    scription of Saratoga Springs, 174
Howe, Elias, 118
Howland, William, 124–5
Hudson River Railway, 125
Hugins, Walter, 42
Hunt, John, 74
Huntington, Charles B., 126

I

Immigrants: labor of, 33; exploita-
    tion of, 87–90; attempts to aid,
    90–91; in urban areas, 92–7; in
    rural areas, 97–9; regarded as in-
    ferior, 102; difficulties of advance-
    ment, 103–4; second-generation,
    104; blamed for social ills, 132;
    housed in cellars, 136; hurt by
    depression of 1857, 149; made
    laboring less respectable, 153;
    and draft riots, 185–7. See also
    Chinese; Germans; Immigration;
    Irish; Italians

Immigration: caused social stratifi-
    cation, 81–2, 84, 100, 102; limited,
    before 1830, 82–4; reasons for,
    85–7; Handlin thesis of, 99–100;
    adverse economic effects of, 100–2
Industrialism: impact of, 106–7,
    119–20, 121; beginnings of, 107–
    8; state aid to, 109–10; aided by
    Erie Canal, 110–11; investment
    in, 111; state of, in Jacksonian
    era, 111–13; cotton manufactur-
    ing, 112; woolen manufacturing,
    112; rapid growth of, 1840's and
    1850's, 113–14, 121; becomes self-
    sustaining, 114; railroads aid,
    114–16; regional specialization of,
    116–18; iron manufacturing, 116–
    17; lumber manufacturing, 117;
    leather manufacturing, 117;
    flour-milling, 118; status of,
    1850's, 118; creates wealthy elite,
    120, 121, 122, 127; threatened
    skilled artisans, 131–2. See also
    Corporations; Labor
Inequality: taken as personal fail-
    ure, 24; visibility of, 122, 138–9;
    labor's acceptance of, 148; created
    by manufacturing, 187
Irish: construction workers, 1830's,
    51–2; flee famine, 86–7; urban
    concentration of, 91–2; life of,
    N.Y.C., 93–5; in upstate N.Y., 98–
    9; as servants, 102–3; second-
    generation, 104; in Astor Place
    Opera House riot, 184; hatred
    of Negroes, 185. See also Immi-
    grants; Immigration
Italians, 93

J

Jackson, Andrew: first inauguration,
    4, 14; election of 1828, 11, 14;
    as hero, 15; on manners, 17; as
    example of success, 23; veto of
    Bank, 45; on American ideals,
    188
Jacksonian era, ideals of, 188

Jefferson, Thomas, 58–9, 70
Johnson, John Taylor, 162

K

Kent, James, 12–13, 14
Kip, William (Bishop), 168–9
Knickerbocker society: described,
  73; compared with aristocracy of
  1860, 158; architecture of, 160;
  mentioned, 58, 72, 168–9, 170
Kossuth, Louis, 160
Kyle, Alexander, 126

L

Labor: respect for, early 1830's, 26;
  farm, 28, 145–6; those composing
  working class, 29–30; apprenticeship system, 29, 30–34; deteriorating conditions of, 31–5; reacts to
  deteriorating conditions, 33–5;
  demands of, 35–9; organizes politically, 39–42; middle-class aspirations of, 41–3; gains support, 43–
  5; organizes unions, 1830's, 45–7;
  1850's, 147–8; hurt by depression,
  1837, 49–50, 128–30; 1857, 149–
  50; bad conditions for unskilled,
  50–54; undermined by immigration, 101–2; reduced wages of,
  130–34; challenged by mechanization, 131–2; living costs of, 132–
  3; living conditions of, N.Y.C.,
  134–8; and middle-class reformers, 140–46; conditions of, 1830's
  compared to 1850's, 150–51; loss
  of status of, 152–4, 181–2; lack
  of power of, 182; class conflicts
  of, 184–7; hurt by Civil War, 185.
  See also Immigrants; Unions;
  Wages
Landed aristocracy. See Aristocracy
Land Reform movement, 142–6
Langdon, Woodbury, 159, 161
Lawrence, Cornelius, 14–15
Leary, Charles, 158

Leisure: rare in Jacksonian era, 26;
  among fashionable women, 176–7
Lenox, Robert, 73
Leonard, Daniel, 66
Libraries, private, 162
Livingston, Edward P., 174
Log Cabin campaign, 16–17
Lyell, Sir Charles, 163

M

McAllister, Ward, 175, 180–81
Macomb, Alexander, 20
Macready, William Charles, 184
Manors, 63–5
Mansions: of N.Y.C. elite, 1830's,
  74–6, 77; costliness of, 160–61;
  lavish interiors of, 161–2
Manufacturing. See Industrialism
Mapleson, Gwilt, 165
Marcy, William, 66
Marx, Henry, 74
Mechanics' Press, 38, 119
Merchant-capitalist, 31–2
Methodist Church, 9–10
Metropolitan Museum of Art, 162
Millionaires, 122
Mohawk and Hudson Railroad,
  114–15
Morris, Robert, 20
Mott, Valentine (Dr.), 74
Mowatt, Anna Cora, Fashion, 164,
  178
Murray, Charles Augustus, 62

N

National Reform Association, 143,
  144, 146
National Trades' Union, 47
National Typographical Union, 147
Newport, R.I., 175
Newspapers. See titles of individual
  papers
New York and Harlem Railroad,
  94, 126
New York and New Haven Rail-
  road, 124, 126

New York Central Railroad, 115
New York City: becomes more democratic, 14–15; description of, 70–72; major port of entry, 88–9; Irish in, 91–2; Germans in, 92; as manufacturing center, 117, 118; density of population, 135; Five Points section described, 136
New York Herald, 165–6
New York Sun, 144
New York Times: working-class family budget of, 132–3; on inequality, 139; supports land reform, 144; on aristocracy at Prince of Wales grand ball, 156–7
New York Tribune: on immigrants, 87–8, 95; working-class family budget of, 133; supports land reform, 144; on strikes, 148; on aristocracy at the opera, 167; advertisements for servants in, 178
North American Phalanx, 142

O

Oviedo, Don Estaban Santa Cruz de, 164
Owen, Robert, 140
Owen, Robert Dale, 41

P

Parks, John, 27
Parton, Mrs. James (Fanny Fern), 171–2
Patroonships, 63. *See also* Manors
Paulding, James Kirke, 79
Paupers, 152. *See also* Beggars
Penniman, James F., 161
Phelps, John Jay, 125
Philanthropy, 183–4
Politics: democratization of, 11–18; of labor, 39–42; in 1860, 155
Potter, David, 19
Poverty: absence of, late 1820's, 28; increased with immigration, 96–7; extensive during depression, 1837, 130; among working-class

families, 133–4; reflected in working-class living conditions, 134–8; increasing signs of, 151–2. *See also* Beggars; Paupers
Presbyterian Church, 9–10
Prime, Nat, 73
Prince of Wales (later Edward VII), 155–8, 164, 166
Pulszky, Francis and Theresa, 160
Pulteney, Sir William, 20

R

Railroads, 114–16. *See also names of individual railroads*
Religion, 9–10. *See also different church sects*
Rensselaerwyck, 65, 67, 69, 70
Renwick, James, 167
Resorts, summer, 173–5
Rhinelander, F. W., 175
Riis, Jacob, 134
Roman Catholic Church, 9, 92
Root, Erastus, 13
Rothschild, Baron Salomon de, 156, 157, 174–5
Royall, Mrs. Anne, 71–2
Ruggles, Samuel, 76

S

Saratoga Springs, 173–5
Saxe Weimar, Duke of, 4–5
Schermerhorn, William, 175
Schlesinger, Arthur, 171
Schuyler, Robert, 121, 124, 126
Scott, Winfield (General), 156, 174
Sedgwick, Catherine M., 171
Servants: egalitarian pretentions of, 5–7; changing status of, 102–3; growing number of, 178–9
Seward, William, 67, 174
Shaw, Lemuel (Judge), 49
Skidmore, Thomas, 40, 41, 42
Social mobility, 22–4, 182
Social stratification: increased through immigration, 81–2, 100, 102; caused by industrialization,

120; reasons tolerated, 182–4. *See also* Class distinctions

Society for the Encouragement of Faithful Domestic Servants, 5

Spas. *See* Resorts, summer

Spirit of the Age, 37

Stewart, Alexander T.: dry goods fortune, 123; art collection of, 162; one-generation aristocrat, 170; built mansion, 172; philanthropy of, 183

Stock exchange, 125–7

Strong, George Templeton: on stock forgery, 126; on cholera epidemic, 1854, 138; on visit of Prince of Wales, 156, 157, 158; on aristocratic extravagance, 158–9, 161; on uptown movement of fashion, 160; art collection and library of, 162; on servants, 179; on philanthropy, 183; on draft riots, 186

Stuart, Alexander, 183

Stuart, Robert, 183

Suffrage, universal male, 11–14

T

Tariffs, 108–9

Tenement houses, N.Y.C., 89–90, 134–8

Thackeray, William Makepeace, 163

Tocqueville, Alexis de: on equality, 3–4, 5; on withdrawal of aristocracy from politics, 18; on desire to advance, 19–20; on farming, 21–2; on social mobility, 22–3; on inability to achieve equality, 24–5; on contempt for equality of property, 56–7; predicts manufacturing aristocracy, 106, 119, 120, 187

Townsend, Samuel ("Sarsaparilla"), 172

Trade Unions. *See* Unions

Trinity Church, 76

Trobriand, Baron M. de, 163

Trollope, Anthony, 164

Trollope, Mrs. Frances, 70–71, 72

Typographical Association, N.Y.C., 45

U

Union Club, 77

Union League Club, 186

Unions: first, 30–31; organized, 1820's, 35; 1830's, 45–7; 1850's, 147; opposed by courts, 39, 47–9; opposed by employers, 47; legality of, established, 49; collapse of, late 1830's, 49–50; late 1850's, 148–9; difficulties reviving, after 1837, 140; "bread and butter" objectives of, 147–8; use of strike, 148

Upper classes. *See* Aristocracy

V

Van Buren, John, 66–7

Van Buren, Martin, 12, 15, 17, 174

Vanderbilt, Cornelius, 121, 162, 170

Van Rensselaer, Henry, 175

Van Rensselaer, Kiliaen, 63

Van Rensselaer, Stephen, III: lord of manor, 65; death of, 65; will of, 66; as railroad president, 115

Van Rensselaer, Stephen IV, 66, 68–9

Van Rensselaer, William, 66

W

Wages: higher in America than Europe, 26–7; of laborers, 51, 130–34; reduced by immigration, 100–1

Ware, Norman, 152

Wealth: criterion for high social standing, 19, 22, 57–8, 158–64, 170, 172–3; growth of, 121–4; visible contrast with poverty, 138–9; conferred power and honor, 168–9; fluctuation of, 172; persons catering to, 178

Webster, Daniel, 115

Wecter, Dixon, 17
Weed, Thurlow, 15, 16
Whitney, Stephen, 73
Willis, Nathaniel: coins phrase "Upper Ten Thousand," 169; on rapid rise of aristocracy, 170; on persons catering to wealth, 178; mentioned, 165
Women: laborers, 52–3; dress of fashionable, 163; of fashion, 176–8

Working class. *See* Labor
Working Man's Advocate, The, 26, 142
Working Men's party, 29, 40–42, 43
Wright, Silas, 67
Wyse, Francis, 103–4

Y

Young, John, 68

COMMUNITY COLLEGE OF ALLEGHENY COUNTY
ALLEGHENY CAMPUS
808 RIDGE AVENUE
PITTSBURGH, PA.
15212
LIBRARY